CAMBRIDGE LIBRARY COLLECTION

Books of enduring scholarly value

Travel and Exploration

The history of travel writing dates back to
and the Crusaders, and its many themes
recreation. Explorers from Columbus to
visited by Western travellers, and were fo
and colonists, who wrote accounts of the
steam power in the nineteenth century p
numbers of 'ordinary' people to travel further, more economically, and more
safely, and resulted in great enthusiasm for travel writing among the reading
public. Works included in this series range from first-hand descriptions of
previously unrecorded places, to literary accounts of the strange habits of
foreigners, to examples of the burgeoning numbers of guidebooks produced
to satisfy the needs of a new kind of traveller - the tourist.

The Canarian

The publications of the Hakluyt Society (founded in 1846) made available
edited (and sometimes translated) early accounts of exploration. The first
series, which ran from 1847 to 1899, consists of 100 books containing
published or previously unpublished works by authors from Christopher
Columbus to Sir Francis Drake, and covering voyages to the New World,
to China and Japan, to Russia and to Africa and India. The Canary Islands
have been known to European countries since the Roman era. In 1402, the
kingdom of Castile sent an expeditionary force, led by French explorers
Jean de Bethancourt (1362–1475) and Gadfier de la Salle (1340–1415), to
conquer the islands. This volume, first published in English in 1872, contains
a contemporary account of the conquest written by Pierre Bontier and Jean
le Verrier, both members of the expedition; it contains valuable details of the
indigenous inhabitants of the islands.

Cambridge University Press has long been a pioneer in the reissuing of out-of-print titles from its own backlist, producing digital reprints of books that are still sought after by scholars and students but could not be reprinted economically using traditional technology. The Cambridge Library Collection extends this activity to a wider range of books which are still of importance to researchers and professionals, either for the source material they contain, or as landmarks in the history of their academic discipline.

Drawing from the world-renowned collections in the Cambridge University Library, and guided by the advice of experts in each subject area, Cambridge University Press is using state-of-the-art scanning machines in its own Printing House to capture the content of each book selected for inclusion. The files are processed to give a consistently clear, crisp image, and the books finished to the high quality standard for which the Press is recognised around the world. The latest print-on-demand technology ensures that the books will remain available indefinitely, and that orders for single or multiple copies can quickly be supplied.

The Cambridge Library Collection will bring back to life books of enduring scholarly value (including out-of-copyright works originally issued by other publishers) across a wide range of disciplines in the humanities and social sciences and in science and technology.

The Canarian

Or, Book of the Conquest and Conversion of the Canarians in the year 1402, by Messire Jean de Bethencourt, Kt

PIERRE BONTIER
JEAN LE VERRIER

CAMBRIDGE
UNIVERSITY PRESS

CAMBRIDGE UNIVERSITY PRESS

Cambridge, New York, Melbourne, Madrid, Cape Town, Singapore,
São Paolo, Delhi, Dubai, Tokyo

Published in the United States of America by Cambridge University Press, New York

www.cambridge.org
Information on this title: www.cambridge.org/9781108011396

© in this compilation Cambridge University Press 2010

This edition first published 1872
This digitally printed version 2010

ISBN 978-1-108-01139-6 Paperback

WORKS ISSUED BY

The Hakluyt Society.

HISTORY

OF THE

CONQUEST OF THE CANARIES.

M.DCCC.LXXII.

PORTRAIT OF MESSIRE JEAN DE BETHENCOURT,
KING OF THE CANARIES.

THE CANARIAN,

OR, BOOK OF THE

CONQUEST AND CONVERSION

OF

THE CANARIANS

IN THE YEAR 1402,

BY

Messire JEAN DE BETHENCOURT, K^T.,

*Lord of the Manors of Bethencourt, Riville, Gourrel, and Grainville la Teinturiere,
Baron of St. Martin le Gaillard, Councillor and Chamberlain in Ordinary
to Charles V and Charles VI,*

COMPOSED BY

PIERRE BONTIER, AND JEAN LE VERRIER,
MONK. PRIEST.

TRANSLATED AND EDITED,

With Notes and an Introduction,

BY

RICHARD HENRY MAJOR, F.S.A., ETC.,

KEEPER OF THE DEPARTMENT OF MAPS AND CHARTS IN THE BRITISH MUSEUM,
AND HON. SEC. OF THE ROYAL GEOGRAPHICAL SOCIETY.

LONDON:

PRINTED FOR THE HAKLUYT SOCIETY.

M.DCCC.LXXII.

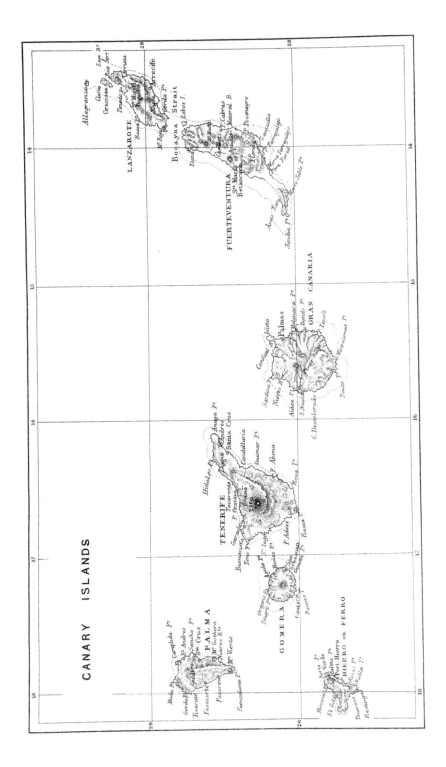

CANARY ISLANDS

INTRODUCTION.

It is a remarkable fact that in the proud list of the glories of noble France there is one class of achievements for which she has claimed more, and at the same time received less, honour than she really deserves. She has put forth a claim to having preceded even Prince Henry of Portugal in lifting the veil from the Sea of Darkness, the mysterious Atlantic, and in colonising the west coast of Africa; but although the most illustrious of her claimants to this distinction, the learned M. d'Avezac, still clings lovingly to his patriotic convictions on this head, the present writer has already demonstrated that that claim can by no means be maintained.[1] At the same time France is very far from having received the amount of honour which is her due for the boldness of her maritime explorations at a somewhat later but still very early period. There can be no doubt that in the first half of the sixteenth century France was the nation which followed most boldly in the footsteps of Portugal, and it is possible

---

[1] See *Life of Prince Henry the Navigator and its Results*, London, 1868, chapter of "The Sea of Darkness," pp. 117-128.

that we have yet much to learn from unexamined
manuscripts as to the exploits of the adventurous
Dieppese at that interesting period in the history of
navigation. The voyage treated of in the present
volume holds an isolated and highly distinguished
position midway as to date between the pretended
and the real early achievements of the French
nation at sea; for whereas the former were said to
have taken place in the fourteenth, and the latter
unquestionably did take place in the sixteenth, this
voyage of De Bethencourt was made at the very
commencement of the fifteenth century. It is consequently the earliest authenticated distant voyage
made by Frenchmen to the south. Had it been
directed to unexplored latitudes it would have
eclipsed the glory even of Prince Henry himself,
whose first expedition it preceded at least by
thirteen years, if not more. But though its destination was only to the Canaries, a group of islands
whose position was well known, and which had been
the subject of poetical allusion for more than two
thousand years, yet as an early attempt at colonisation, which has made the name of its originator
illustrious, it possesses a strong claim to insertion
among the series of our Society's publications. As a
mere maritime feat, the expedition was in no way
remarkable. The track was a beaten one. For a
century the Venetians had already been in the
habit of making the voyage to Flanders, and the

---

[1] Our learned compatriot, Mr. Rawdon Brown, who has for
so many years been an unwearied student of Venetian records,

Spaniards and the Genoese not unfrequently visited the Canaries for goat's-flesh, making their way by the west coast of Africa down to Cape Cantin, and so by a short traverse to Lancerote or Fuerteventura. And while it is true that in this expedition originated that colonisation of the Canaries from which sprung their present European population, yet it is not correct to suppose, as hitherto it has been generally asserted, that the principal islands of the group then received for the first time the names which they at present bear. But in order that the reader may form an idea of the true position and value of this expedition in the history of discovery, it will be necessary to take a brief survey of what had been previously known of these islands. In the poems of Homer the ocean is treated as a river beyond which at the earth's confines were the Elysian fields which Hesiod and Pindar made to be surrounded by water, so that the habitations of the blest were transformed into islands, and hence, probably, originated the name of the Insulæ Fortunatæ or Fortunate Islands. On this point Strabo says, lib. 3 :—" The poets make mention of the Islands of the Blest, and we know that even now they are to be seen not far from the extremity of Mauritania, opposite Gades (Cadiz). Now I say that those who pointed out these things were the Phœnicians who,

has published, in his *L'Archivio di Venezia con riguardo speciale alla Storia Inglese*, Venezia e Torino, 1865, 16mo, pp. 274-279, a list of the captains in the Flanders voyages from 1317 down to 1533.

before the time of Homer, had possession of the best part of Africa and Spain." Here we see the Canaries evidently alluded to, and the inference suggested that they were known to the Phœnician colony of Carthaginians established at Cadiz three thousand years ago. About eighty-two years before our era, we find these islands afresh brought under notice. Some Lusitanian sea captains who had just returned from them, fell in with Sertorius, who, in his flight from the ships of Annius, had passed through the straits and landed near the mouth of the Quadalquivir. Their glowing account of the fertility of the soil, the purity of the air, and the happiness of the people, inspired Sertorius with an ardent desire to withdraw from the business of life, and seek repose there, but fate decreed otherwise. It is to Plutarch (see Plutarch's *Life of Sertorius*) that we are indebted for this account. Two islands only were mentioned, probably Lancerote and Fuerteventura.

Twenty years after the death of Sertorius, we have five islands specified by distinct names in a vague itinerary drawn up by one Statius Sebosus from the accounts of navigators of his time, and preserved to us by Pliny. He represents the group, to which he gives the name of Hesperides, as one day's sail from the western promontory (Cape Non). He names them (1) Junonia, at 750 miles from Gades (Cadiz), (2) Pluviālia, and (3) Capraria, 750 miles west of Junonia, and 250 miles beyond, to the left of Mauritania and towards the ninth hour of the sun, were the great Fortunate Islands, one called (4)

Convallis and the other (5) Planaria, on account of their form ; but all these indications are too indistinct to supply us with any information beyond the fact that in the time of Sebosus five islands of the Canary group had received individual names.

Happily we are supplied also by Pliny with information of a far more distinct character respecting these islands. When King Juba the Second was reinstated by Augustus on the throne which his father had lost, on his return to Mauritania he turned to account the geographical knowledge which he had acquired through his education in Italy, and sent out an expedition for the express purpose of exploring the Fortunate Islands. On the return of the navigators he wrote a narrative of the voyage from their report, and sent it to the emperor. A fragment only of that narrative survives, and has been transmitted to us by Pliny in the following shape: "The Fortunate Islands lie to the south-west, at 625 miles from the Purpurariæ. To reach them from the latter they first sailed 250 miles westwards and then 375 miles to the east.[1] The first is called Ombrios, and contains no traces of buildings. There is in it a pool in the midst of mountains, and trees like ferules, from which water may be pressed, which

---

[1] The "three hundred" is omitted in some editions of Pliny, but that they are necessary is evident from the account of Pliny himself. It is clear that the 625 miles are reckoned in making the periplus of the whole group, the 250 tallying with the distance from Fuerteventura, one of the Purpurariæ, to Ombrios or Palma. The 375 would be the length of the eastern return track from Palma round the group.

is bitter from the black kinds, but from the lighter ones pleasant to drink (sugar-cane). The second is called Junonia, and contains a small temple built entirely of stone. Near it is another smaller island having the same name. Then comes Capraria, which is full of large lizards. Within sight of these islands is Nivaria, so called from the snow and fogs with which it is constantly covered. Not far from Nivaria is Canaria, so called on account of the great number of large dogs therein, two of which were brought to King Juba. There were traces of buildings in this island. All the islands abound in apples and in birds of every kind, and in palms covered with dates, and in the pine nut. There is also plenty of honey. The papyrus grows there, and the Silurus fish is found in the rivers." (See Pliny, *Nat. Hist.*, lib. 6, cap. 37.) In Ombrios we recognise the Pluvialia of Sebosus, the words being synonymous. Convallis becomes Nivaria, and Planaria is replaced by Canaria, which name is still borne by the large central island, and has now been given to the whole Archipelago. There is no difficulty in fixing the island named Nivaria, a name which clearly indicates the snowy peak of Teneriffe, almost constantly capped with clouds. In Ombrios or Pluvialia, with its pool in the midst of mountains, we recognise the island of Palma, with its famous Caldera or cauldron, the crater of an old volcano. The distance also of this island from Fuerteventura agrees with that of the 250 miles indicated by Juba's navigators as existing between Ombrios and the Purpurariæ. It has been

already seen that the latter agree with Lancerote and Fuerteventura in respect of their distance from the continent and from each other, as described by Plutarch. That the Purpurariæ are not, as M. Bory de St. Vincent supposed, the Madeira group, is not only shown by the want of inhabitants in the latter, but by the orchil, which supplies the purple dye, being derived from and sought for specially from the Canaries and not the Madeira group, although it is to be found there. Junonia, the nearest to Ombrios, will be Gomera. It may be presumed that the temple found therein was, like the island, dedicated to Juno. Capraria, which implies the island of goats, agrees correctly with the island of Ferro, which occurs next in the order of the itinerary, for these animals were found there in large numbers when the island was invaded by Jean de Bethencourt in 1402. But a yet more striking proof of the identity of this island with Capraria is the account of the great number of large lizards found therein. Bethencourt's chaplains, describing their visit to the island in 1402, state :—" There are lizards in it as big as cats, but they are harmless, although very hideous to look at."

It was probably the desire to bring these mysterious islands within the grasp of history that induced King Juba to send out this expedition; and although the blessedness that was looked for formed no part of the discovery, yet as these were the only islands that were lighted upon in the ocean where they were sought for, they were assumed to be the genuine Insulæ Fortunatæ, and accordingly retained the name.

For thirteen centuries from the time of which we have been speaking, the Fortunate Islands were destined again to be almost buried in oblivion. The destruction of the Roman Empire re-plunged Europe into ignorance; and, although the Fortunate Islands were vaguely known to the Moors of Spain under the designation of the Islands of Khaledat, it has been elaborately shown by the eminent Portuguese *savant*, Senhor Joaquim José da Costa de Macedo, that the Arabs had no practical knowledge of the Canaries before the times of the Portuguese discoveries. He maintains that the only notions they had respecting them were such as they derived from Greek and Latin authors, and he seems satisfactorily to have proved his point.

It was not till the beginning of the fifteenth century, when the Norman Jean de Bethencourt, the subject of the present narrative, established himself in the Canaries, that something like substantial information respecting these islands was made accessible to Europeans. Much earlier expeditions, it is true, had been attempted, but of the navigators who visited them before the fifteenth century, some only landed accidentally, and others went for the purpose of taking slaves, or goats' flesh, or else to gather orchil for dyeing, and dragon's blood, or other products that might be useful in commerce.

In the Bibliotheca Laurentiana, in Florence, is a portulano of the date of 1351, known as the Portulano Mediceo, which, although anonymous, has been satisfactorily proved by Count Baldelli Boni, in his

valuable edition of the *Milione of Marco Polo*, published in Florence in 1827, to be of Genoese construction. On one of the maps in this Portulano, against the island of Lancerote in the Canaries, is inserted the shield of Genoa, distinctly claiming the priority of discovery in favour of that republic; and Count Baldelli with reason remarks that no Venetian or Pisan or Catalan would be the first to lay down, on a map so important, a fact in favour of their rivals the Genoese. It is right, however, to observe that on the later Venetian map by the brothers Pizzigani of 1367, and in the Catalan map of 1375, this remarkable indication is inserted. Perhaps a stronger argument is derived from the use of the Genoese dialect in the names in preference to that of Venice or Pisa. M. d'Avezac, with his usual untiring research, has bestowed great labour upon the inquiry into the discovery and naming of the island of Lancerote. He has shown that the discoverer was of the ancient, but now extinct, Genoese family of Malocello. In the visit of the Norman knight Jean de Bethencourt to that island in 1402, it is said that they stored their grain in an old castle reputed to be built by Lancelot Maloisel. In a Genoese map of the date of 1455, made by Bartolommeo Pareto, are inserted against the same island the words "Lansaroto Maroxello Januensis"; and, further, we are led to believe that the discovery was made as early as the thirteenth century from a passage in Petrarch, which declares that *a patrum memoriâ, i. e.,* a generation back, an armed fleet of

Genoese had penetrated as far as the Fortunate Islands. Now as Petrarch was born in 1304, if, as is highly probable, Lancelote Malocello's voyage was the one alluded to, it will have taken place at the latest in the close of the thirteenth century. We thus find a reason for the reservation by Genoese map makers of the claim of their country to the island of Lancerote.

That the Canaries were visited, but visited only, by the Portuguese, even earlier than the year 1345 is proved by a passage in a letter from Affonso IV, King of Portugal, to Pope Clement VI, which was written under the following circumstances. When Alfonso, the eldest son of the Infant Don Ferdinand, and grandson of King Alfonso the Wise, was deprived by his uncle Don Sancho of the succession to the Crown of Castile, he retired in indignation to France to the Court of his uncle Philippe le Bel. He there married Marhaut or Mafalda, daughter of Amery VI, Viscount of Narbonne, by whom he had Luis of Spain, called by almost all the Spanish historians Luis de la Cerda, Count of Talmond, and Admiral of France. On the death of John III, Duke of Brittany, a civil war divided the country into two parties. England took the part of the Count de Montfort, the Duke's brother, while the King of France maintained that of his nephew the Count de Blois, who had been called to the succession by the Duke himself. In this contest Don Luis commanded in several engagements against England, till at length Pope Clement VI obtained a truce, signed at Malestroit on the 19th

January, 1343, which was to last three years, so that terms of peace might in the interval be negotiated in the Pope's presence at Avignon. One of the plenipotentiaries was Luis de la Cerda, and as the negotiations were greatly protracted by repeated delays on the part of the King of England, he remained there till the beginning of the year 1345.

During his stay at Avignon, Don Luis represented to the Pope that there were islands in the ocean, named the Fortunate Islands, some of which were inhabited and others not, and that he wished to obtain possession of these for the exaltation of the Faith and the spread of Christianity, and for this purpose he prayed his Holiness to grant him the necessary authority and the title of King of these islands. The Pope granted his request, and by a Bull dated from Avignon, November 15th, 1334, bestowed on him the lordship of the fortunate Islands with the title of Prince of Fortune, to remain in perpetual fief to the Apostolic See, to which it should pay annually 400 florins of good and pure gold of Florentine coinage; and Don Luis gave an acknowledgment of the fief on the 28th of November of the same year. At the same time the Pope wrote letters to the Kings of France, of Sicily, of Aragon, of Castile, and Portugal, as well as to the Dauphin, and to the Doge of Genoa, desiring them to help the new king in this enterprise. The reply of the King of Portugal contains the passage to which allusion has been made. While submitting, from habitual reverence, to the desire of his Holiness, he reminded

him that he had already sent out expeditions to those islands, and was only prevented from sending out a large armada by the wars in which he became involved, first with the King of Castile, and afterwards with the Saracens. The letter finished with the King's excusing himself on account of the exhausted condition of his treasury from supplying Don Luis with ships and soldiers, but expressing his willingness to furnish him to the extent of his power with provisions, and other supplies. This letter was dated from Monte Mor, 12th of February, 1345. The war with Spain, to which the King referred, broke out at the close of 1336, whence it follows that his assertion that he had thereby been prevented from sending out a large armada to those islands, either means that previously to that year the Portuguese had sent out expeditions to the Canaries, or that expeditions which he had sent out during the war would, but for the war, have been equipped on a grander scale.

By a treaty concluded in 1317, Denis the Labourer, King of Portugal, secured the services of the Genoese Emmanuele Pezagno as hereditary admiral of his fleet, with a distinct understanding that he and his successors should make unfailing provision of twenty Genoese captains experienced in navigation to command the king's galleys.

In the year 1326 we find this same Emmanuele Pezagno sent by Affonso IV as ambassador to our own King Edward III, who regarded him with such favour, that on July 24, 1332, he addressed a letter

to Affonso, recommending both Emmanuele and his son Carlo to his especial patronage. Even so late as 1373, we find the rank of admiral of the Portuguese fleet remaining in the hands of Lancelot, son of Emmanuele Pezagno, who received it from Peter I by letters patent dated 26th June, 1357. So that in these facts we have a remarkable light thrown upon the declaration of Affonso IV to Pope Clement VI, that previous to 1334 he had already sent out expeditions to these islands.

Meanwhile we have evidence to show that in 1341 a voyage was made to the Canaries, under the auspices of the King of Portugal, in a narrative for which we are indebted to the poet Boccaccio, and which has been rescued from oblivion so recently as 1827 by the learned Sebastiano Ciampi. It was derived from letters written to Florence by certain Florentine merchants established at Seville, under date of the 17 kalend of December, 1341.

The narrative records that "On the 1st of July of that same year, two vessels, furnished by the King of Portugal with all the necessary provisions, and accompanied by a smaller vessel, well armed and manned by Florentines, Genoese, Castilians, and other Spaniards, among whom were naturally included Portuguese, for the word Hispani included all inhabitants of the Peninsula, set sail for Lisbon, and put out into the open sea.[1] They took with them horses,

---

[1] "The Florentine who went with these ships was Angelino del Tegghia dei Corbizzi, a cousin of the sons of Gherardino Gianni," according to what we learn from a marginal note by Boccaccio.

arms, and warlike engines for storming towns and castles, in search of those islands commonly called the "Rediscovered." The wind was favourable, and on the 5th day they found land. They did not return till the month of November, when they brought back with them four of the natives, a large quantity of goat skins, the fat and oil of fish, and seal skins; red wood which dyed almost as well as the verzino (Brazil wood), although connoisseurs pronounced it not to be the same; the barks of trees to stain with a red colour; red earth and other such things. Nicoloso de Recco, a Genoese, the pilot of this expedition, stated that this archipelago was nearly nine hundred miles from the city of Seville; but that reckoning from what now is called Cape St. Vincent, the islands were much nearer to the continent, and that the first of those which they discovered [most probably Fuerteventura] was a hundred and fifty miles in circumference; it was one mass of uncultivated stony land, but full of goats and other beasts, and inhabited by naked men and women, who were like savages in their appearance and demeanour. He added that he and his companions obtained in this island the greater part of their cargo of skins and fat, but they did not dare to penetrate far into the country. Passing thence into another island [Great Canary], somewhat larger than the first, a great number of natives of both sexes, all nearly naked, came down to the shore to meet them. Some of them, who seemed superior to the rest, were covered with goats' skins covered yellow and red,

and, as far as could be seen from a distance, the skins were fine and soft, and tolerably well sewn together with the intestines of animals. To judge from their gestures they seemed to have a prince, to whom they showed much respect and obedience. The islanders showed a wish to communicate with the people in the ship, but when the boats drew near the shore, the sailors who did not understand a word that they said did not dare to land. Their language however was soft, and their pronunciation rapid and animated like Italian. Some of the islanders then swam to the boats, and four of them were taken on board and afterwards carried away. On the northern coasts of the island, which were much better cultivated than the southern, there were a great number of little houses, fig trees and other trees, palm trees which bore no fruit, and gardens with cabbages and other vegetables. Here twenty-five of the sailors landed, and found nearly thirty men quite naked, who took to flight when they saw their arms. The buildings were made with much skill of square stones, covered with large and handsome pieces of wood. Finding several of them closed, the sailors broke open the doors with stones, which enraged the fugitives, who filled the air with their cries. The houses were found to contain nothing beyond some excellent dried figs, preserved in palm baskets, like those made at Cesena, corn of a much finer quality than the Italian, not only in the length and thickness of its grain but its extreme whiteness, some barley and other grains. The houses

were all very handsome and covered with very fine wood, and as clean inside as if they had been white-washed. The sailors also came upon a chapel or temple, in which there were no pictures or ornament, but only a stone statue representing a man with a ball in his hand. This idol, otherwise naked, wore an apron of palm-leaves. They took it away and carried it to Lisbon. The island seemed to be thickly peopled and well cultivated ; producing not only corn and other grain, but fruits, principally figs. The natives either ate the grain like birds, or else made it into flour, and ate it with water without kneading. On leaving this island they saw several others, at the distance of five, ten, twenty, or forty miles, and made for a third, in which they remarked nothing but an immense number of beautiful trees shooting straight up to the skies [most probably Ferro, remarkable for its magnificent pines]. Thence to another, which abounded in streams of excellent water and wood [Gomera]. They found also many wild pigeons, which they killed with sticks and stones. They were larger and of better flavour than those in Italy. Falcons and birds of prey were numerous. The sailors ventured but a very little way into the country. At length they discovered another island, the rocky mountains of which were of immense height and almost always covered with clouds, but what they could see during the clear weather seemed very agreeable, and it appeared to be inhabited [Palma]. They afterwards saw other islands, making in all thirteen, some of them inha-

bited and some not, and the further they went the more they saw. They remarked the smoothness of the sea which separates these islands, and found good anchorage, although there were but few harbours, but all the islands were well provided with water. Of the thirteen islands five were inhabited, but some were much more populous than others.[1] The languages of these people were said to be so different, that those of one island did not understand those of another, and they had no means of communication except by swimming. A phenomenon which they witnessed on one of these islands [Teneriffe] deterred them from landing. On the summit of a mountain which they reckoned to be more than thirty thousand feet high they observed what from its whiteness looked like a fortress. It was, however, nothing but a sharp point of rock, on the top of which was a mast, as large as a ship's mast, with a yard and a lateen sail set upon it. The sail when blown out by the wind took the form of a shield, and soon afterwards it would seem to be lowered, together with the mast, as if on board a vessel, then again it was raised and again would sink, and so alternately.

"They sailed round the island, but on all sides they saw the same phenomenon, and thinking it the effect of some enchantment, they did not dare to land. They saw many other things also, which

---

[1] Thirteen is correct if the desert islands be added to the seven inhabited ones. Those inhabited are here counted five instead of seven, doubtless from defective exploration.

Niccoloso refused to relate. At any rate the islands do not seem to have been very rich, for the sailors hardly covered the expense of the voyage.

"The four men whom they carried away were young and beardless, and had handsome faces. They wore nothing but a sort of apron made of cord, from which they hung a number of palm or reed fibres of a hair's-breadth and a half or two hairs'-breadth, which formed an effectual covering. They were un-circumcised. Their long light hair veiled their bodies down to the waist, and they went barefooted. The island whence they were taken was called Canary, and was more populous than the others. These men were spoken to in several languages, but they under-stood none of them. They did not exceed their captors in stature, but they were robust of limb, courageous, and very intelligent. When spoken to by signs they replied in the same manner, like mutes. There were marks of deference shown from one to another; but one of them appeared more honoured than the rest. The apron of this chief was of palm leaves, while the others wore reeds painted in yellow and red. They sang very sweetly, and danced almost as well as Frenchmen. They were gay and merry, and much more civilised than many Spaniards. When they were brought on board, they ate some bread and figs, and seemed to like the bread, though they had never tasted it before. They absolutely refused wine, and only drank water. Wheat and barley they ate in plenty, as well as cheese and meat, which was abundant in the islands,

and of good quality, for although there were no oxen, camels, or asses, there were plenty of goats, sheep, and wild hogs. They were shown some gold and silver money, but they were quite ignorant of the use of it; and they knew as little of any kind of spice. Rings of gold and vases of carved work, swords and sabres, were shown to them; but they seemed never to have seen such things, and did not know how to use them. They showed remarkable faithfulness and honesty, for if one of them received anything good to eat, before tasting it, he divided it into portions which he shared with the rest. Marriage was observed among them, and the married women wore aprons like the men, but the maidens went quite naked, without consciousness of shame."

Meanwhile the Prince of Fortune made but little progress towards the acquirement of the royal domain with which the Pope had endowed him. In short, the whole project proved a mere abortion, and neither the treasury of the Pope, the property of Don Luis, nor the knowledge of the geography of the Canaries, were advanced one iota thereby.

The enterprise undertaken a century and a half later by Jean de Bethencourt, of which this volume treats, was of a far more persistent and effectual character. During the century which preceded it, however, the Canaries were exposed to frequent ravages from corsairs and from adventurers of all sorts.

On one occasion chance led to the landing of a party on the Great Canary, which, as it seems to be

referred to in the present work, deserves particular mention. In a MS. account by a Canarian writer, Don Pedro del Castillo (quoted at p. 41 of the *Histoire Naturelle des Iles Canaries,* par MM. Barber Webb and Sabin Berthelot, Paris, 1842, 4to), is recorded an expedition, by Captain Francisco Lopez, from Seville to Galicia, in which his vessel was carried southward by a tempest and took refuge, on June 5th, 1382, at the mouth of the Guiniguada in the Great Canary, where the capital has since been founded. Lopez and twelve of his companions were treated at first with humanity by the natives of this part of the island, and passed seven years peacefully occupied with the care of the flocks that had been granted them. They profited by this enforced sojourn to give Christian instruction to many young Canarians, some of whom had learned the Castilian language ; but suddenly the natives changed their conduct towards them, and killed them all without exception. It seems, however, that before their death the unhappy Spaniards confided a written document to one of their pupils, and there is no doubt that it is this event that Bethencourt's chaplains have mentioned in their history of the first attempt by the Chevalier Gadifer de la Salle upon the Grand Canary (see Chap. XL). A young islander had come on board Gadifer's ship to give him a parchment that was tied round his neck. "We have found," said the chaplains, "the testament of the Christian brothers, thirteen in number, whom they killed twelve years ago, which testament says also that

none ought to trust them for their fair outside demeanour, for they were traitors by nature." There can be little doubt that the party in question was that of Lopez (1382), mentioned by Castillo. It is probable that the mistrust aroused in the Canarians by the relations of their guests with the adventurers who frequented their shores, and the fear of some surprise on the part of the Europeans, determined them to get rid of these strangers, to whom they had shown themselves at first so friendly ; but, according to the historians of the conquest, the Canarian pretence was that the Spaniards had sent letters to the land of the Christians adverse to those with whom they had dwelt for seven years.

M. d'Avezac, in his valuable work on the "Iles d'Afrique," in the *Univers Pittoresque*, tells us that an official document, preserved in the Escurial, and embodying the results of an inquiry instituted in 1476 by Queen Isabelle of Castile as to the respective rights of the various pretenders to the possession of the Canaries, declares formally that Jean de Bethencourt had received information in Normandy respecting these islands from two French adventurers, who had made incursions on them in company with a Spaniard named Alvaro Becerra, and that he was thereby induced to undertake the conquest, of which we will now proceed to give the summary.

Messire Jean de Bethencourt, Lord of Grainville la Teinturière, in the Pais de Caux in Normandy, having conceived the project of conquering the

Canaries, which were then only frequented by merchants or Spanish pirates, assembled a body of adventurers, among whom was a knight named Gadifer
de la Salle, who joined him at Rochelle. M. de
Bethencourt took with him his two chaplains, Brother
Pierre Bontier, a monk of St. Jouin de Marnes, and
Jean le Verrier, a priest, who were the historians of
the expedition. They started from Rochelle on the
1st of May, 1402, putting in at Corunna and at Cadiz,
where they stayed till the month of July, the party
meanwhile becoming reduced by the desertion of
twenty-seven men to only fifty-three in number.
Eight days from Cadiz brought them to the island
of Graciosa; thence they went to Lancerote, where
they were well received and obtained permission to
build a fort, which they named Rubicon. Leaving
Bertin de Berneval in charge, Bethencourt went
with Gadifer to Fuerteventura, but was obliged to
return to Lancerote on account of mutiny among his
sailors and want of provisions.

It was then resolved that Bethencourt should go
to Spain to get together what was necessary to
complete the enterprise. Gadifer remained as lieutenant, and while he was absent at the Isle of Lobos,
Bertin excited disaffection against him, drew together
a faction of his own, with which he pillaged the
castle of Rubicon and took a number of natives
prisoners, including Guadarfia, the King of Lancerote,
who had already made friendly submission to Bethencourt. Two Spanish ships had arrived meanwhile,
and Bertin having gained over Ferdinand Ordoñez,

captain of the *Tranchemar*, took his spoils and prisoners on board, abandoned his ill-fated followers to perish miserably in Africa, and went himself to Spain. The unfortunate Gadifer was left by this treachery in the island of Lobos, without the supplies he expected to follow him, until the captain of the other Spanish ship, the *Morelle*, sent a canoe to his rescue, and he returned to Rubicon. Here he found affairs in a sad state, no provisions, no stores, and an insufficient number of men to keep the natives in check.

Meanwhile Bethencourt was obtaining from Henry III, King of Castille, the supplies he wanted, on condition of doing homage; and having sent home his wife in the charge of Enguerrand de la Boissière, he preferred to return to Lancerote. He had learned the state of affairs on the arrival of the ship *Morelle*, which preceded by a short time the *Tranchemar*, in which the traitor Bertin arrived with his captives, and sent help to Gadifer from the king, with directions to follow up the explorations. During Bethencourt's absence, there had been a rebellion against the King of Lancerote, which had been quelled, and the traitor put to death.

Gadifer had been to Fuerteventura, the Grand Canary, Ferro, Gomera, and Palma, and returned to Rubicon after a voyage of three months. He had sent a ship to Spain with the account of his expedition, but Bethencourt himself now arrived at Rubicon, where he was received with great demonstrations of

joy. He proceeded vigorously with the conquest of the natives, and in a few days the king submitted and asked for baptism, which he received with many of his people. After this, Bethencourt and Gadifer were only withheld from further conquest by want of aid from the courts of France and Spain, though application was made especially to the former. On their return from an expedition to the coast of Africa, Gadifer showed discontent that Bethencourt had not considered his interests when he did homage to the King of Castile for the government of the islands. However, he took part in an expedition against the Grand Canary in 1404, but the dispute was afterwards renewed, and they set out for Spain to settle the question, travelling in different ships. Finally, however, Gadifer, knowing Bethencourt's greater interest at the court of Castile, gave up his own cause in despair, and returned to France. Bethencourt proceeded to Castile and was solemnly invested with the government of the islands. On his return to the Canaries he had several encounters with the natives, but maintained his authority successfully, and the two kings of Fuerteventura, together with their people, became Christian. He then went to France, to obtain the materials for forming a colony, was warmly welcomed at Grainville, and obtained all he required. He returned to Lancerote with his nephew Maciot de Bethencourt, and was received with great joy by his own people, as well as by the inhabitants of Fuerteventura. In October 1405 he set out on his expedition to the Grand Canary, which was unsuccessful from vari-

ous causes; but in Palma and Ferro, after some opposition, he formed colonies. Returning to Lancerote, he arranged everything for the good government of the islands which he had conquered and civilised, and leaving his nephew Maciot as his lieutenant-general, he departed universally regretted. He went thence to Spain, where the king received him warmly and gave him letters of recommendation to the Pope, from whom he was anxious to obtain the appointment of a bishop for the islands. At Rome he was well received by the Pope, who granted all he required. He then returned to France, by way of Florence, where he was fêted by the government. Thence he went to Paris and so to his own house. Here he remained for several years, receiving from the bishop news of the islands and the good government of his nephew, till, as he was preparing to visit them once more, he died at his house of Grainville in 1425.

It will be observed that the text of the MS. places the death of Bethencourt in 1422, but Bergeron, who was not an idle investigator, in fixing the date at 1425, says, "comme il appert par plusieurs actes." So that we may reasonably accept his decision. With respect to the sepulture of Bethencourt, every memento would have been lost in the dim gloom of the past, had it not been for the laudable enthusiasm of a Norman antiquary, the Abbé Cochet, who seems to have been the only man of the age to take an interest in the local glory of the conqueror of the Canaries. Describing his visit to Grainville

in 1831 (see *Les Eglises de l'Arrondissement d'Yvetot,* par M. l'Abbé Cochet, Paris, 1832, tom. i, p. 151), he says, " In the church I looked with eagerness for the name of the hero whose memory had led my steps to the spot. To my sorrow I found not a single word, a single stone that spoke to me of him. His very name had perished from the traditions of the old gossips of the place, and there remained but a vague memory of his greatness, which faded like a distant echo. From that moment I resolved to labour at the restitution of that great memory, and I have had the happiness to convert the thought into a reality. At my request, supported by the Commission des Antiquités, M. E. Leroy, the honoured and enlightened Prefect of the Seine Inférieure, was pleased to grant a sum of two hundred francs from the historical funds (sur les fonds historiques) of his Department. With this small sum, managed with prudence, I have been able to have a commemorative inscription, surmounted by the arms of Bethencourt, made by Caulier, a sculptor at Dieppe. A black marble slab, embedded in a carved stone frame, bears the following inscription in gilt letters—

A LA MEMOIRE

DE JEHAN

DE BETHENCOURT

NAVIGATEUR CÉLÈBRE

ET ROI DES CANARIES

INHUMÉ DANS LE CHŒUR

DE CETTE EGLISE

EN 1425.

PRIEZ DIEU POUR LUI.

With the authorisation of the Building Committee of Grainville and the permission of the Archbishop of Rouen and of the minister of public worship, this inscription was placed on one of the pilasters of the choir on the 16th of December, 1851."

There is much of picturesque beauty about the quaint old narrative of the adventures of the Sire de Bethencourt. We find ourselves in an atmosphere of romance, albeit the story is most essentially true. The mind's eye becomes familiar with the habergeon, the corslet, and the pennon, and the mind's ear—an organ, by the way, too little recognised—with the sound of the clarion and trumpet as realities which lend the charm of chivalry to an expedition of dis- covery undertaken at a period when chivalry was itself a reality. Of the manor-house of Grainville la Teinturière, in the lovely valley of the Durdent, there remain only a moat filled with water, a vaulted cell, which was doubtless the donjon, and an old gate covered with ivy, seen by the Abbé Cochet in 1831, but which probably by this time has disappeared also.

Here it will be interesting to note the account given of the Canaries a few years later by Gomez Eannes de Azurara, who, in 1448, drew up a narra- tive of the conquest of Guinea under the direction of Prince Henry the Navigator. It was compiled from the rough narrative of one of Prince Henry's sailors, Affonso de Cerreira, and consequently, though we do not know the exact year, was some time earlier than the date of Azurara's chronicle.

In 1443 an expedition of six caravels, formed un-

der the auspices of the Prince, explored the Bay of Arguin and part of the neighbouring coasts, two of which separated and turned northward. On their way they met with the caravel of Alvaro Gonzalves de Atayde, the captain of which was one João de Castilha, going to Guinea, whom they dissuaded from that voyage, and induced him to join them in an expedition to the island of Palma. On reaching Gomera they were well received, and two chieftains of the island, named Bruco and Piste, after announcing themselves as grateful servants of Prince Henry, from whom they had received the most generous hospitality, declared their readiness to do anything to serve him. The Portuguese told them they were bound to the island of Palma for the purpose of capturing some of the natives, and a few of the chieftain's subjects would be of great use as guides and assistants, where both the country and the people's mode of fighting were alike unknown. Piste immediately offered to accompany them, and to take as many Canarians as they pleased, and with this help they set sail for Palma, which they reached a little before daybreak. Unsuitable as the hour might seem, they immediately landed, and presently saw some of the natives fleeing, but, as they were starting in pursuit, one of the men suggested that they would have a better chance of taking some shepherds, chiefly boys and women, whom they saw keeping their sheep and goats among the rocks. These drove their flocks into a valley that was so deep and dangerous that it was a wonder that they

could make their way at all. The islanders were naturally sure-footed to a wonderful degree, but several of them fell from the crags and were killed. The page Diogo Gonsalves, who had been the first to swim to the shore in the encounter near Tider, again distinguished himself. It was hard work for the Portuguese, for the Canarians hurled stones and lances with sharp horn points at them with great strength and precision. The contest ended in the capture of seventeen Canarians, men and women. One of the latter was of extraordinary size for a woman, and they said that she was the queen of a part of the island. In retiring to the boats with their capture they were closely followed by the Canarians, and were obliged to leave the greater part of the cattle that they had had so much trouble in taking.

On their return to Gomera they thanked the island chieftain for the good service he had rendered them, and afterwards, when Piste, with some of the islanders, went to Portugal, they were so well received by the Prince that he and some of his followers remained for the rest of their lives.

As João de Castilha, the captain of the caravel of Gonsalvez de Atayde, had not reached Guinea as the others had done, and consequently had less booty than they to carry back to Portugal, he conceived the dastardly idea of capturing some of the Gomerans, in spite of the pledge of security. As it seemed too hideous a piece of treachery to seize any of those who had helped them so well, he removed to another

port, where some twenty-one of the natives, trusting to the Portuguese, came on board the caravel and were straightway carried to Portugal. When the Prince heard of it he was extremely angry, and had the Canarians brought to his house, and with rich presents sent them back to their own country.

Alvaro Dornellas, after an unsuccessful attempt to make a capture in the Canary Islands, which resulted in his only taking two captives, remained at the islands, not caring to return to Lisbon without more booty. He sent Affonso Marta to Madeira to procure stores by the sale of the two Canarians. The weather prevented Marta making the island, and he was obliged to put in at Lisbon, where at that time was João Dornellas, squire to the king, and cousin to Alvaro. João had a joint interest in the caravel, and hearing of his cousin's difficulties, hastened to his assistance. Together they made a descent upon the island of Palma, having obtained help from the people of Gomera in the name of Prince Henry, and in a night attack, after a fierce encounter, took twenty captives. They returned to Gomera, where Alvaro had to remain, and his cousin left for Portugal. In the homeward passage, such a dearth of victuals supervened that they were well-nigh compelled to eat some of their captives, but happily, before they were driven to that extremity, they reached the port of Tavila, in the kingdom of Algarve.

It has been already seen that Jean de Bethencourt, retiring to France in 1406, had left his nephew,

Maciot de Bethencourt, as governor-general of his conquests in the Canaries, comprising Lancerote, Forteventura, and Ferro. Azurara gives the Christian population of Lancerote, Fuerteventura, and Ferro, in his time, as follows: "In Lancerote sixty men, in Fuerteventura eighty, and in Ferro twelve. They had their churches and priests.

"In the Pagan islands the numbers were, in Gomera[1] about seven hundred men, in Palma five hundred, in Teneriffe six thousand bearing arms, and in the Great Canary five thousand fighting men. These had never been conquered, but some of their people had been taken, who gave information respecting their customs.

"The Great Canary was ruled by two kings and a duke, who were elected, but the real governors of the island were an assembly of knights, who were not to be less than one hundred and ninety, nor so many as two hundred, and whose numbers were filled up by election from the sons of their own class. The people were intelligent, but little worthy of trust; they were very active and powerful. Their only weapons were a short club and the stones with which their country abounded, and which supplied them also with building materials. Most of them went entirely naked, but some wore petticoats of palm leaves. They made no account of the precious metals, but set a high value on iron, which they worked with stones and made into fishing-hooks;

[1] Maciot attempted, with the assistance of some Castilians, to subdue the island of Gomera, but without success.

they even used stones for shaving.   They had abundance of sheep, pigs, and goats, and their infants were
generally suckled by the latter.   They had wheat,
but had not the skill to make bread, and ate the
meal with meat and butter.   They had plenty of
figs, dragon's-blood, and dates, but not of a good
quality, and some useful herbs.   They held it an
abomination to kill animals, and employed Christian
captives as butchers when they could get them.
They kindled fire by rubbing one stick against another.
They believed in a God who would reward and
punish, and some of them called themselves Christians.

" The people of Gomera were less civilised.   They
had no clothing, no houses.   Their women were
regarded almost as common property, for it was a
breach of hospitality for a man not to offer his wife
to a visitor by way of welcome.   They made their
sisters' sons their heirs.   They had a few pigs and
goats, but lived chiefly on milk, herbs, and roots,
like the beasts ; they also ate filthy things, such as
rats and vermin.   They spent their time chiefly in
singing and dancing, for they had to make no exertion to gain their livelihood.   They believed in a
God, but were not taught obedience to any law.
The fighting men were seven hundred in number,
over whom was a captain with certain other officers.

" In Teneriffe the people were much better off,
and more civilised.   They had plenty of wheat and
vegetables, and abundance of pigs, sheep, and goats,
and were dressed in skins.   They had, however,
no houses, but passed their lives in huts and caves.

Their chief occupation was war, and they fought with lances of pine-wood, made like great darts, very sharp, and hardened in the fire. There were eight or nine tribes, each of which had two kings, one dead and one living, for they had the strange custom of keeping the dead king unburied till his successor died and took his place : the body was then thrown into a pit. They were strong and active men, and had their own wives, and lived more like men than some of the other islanders. They believed in the existence of a God.

" The people of Palma had neither bread nor vegetables, but lived on mutton, milk, and herbs ; they did not even take the trouble to catch fish like the other islanders. They fought with spears like the men of Teneriffe, but pointed them with sharp horn instead of iron, and at the other end they also put another piece of horn, but not so sharp as that at the point. They had some chiefs who were called kings. They had no knowledge of God, nor any faith whatever."

The following is the account given half a century after the date of Bethencourt's conquest, by the Venetian Alvise Cadamosto, who, in 1455, visited them while in the service of Prince Henry the Navigator.

" Four of them," he says, " Lancerote, Fuerteventura, Gomera, and Ferro, were inhabited by Christians ; the other three, Grand Canary, Teneriffe, and Palma, by pagans. The governor of the former was a knight named Herrera, a native of Seville, and a subject of

d

the King of Spain. They had barley-bread, goats'-flesh, and milk in plenty, for goats were very numerous; they had no wine nor corn, except what was imported, and the islands produced but little fruit. There were great numbers of wild asses, especially in the island of Ferro. Great quantities of orchil for dyeing were sent from these islands to Cadiz and Seville, and thence to other parts both east and west. The chief products were goats'-leather, very good and strong, tallow, and excellent cheeses. The inhabitants of the four Christian islands spoke.different languages, so that they could with difficulty understand each other. There were no fortified places in them, only villages; but the inhabitants had retreats in the mountains, to which the passes were so difficult that they could not be taken except by a siege. Of the three islands inhabited by pagans, two were the largest and most populous of the group, viz., the Grand Canary, in which were about eight or nine thousand inhabitants, and Teneriffe, the largest of all, which contained from fourteen to fifteen thousand. Palma was not so well peopled, being smaller, but a very beautiful island. The Christians have never been able to subdue these three islands, as there were plenty of men of arms to defend them, and the mountain heights were difficult of access. Teneriffe, of whose peak Cadamosto speaks as being visible, according to some sailors' accounts, at a distance of two hundred and fifty Italian miles, and sixty miles high from the foot to the summit, was governed by nine chiefs, bearing

the title of dukes, who did not obtain the succession
by inheritance, but by force. Their weapons were
stones, and javelins pointed with sharpened horn instead of iron, and sometimes the wood itself hardened
by fire till it was as hard as iron itself. The inhabitants went naked, except some few who wore goats'-
skins. They anointed their bodies with goats'-fat
mixed with the juice of certain herbs, to harden
their skins and defend them from cold, although the
climate is mild. They also painted their bodies with
the juice of herbs, green, red, and yellow, producing
beautiful devices, and in this manner showed their
individual character, much as civilised people do by
their style of dress. They were wonderfully strong
and active, could take enormous leaps, and throw
with great strength and skill. They dwelt in caverns
in the mountains. Their food was barley, goats'-
flesh, and milk, which was plentiful. They had some
fruits, chiefly figs, and the climate was so warm that
they gathered in their harvest in March or April.
They had no fixed religion, but some worshipped the
sun, some the moon, and others the planets, with
various forms of idolatry. The women were not
taken in common among them, but each man might
have as many wives as he liked. No maiden, however, was taken till she had passed a night with the
chief, which was held a great honour. These accounts
were had from Christians of the four islands, who
would occasionally go to Teneriffe by night and
carry off men and women, whom they sent to Spain
to be sold as slaves. It sometimes happened that

d 2

the Christians were captured in these expeditions,
but the natives, instead of killing them, thought it
sufficient punishment to make them butcher their
goats, and skin them, and cut them up, an occupation which they looked upon as the most degrading
that a man could be put to; and at this work they
kept them till they might be able to obtain their
ransom. Another of their customs was, that when
one of their chiefs came into possession of his estate,
some one among them would offer himself to die in
honour of the festival. On the day appointed they
assembled in a deep valley, when, after certain
ceremonies had been performed, the self-devoted
victim of this hideous custom threw himself from a
great height into the valley, and was dashed to
pieces. The chief was held bound in gratitude to do
the victim great honour, and to reward his family
with ample gifts." Cadamosto was told of this in-
human custom, not only by the natives, but also by
Christians who had been kept prisoners in the island.
Cadamosto visited the islands of Gomera and Ferro,
and also touched at Palma, but did not land, because
he was anxious to continue his voyage.

In 1414, the exactions and tyranny of Maciot de
Bethencourt had caused Queen Catherine of Castile
to send out three war caravels under the command
of Pedro Barba de Campos, Lord of Castro Forte, to
control him. Maciot, although only regent, for Jean
de Bethencourt was still alive, ceded the islands to
Barba and then sailed to Madeira, where he sold to
Prince Henry of Portugal, surnamed the Navigator,

these very islands of which he had just made cession
to another, together with those which still remained to
be conquered. Maciot subsequently sold them to the
Spanish Count de Niebla. Pedro Barba de Campos
sold them to Fernando Perez of Seville, and the latter
again to the aforesaid Count de Niebla, who disposed
of them to Guillem de las Casas, and the latter to
his son-in-law Fernam Peraza. Meanwhile, the legitimate proprietor, Jean de Bethencourt, left them
by will to his brother Reynaud. But as yet there
still remained unconquered the Great Canary, Palma,
Teneriffe, and the small islands about Lancerote,
and, in 1424, Prince Henry sent out a fleet under
the command of Fernando de Castro, with two
thousand five hundred infantry and a hundred and
twenty horse, to effect the conquest of the whole of
the islands ; but the expense entailed thereby, combined with the expostulations of the King of Castile,
caused him to withdraw for a time from the undertaking.

Subsequently, in the year 1446, he resumed his
efforts at this conquest, but before taking any step
he applied to his brother, Dom Pedro, who was then
regent, to give him a charter prohibiting all Portuguese subjects from going to the Canary Islands,
either for purposes of war or commerce, except by
his orders. This charter was conceded, with a further
grant of a fifth of all imports from those islands.
The concession was made in consideration of the
great expenses which the Prince had incurred. In
the following year, 1447, the Prince conferred the

chief captaincy of the island of Lancerote on Antam Gonsalves, who went out to enforce his claim; but unfortunately, Azurara, from whom we derive this date, and who, as it was very near the period of his writing, would be little likely to be in error, fails to tell us the result of Gonsalves' expedition. If we were to follow Barros and the Spanish historians, the date of this expedition would be much earlier. Be this as it may, when, in 1455, King Henry IV of Castile was married to Joanna, the youngest daughter of Dom Duarte, King of Portugal, Dom Martinho de Atayde, Count d'Atouguia, who escorted the Princess to Castile, received from King Henry the Canary Islands as an honorary donation. De Atayde sold them to the Marques de Menesco, who again sold them to Dom Fernando, Prince Henry's nephew and adopted son. In 1466 Dom Fernando sent out a new expedition under Diogo da Silva, but if we are to believe Viera y Clavijo, it was as unfortunate as its predecessors. But meanwhile, at the death of Fernam Peraza, his daughter Iñez, who had married Diogo Garcia de Herrera, inherited her father's rights in the Canaries, and one of her daughters married Diogo da Silva. Still Spain maintained its claims, and it was not till 1479, when, on the 4th of September, the treaty of peace was signed at Alcaçova, between Affonso V of Portugal and Ferdinand and Isabella of Castile, that the disputes of the two nations on this point were settled. The sixth article of that treaty (Torre do Tombo, Gav. 17, Maç. 6, n.

16) provided that the conquests from Cape Non to the Indies, with the seas and islands adjacent, should remain in possession of the Portuguese, but the Canaries and Granada should belong to the Castilians. An ethnological examination of the inhabitants of the Canaries at the time of Bethencourt's conquest, as based upon the descriptions of their persons and manners, the peculiarities of their languages and the characteristics of the mummies which have been found, leaves little reason to doubt that the archipelago was peopled by two distinct races, viz., Berbers and Arabs, and that the tribes of the latter, which were in the minority in the western islands, had maintained the superiority in numbers and gained political supremacy in the eastern. The chaplains describe the natives of Lancerote and Fuerteventura as tall. Those of Great Canary and of Palma seem to have been of middle stature. The people of Gomera and Ferro are described by Galindo as small, while the mummies of the Guanches of Teneriffe show that they did not much exceed the latter in height. The natives of Lancerote and Fuerteventura had very brown complexions, while most of the inhabitants of Canary, Teneriffe, Gomera, Palma, and Ferro were more or less fair, or even quite blonde. In Lancerote, and perhaps in Fuerteventura, polyandry existed, and a woman would often have as many as three husbands ; while in the other islands monogamy was strictly maintained by law. The inhabitants of Fuerteventura buried their dead

*

in stone tombs. Those of Great Canary enclosed theirs in mounds of a conical or pyramidal shape. The Guanches of Teneriffe and of Palma embalmed the bodies of their relatives or simply deposited them in sepulchral caverns.

The archipelago presented also great variety in the form of government. In the east, despotism and hereditary right, without distinction of sex, prevailed. In the west, women were entirely excluded from authority, and there existed a sort of aristocratic republicanism, in which authority was recognised and religiously preserved in certain families, but yet subjected, as each event occurred, to the sanction of a privileged body. The territory of the tribe was a sort of common patrimony, of which each member cultivated his own part and enjoyed the proceeds, but the administration belonged only to the chief. Veneration for age and submission to the experience of the head of the family was the principle which underlay this system of government.

Don Antonio de Viana, who published in 1604 at Seville a work on the *Antiguedades de las Islas Canarias*, gives the following faithful summary of the characteristics of the Guanches. He says—"They were virtuous, honest, and brave, and the finest qualities of humanity were found united in them: to wit, magnanimity, skill, courage, athletic powers, strength of soul and of body, pride of character, nobleness of demeanour, a smiling physiognomy, an intelligent mind, and patriotic devotedness."

Bontier and Le Verrier, however, dwelt much

more upon the doings of the Norman baron and the adventurers whom he had brought in his suite than on the history of the conquered people themselves. Their narrative treats of successes obtained in this first invasion, of the occupation of Lancerote, Fuerteventura, and Ferro, of the different excursions of the Normans in other parts of the archipelago, of an expedition of the conqueror to the coast of Africa,[1] and of his voyages to Europe. The two authors speak at length of the quarrels of the adventurers, of their combats with the natives, and of the system of administration established by Bethencourt in the conquered islands. One of them, Father Bontier, who, as we have said, was a Franciscan monk of St. Jouin de Marnes, officiated at Lancerote in the church of St. Martial de Rubicon, which Bethencourt had built in the castle of that name. The second, Le Verrier, who was a priest, was installed first at Fuerteventura, as vicar in the chapel of Ste. Marie de Bethencourt, and returned afterwards to France with his lord, whom he attended at his death-bed as his chaplain. The MS. record of their recollections, begun in 1402 and finished in 1406, seems to have been written by Bontier and finished by Le Verrier, for Bontier says, on the last page, in speaking of his companion, "Messire Jean le Verrier, his chaplain (Bethencourt's), whom he had taken to and from the Canary Isles, wrote his will, and was with him all the time of his last illness"; so that it would seem highly

---

[1] This excursion, described on pp. 180-181, is, among others, the basis of the claim referred to on p. 1 of this Introduction.

probable that the latter would record that of which he was the eye-witness. The MS. was brought to light by Galien de Bethencourt, Councillor of the parliament of Rouen, and edited in Paris, in 1630, by Bergeron, whose opinion on the merits of this work is stated in the following terms in a *Traicté des Navigations* printed at the end of his edition, a learned and valuable piece of labour, but not free from inaccuracies. "With regard to this history, written according to the ignorance and simplicity of the time, it seems better to leave it in its rude and *naïve*, but sufficiently intelligible language, than to turn it into a more elegant form, as this gives one more confidence in its truth than all that one could now say. It has been taken from an ancient MS. made at the time, well painted and illuminated, and preserved in the library of M. de Bethencourt, which he has been so good as to communicate to the public, an act for which he deserves the gratitude of all, on account of the interest that France must take in it."

And here it will be well that we make some inquiry into the antecedents and personal history of this Norman gentleman, in whose doings it was so justly said that "France must take an interest." Messire Jean de Bethencourt, Knight, was of noble birth, and held the title of Baron in right of the Barony of St. Martin le Gaillard in the Comté d'Eu, where he had a strong castle, which was taken and retaken several times in the wars with England. Monstrelet speaks of its final siege and ruin in 1419. It came by inheritance to Messire de Bethen-

court from his grandmother Dame Isabeau de St. Martin. The earliest of his ancestors of whom we find mention was Philippe, Seigneur de Bethencourt and de St. Vincent de Rouvray, Knight, of the time of Louis VIII, who was buried in the church of the Priory of Sigy, where his tomb, and those of others of the family of yet older date, had been seen, as Bergeron tells us, by persons living in his time, that is, in the early part of the seventeenth century, but were demolished in the civil wars. This Philippe was the father of Regnault de Bethencourt, lord of the same places, as recorded in a Latin charter of the year 1282. Regnault was the father of Jean I, mentioned in a deed of exchange of the date of 1346, which latter married the above-mentioned Isabeau de St. Martin, by whom he had Jean II, as shown by other deeds of exchange of the date of 1358. Jean I perished at Honfleur in the company of Marshal de Clermont about the year 1357, and his widow married Mathieu de Bracquemont. Jean II married, in 1358, Madame Marie, daughter of Messire Regnault de Bracquemont,[1] who died in the affair at Cocherel, in 1364, in the company of Messire Bertrand du Guesclin. The offspring of this marriage were Jean III, the conqueror of the Canaries, and Messire Regnault de Bethencourt, surnamed

[1] Marie de Bracquemont's brother Robert became greatly renowned in the histories of France and Spain, and was made Admiral of France in 1418 ; and it was to him that his nephew, the subject of the present story, mortgaged his lands of Bethencourt and Grainville, apparently for the very purpose of fitting out the expedition here treated of.

Morelet or Moreau. The hero of the present history was Lord of Grainville la Teinturière, and of other lands mentioned in this narrative, viz., Bethencourt, St. Saire, Lincourt, Riville, Grand Quesnoy, Huqueleu, St. Martin, etc. His wife was of the house of Fayel, in Champagne. They had no offspring; and an indiscreet, though perfectly innocent, word from Madame de Bethencourt with reference to her brother-in-law, Messire Regnault de Bethencourt, produced an estrangement between her and her husband, whose jealous cruelty would seem to have brought about her early death, while a feeling of revenge led him to impoverish as far as possible the property to which his brother would be the successor. It is but justice to say that before his death he saw his error, and on his death-bed was anxious to declare his repentance to the brother whom he had injured. Regnault became his successor, and from him and his second wife, Philipote de Troyes (his first wife having been Marie de Breauté, Dame de Rouvray), are descended all the Bethencourts of Normandy; and if, as is to be supposed, Maciot de Bethencourt was one of his sons, from him also must be descended all those of the name in Spain, the Azores, the Madeira group, and the Canaries. Regnault's lineal descendant in the seventh generation was Galien de Bethencourt, Councillor of the Court of Parliament of Rouen, and to him it is that we are indebted for the first publication of the present narrative, in 1630. The editor, Pierre Bergeron, tells us, as we have said, that "it is derived from an ancient manuscript,

made at the time, well painted and illuminated, which is preserved in the library of Monsieur de Bethencourt, Councillor of the Parliament of Rouen," and to him the work is dedicated. From him, also, Bergeron states that he received communication of several memoirs concerning this history, the genealogy of the Bethencourts, as well as the originals of the letters from the Bethencourts of the Canaries.

And now that I come to speak of the text of this work, I have to acknowledge a debt of gratitude which would leave me utterly bankrupt, if I had not learnt from experience that a simple statement of facts is a thousand times more eloquent than the most fervid expression of sentiment, however sincere. Being aware that M. E. Charton, in his *Voyageurs anciens et modernes,* Paris, 1855, 8vo, had had the advantage of seeing an early MS. of this narrative belonging to Madame de Mont Ruffet, who appears to have inherited the volume through the channel of family relationship with the Bethencourts, I applied to my distinguished and much honoured friend, M. d'Avezac, Membre de l'Institut, in the hope that he might be able to borrow it also. Happily, Madame de Mont Ruffet proved to be a friend of M. d'Avezac's of old standing, and the MS. was kindly entrusted to his care; but as, on the occasion of a previous loan, this valuable document appears to have been not too gently dealt with, Madame de Mont Ruffet very naturally limited her present most obliging act of kindness to M. d'Avezac's retention of the volume in his own custody, and her permission

that photographs of two out of the numerous drawings
which illustrate the volume might be made for the
purposes of the present edition. This was a great
step gained, but with the above very reasonable
embargo laid upon the employment of the MS., the
result would have been but small, had it not been
for such an exertion of friendship and of literary
zeal on the part of M. d'Avezac as I, for one, never
hope to find equalled in all my experience. Seventy
winters had not sufficiently cooled the generous
blood of this venerable *savant*, the Humboldt of
France, to deter him from the *improbus labor* of
collating the whole of the manuscript with the text
of Bergeron. This collation, written minutely in
lines at distances of less than the eighth of an inch,
and in a hand so firm and clear that I have never
had to doubt the meaning of a single stroke, is a
curiosity of caligraphy. The neatness of the writing
is suggestive of the carefulness of the collation.
Circumstances, which from motives of delicacy I
refrain from describing, gave to this laborious act of
kindness to myself a character of the noblest gene-
rosity. The Hakluyt Society has only to do with
the result, and their thanks are due to M. d'Avezac
for the opportunity of issuing an edition of Bethencourt freed from the modifications of the ancient
edition; but I may be forgiven if I avail myself of
the opportunity to say that the friendship *talis
tantique viri* is one of the events in my life of which
I have the greatest reason to be proud.

Nor is this collation all for which I have to thank

M. d'Avezac. No item of information has he left unexamined or undescribed for my guidance, and all the following facts are from his pen.

The manuscript in Madame de Mont Ruffet's possession is in a volume thirty *centimètres* high and twenty broad, bound in wood, with a dark tawny gauffered cover. It has leather clasps with stamped brass clips, and there are four protruding bands at the back. Under the one cover are two works. 1. The Bethencourt MS. 2. A copy of a book (so says the explicit) without date, printed for Antoine Verard, and of which the following is the very instructive title :—" C'est le livre de la compilacion faicte par celluy qui point ne veult que gloire ne louenge len luy donne, pour son rude entendement et insuffisance, etc." The Bethencourt MS. consists of eighty-eight leaves, the first forty-eight of which have in the filigrane a unicorn passant, placed across waterlines ; the following forty have in the filigrane the well known mark of the ox's head surmounted with a starred flower between the horns. The handwriting, which is unequal both as to carefulness and the distances of the lines, seems in one hand from the beginning down to the rest of leaf 83, where the text closes with what Bergeron reads as 1425 (the date of M. de Bethencourt's death), but which to M. d'Avezac has the appearance of 1422 (mil cccc et xxij). After which follow the words—" Cest livre est a Jehan de Bethencourt Escuier seigneur De bethencourt." The five following leaves, which are devoted to genealogical notices, are in different hands and of different

dates, but the first three pages appear to be in the
same hand as the body of the MS., except that on
the third recto of leaf 85 there are interlinear and
marginal additions made later. The latest date
written by the first hand is the 2nd September,
1482, the date of the birth of the fourth child of
Jean IV de Bethencourt; at the birth of the fifth
child, on the 12th September, 1485, the ink is no
longer the same, and the writing, though perhaps
by the same hand, showed signs of the lapse of a
considerable time. Similar shades of difference between the fifth and the sixth, and again between
the sixth and the seventh, and still more between
the seventh and the eighth. From this circumstance,
of all the first four entries of birth being in one
hand, and that the same as the body of the MS.,
M. d'Avezac concludes that the MS. was executed,
or at any rate finished, as far as the recto of leaf 85,
at a date very little later than the 2nd September,
1482, when the head of the family was Jean IV, son
of Regnault and nephew of Jean III, the conqueror
of the Canaries. Without detailing the intervening
genealogical entries, it will suffice to state that the
most recent addition is a marginal note on the recto
of leaf 85, but undated, which mentions Galien de
Bethencourt, Councillor of the Parliament of Rouen,
who was possessor of the MS. when Bergeron had it
placed in his hands somewhat before 1630. The
distribution of the chapters in the original MS. does
not agree with that adopted by Bergeron, who,
moreover, has altered the headings of many of them.

M. d'Avezac, with the considerate purpose of giving me as the editor the most perfect acquaintance with the differences between the original MS. and Bergeron's edition, has supplied me with a most painstaking and elaborate detail of all the specialities of the former. I cannot speak too gratefully of the conscientiousness which, with this object in view, inspired the execution of so great an amount of hard work, rendered charming by that zealous interest in minute details which could only come from, or be appreciated by, a genuine antiquary. I do not however think it needful to lay before the reader more than a summary of that which was thus fully written for my own enlightenment.

In the original MS. there occurred, at places where no headings or titles were supplied, "coupures" or divisions in the chapters, as if suggestive of new chapters being there intended. The rubricated titles in the original were of the same period as the body of the MS., although, like the illuminated capitals, inserted subsequently, and often in spaces insufficiently large. These titles are numbered up to Chapter L inclusive, but the numbering is evidently a later addition, probably by Galien de Bethencourt, whose handwriting M. d'Avezac thinks he recognises therein. But this brings me to speak of another manuscript document connected with the edition prepared in 1625 by Galien de Bethencourt, but published only in 1630 under the editorial care of Pierre Bergeron. It is written on paper folio size and covered with parchment. It had passed in 1732 from the Coislin

Library (*olim* Segueriana) to that of St. Germain des Prés, whence it migrated at the Revolution to the National Library, where it bears the No. 18629 among the French MSS. It is a series of notes and accessory pieces, which Bergeron appears to have thought useless, as he says nothing of them; fourteen pieces of verse in Latin, French, and Greek, addressed generally " nobilissimo clarissimoque Viro Domino de Bethencourt, Senatus Rothomagensis Consiliario Regio," and beginning with a sextuple acrostic on the theme " Galenus Bethencurtius," in twenty verses, each of which repeats six times his initial letter, "Grande Genus Graio Generate Galene Galerio," and so on. Pro totâ operis votivâ dedicatione Exachrosticon (*sic*). The author of most of these pieces is D. D. Petrus Quevilly, Rector of the church of Le Bosguérard.

After the twelve leaves devoted to this poetical garland, formerly so much in fashion, follow five leaves, bearing above the left border the title, "Suitte des chapitres de l'Histoire." And here is an important point to notice : Bergeron, altering the original series of chapters and their titles after his own ideas, numbered them up to 93, while Galien de Bethencourt in this document makes them tally with the original MS., and, continuing the numbers (interrupted at No. 50 in the MS.), reaches a total of only 87 numbered chapters. He does not fail, however, to take scrupulous account of the "coupures," some of which Bergeron had entirely disregarded. The result is, that chapters 52, 56, 63, 74, 76, 80,

84 of Bergeron, are in the MS. 52, 55, 61, 71, 72, 76, 80, each in two parts, of which the first only bears a number, and thus chapter 93 of Bergeron is chapter 87 and last of the MS. In compliance with a suggestion of M. d'Avezac, however, I have paid regard to every "coupure" in the original MS., restored the titles to their original form and place, as supplied to me by him, and, in the few places where titles were wanting, have supplied them in the concisest form possible, enclosing them in brackets to prevent any mistake as to their origin. The following table will show the mutual correspondence in the numeration of the chapters adopted respectively by M. d'Avezac, Bergeron, and Galien de Bethencourt, A standing for the first, B for the second, and G for the third. It must be premised that all three are in unison with respect to chapters 5 to 51 inclusive. These chapters therefore are omitted. With Bergeron's edition in hand, it is hoped that the bibliographer, who takes an interest in the matter, will be enabled by the table clearly to recognise the modifications in each case.

A.	B.	G.	A.	B.	G.	A.	B.	G.	A.	B.	G.
1	1 a	...	61	61	59	74	74	71a	87	85	80b
2	1 b + 2 a	...	62	62	60	75	75	71b	88	86	81
3	2 b + 3	...	63	63	61a	76	76a	72a	89	87	82
4	4	...	64	64	61b	77	76b	72b	90	88	83
52	52	52a	65	65	62	78	77	73	91	89	84
53	53	52b	66	66	63	79	78	74	92	90	85
54	54	53	67	67	64	80	79	75	93	91	86a
55	55	54	68	68	65	81	80a	76a	94	92	86b
56	56	55a	69	69	66	82	80b	76b	95	93a	87a
57	57	55b	70	70	67	83	81	77	96	93b	87b
58	58	56	71	71	68	84	82	78	97	93c	87c
59	59	57	72	72	69	85	83	79			
60	60	58	73	73	70	86	84	80a			

The collation of the text which M. d'Avezac has
made does not profess to be literal, but only verbal ;
and, although in the first instance he had not
anticipated that our Society would care to print the
foreign text concurrently with the English version,
I was happy to find that, in spite of the absence of
absolute literal revision, the plan met with his strong
approval. Speaking of the orthography of the original, he says, "It is very variable, and often faulty.
To meet the requirements of some hypercritical philo-
logists, it would be requisite to reproduce the MS.
scrupulously with all its varieties and orthographical
errors. I do not share that opinion, and think it
wiser to hold a uniform orthography, derived from
the most frequent and best established examples in
the MS. ; although for the proper names I would
retain exactly the different spellings employed." In
conforming practically to these suggestions, I have
not simply acted from deference to M. d'Avezac, but
from entire concurrence with his judgment.

And here I may reasonably be asked why this manuscript, executed in 1482, or thereabouts, should be described as original, when the events recorded took place
nearly sixty years earlier. It must be granted that
the expression should be used in a modified sense.
This MS. is the *earliest fair transcript* of the original
rough draft of the narrative of Bethencourt's chaplains. It may well be conceived that that rough
draft, precious indeed as it would be if it could be
found, having been drawn up in the actual course of
the expedition, and consequently under circumstances

the most unfavourable, would exhibit but little of the symmetry, beauty, and dignity, which we should look for in a monumental record of a great achievement. We may also venture on a shrewd guess that Regnault de Bethencourt, the successor of the conqueror, who had been left an impoverished inheritance as the consequence of his brother's unmerited jealousy and revenge, would have but little heart, and perhaps less means, for the indulgence of the *dilettante* pleasure of having a costly copy made of the record of that brother's conquest. But when his son Jean [sans terres], fourth of the name, born in 1432, after long legal processes, recovered the domains of which his father had been deprived, it becomes easy to understand that he recollected that his uncle was a conqueror and a king, and that he would take a pride in the execution of this artistic monument to the family glory, which should be an heirloom and at the same time a register of the births of the legitimate inheritors of the hero's name. Furthermore, this MS. is the one which, in due time descending to Galien de Bethencourt, formed the basis of the edition which he prepared in 1625, and which appeared in print under the editorship of Bergeron in 1630. It is on these grounds that I have called it the original MS. It is handsomely illuminated with elaborate initial letters, with the arms of Bethencourt and with 85 illustrative drawings, 61 on a red, and 24 on a grey, ground. Permission being granted by Madame de Mont Ruffet to have two of these photographed for this edition,

M. d'Avezac judiciously selected the one exhibiting the arms of Bethencourt, and a drawing on which were represented the banners of Bethencourt and Gadifer de la Salle, the latter of which bears a cross. M. d'Avezac has taken considerable pains to discover the colours of the arms of the La Salles, but in vain. It may be mentioned that, although it was at La Rochelle that Gadifer de la Salle joined Bethencourt's expedition, the name is connected with more than one Norman locality, a fact which suggests a facility of introduction between the two adventurers.

And now a word as to the title of the work. Bergeron, losing sight of what is said in the original introduction, or, as he calls it, " The Author's Preface," in which occurs the expression " Et pour ce est ce livre nommé le Canarien," made up a title after his own fashion; but Galien de Bethencourt, in his MS. of 1625, drew one up more in conformity with the primary intention. It is that which the reader will find preceding the text, and a translation of which has been adopted for the title of the present edition.

I must not close without recording the Society's indebtedness to the Right Hon. Sir David Dundas for his kindness in lending me his very handsome copy of Bergeron's edition to work from; a copy which has the rare advantage of containing the portrait of Bethencourt, a woodcut copy of which is given as a frontispiece to the present work. There is no warranty for the authenticity of the portrait. The best arguments in favour of the supposition that it may have

been derived from a genuine original are the following.
1. The conqueror survived his return from the Canaries
to Normandy nineteen years.   2. The distinction
which he had earned for himself, as one who was to
live in the minds of men, would suggest the desirable-
ness of a portrait of some kind.   3. The engraved
portrait was issued with the sanction of Galien de
Bethencourt, the hereditary possessor of the family
documents.   4. It exhibits a remarkable distortion
in the left eye which, if unwarranted by a prototype,
would be a needless defect, very unlikely to be
fancifully inserted in the portrait of an otherwise
handsome man.

LE CANARIEN

OU

Livre de la conqueſte et converſion faicte des
Canariens à la foy et Religion catholique apoſto-
lique et Romaine en l'an 1402 : par Meſſire Jehan
de Bethencourt, Chevalier, gentilhomme Cauchois,
Seigneur du lieu de Bethencourt, Riville,
Gourrel, Chaſtelain de Grainville la Tain-
turière, Baron de Sainct Martin le
Gaillard, Conſeiller et Chambellan
ordinaire des Roys
Charles 5 et 6.

COMPOSÉ PAR

PIERRE BONTIER, moyne de Sainc Jouyn
de Marnes,

ET

JEAN LE VERRIER, Preſtre,

SERVITEURS DU DIT DE BETHENCOURT.

ARMS OF
MONSEIGNEUR LE BARON DE BÉTHENCOURT,
OF GRAINVILLE LA TEINTURIÈRE
EN CAUX.

AUTHOR'S PREFACE.

INASMUCH as, through hearing the great adventures, bold deeds, and fair exploits of those who in former times undertook voyages to conquer the heathen in the hope of converting them to the Christian faith, many knights have taken heart and sought to imitate them in their good deeds, to the end that by eschewing all vice, and following virtue, they might gain everlasting life; in like manner did Jean de Bethencourt, knight, born in the kingdom of France, undertake this voyage, for the honour of God and the maintenance and advancement of our faith, to certain islands in the south called the Canary Islands, which are inhabited by unbelievers of various habits and languages. Of these the Great Canary is one of the best, largest, and most amply supplied with men, provisions, and everything else. For this reason this book is called the Canarian

POVRCE qu'il est vray que maints cheualiers en oüant retraire les grands auantures, les vaillances, et les biaux faits de ceux qui au temps passé ont entreprins de faire les voyages et les conquestes sur mescreans, en esperance de les tourner et conuertir à la foy Chrestienne, ont prins cœur hardiment, et volenté de les ressembler en leurs bien faicts, et afin d'euiter tous vices, et estre vertueux, et que à la fin de leurs iours puissent acquerir vie permanable; Jean de Bethencourt, Cheualier, né du Royaume de France, eut entreprins ce voyage à l'honneur de Dieu, et au soustenement et accroissement de nostre foy, és parties Meridiennes, en certaines Isles qui sont sur celle bende, qui se dient les Isles de Canare, habitées de gens mescreans de diuerses loix et de diuers langages, dont la grand' Canare est vne des meilleures, et des plus principales et mieux peuplée de gens et de viures, et de toutes autres choses ; pour ce est ce liure nommé le Canarien,

book; and in it, if so it please God, will be found things which in time to come will be thought very remarkable.

We, Brother Pierre Bontier, monk of St. Jouin de Marnes, and Jean le Verrier, priest, servants of the aforesaid de Bethencourt, have begun to set down in writing most of what happened to him at the outset, and also the form of his government, which we had the opportunity of being thoroughly acquainted with, from the time of his leaving the kingdom of France until his arrival at the islands on the 19th day of April, 1406.[1]

Thenceforward the description has passed into the hands of others, who will carry it to the conclusion of his conquest; and may God, Who sees and knows all things, grant, of His holy grace, to those who shall loyally persist therein, knowledge, understanding, strength, and power to complete the conquest and bring it to a happy end, so that it may be a good example to all those who, from devotion, have the courage and the will to employ their bodily energies for the maintenance and exaltation of the Catholic faith.

---

auquel, s'il plaist à Dieu, on trouuera au temps aduenir de bien estranges choses en escrit. Et nous Frere Pierre Bontier, moine de Sainct Jouin de Marnes, & Jean le Verrier, prestre, et serui-teurs du dit de Bethencourt dessus nommé, auons commencé a mettre en escrit le plus des choses qui luy sont aduenues à son commencement, & aussi la maniere de son gouuernement, dont nous pouuons auoir eu vraye connoissance dès ce qui se partit du Royaume de France, iusques au 19 iour d'Auril, 1406, que le dit Bethencourt est arriué és Isles de par deçà; et la en auant est venue l'escriture en autres mains, qui la poursuiuront iusques à la fin de sa conqueste : & Dieu, qui tous voit & tout cognoist, veueille par sa saincte grace donner à ceux qui loyaument s'y sont maintenus & maintiendront, sens, entendement, force, & puissance de parfaire la conqueste, & mener à bonne fin, en maniere que ce soit bō exemple à tous ceux, qui par deuotion ont courage & voulenté d'employer leur corps & leur cheuance au soustenement & a l'exaltation de la foy Catholique.

[1] This appears to be a mistake, for in chapter 43 Bethencourt is said to first reach the island of Lancerote in the month of July.

HISTORY

CONQUEST OF THE CANARIES.

CHAPTER I.—How Monseigneur de Bethencourt set out from Grainville, and went to La Rochelle, and thence to Spain, and what
befel him.

IT was the custom in old times to record in writing the
deeds of chivalry and marvellous feats of the valiant conquerors of former days, as is seen in our ancient histories.
We here propose to speak of the enterprise undertaken by
the Sieur de Bethencourt, chevalier and baron, born in the
kingdom of France in Normandy, who set out from his
house of Grainville la Teinturière en Caux, and came to
Rochelle, and there fell in with Gadifer de la Sale, a good
and worthy knight, who was then starting on his adventures.
In a conversation between them, Monseigneur de Bethen-

[CHAPITRE I.]—*Comme Monseigneur de Bethencourt se partit de
Grainuile, et s'en alla à la Rochelle, et de là en Espaigne.*

Vn temps jadis souloit-on mettre en escrit les bonnes Cheualeries,
et les estranges choses que les vaillans conquereurs souloient
faire au temps passé, ainsi qu'on trouue és anciennes histoires ;
Voulons nous icy faire mention de l'entreprise que Bethencourt,
Cheualier et Baron, né du Royaume de France en Normandie,
lequel Bethencourt se partit de son hostel de Grainuille la
Taincturiere en Caulx, et s'en vint a la Rochelle, et la trouua
Gadifer de la Sale, vn bon et honneste Cheualier, lequel alloit a
son aduantures, et out parole entre le dit Bethencourt et Gadifer,
et luy demanda Monseigneur de Bethencourt quelle part il

court asked Gadifer what he thought of doing; and when the latter replied that he was going to seek his fortune, Monseigneur de Bethencourt said that he was very glad to have met with him, and, describing to him his own intended enterprise, asked Gadifer if it would be agreeable to him to join him in it. Gadifer was rejoiced to hear of the proposed expedition, and many courteous words passed between the two which it would be tedious here to repeat.

Accordingly, on the first of May, 1402, Monseigneur de Bethencourt, with Messer Gadifer and all his retinue, set sail from La Rochelle for the lands of Canary, to see and explore all the country, with the view of conquering the islands, and bringing the people to the Christian faith. They had a very good ship, well provided with men, victual, and everything requisite for their voyage. They had intended to make for Belle Isle, but at the Isle de Ré they met with a foul wind, and consequently steered a course for Spain, and arrived at the port of Vivières (Vivero in Gallicia), where Monseigneur de Bethencourt and his company stayed

---

vouloit tirer, et le dit Gadifer disoit qu'il alloit à son aduanture, adonc Monseigneur de Bethencourt luy dit qu'il estoit fort ioyeux de l'auoir trouué, et luy demanda s'il luy plaisoit de venir en sa compagnie, en contant au dit Gadifer son entreprinse, et tant que ledit Gadifer fut tout joyeux de l'ouir parler, et de l'entreprinse qui estoit faicte par ledit de Bethencourt. Il y eut trop moult de belles paroles entre eux deux, qui trop longues seroient à raconter. Adonc se partit Monseigneur de Bethencourt et Messire Gadifer, et toute son armée de la Rochelle, le premier iour de May, mil quatre cens et deux, pour venir és parties de Canare, pour voir et visiter tout le pays, en esperance de conquerir les isles, et mettre les gens à la foy Chrestienne, avec tres bon nauire, et suffisamment garny de gens et de vitailles, et de toutes les choses qui leur estoient necessaires pour leur voyage, et deuoient tenir le chemin de Belle-Isle, mais au passer de l'isle de Ré, ils eurent vent contraire, et addresserent leur voye en Espagne, et arriverent au port de Viuieres, et là demeura Monseigneur de Bethencourt et sa compagnie huit

eight days. There was a great deal of disagreement between several of the ship's company, so that the voyage was in great risk of coming to nothing, but the Sieur de Bethencourt and Messer Gadifer succeeded in quieting them.

CHAPTER II.—How Bethencourt and his army arrived at Corunna and there found the Earl of Crauford and the Lord de Hely.

Thence the Sieur de Bethencourt, Messer Gadifer de la Sale and the other nobles, came to la Coulôgne (Corunna), where they found a Scottish earl, the Lord de Hely, Messer Rasse de Renty, and many others, with their retinue.

Here Monseigneur de Bethencourt landed, and went to the town, where he had some business to do, and found that they were stripping many of the fittings from a ship which had been captured—we do not know from whom. When Bethencourt saw this, he begged the earl that he might be allowed to take from the ship anything which might be of service to him, and the earl gave him leave,

iours, et y eut grand discord entre plusieurs gens de la compagnie, tant que le voyage fut en grand danger d'estre rompu, mais ledit Seig. de Bethencourt, et Messire Gadifer les rappaisserent.

[CHAPITRE II.]—*Comme Bethencourt et son armée arrivèrent à la Coulongne et trouverent le Comte de Crafort et le Sire de Hely.*

Adonc se partit de là le sieur Bethencourt, auec luy Messire Gadifer de la Sale, et autres Gentil-hômes, et vindrent à la Coulôgne, et y trouuerent vn Comte d'Escosse, le Sire de Hely, Messire Rasse de Renty et plusieurs autres auec leur armee. Si descendit Monseigneur de Bethencourt à terre, et alla à la ville où il auoit a besongner, et trouua qu'il defaisoient vne nef de plusieurs habillemens qu'ils auoient prinse, nous ne sçauons sur qui. Quand Bethencourt vid cela, il pria le Comte qu'il peust prendre de la nef aucunes choses qui leur estoient necessaires, et

whereupon Bethencourt went to the ship, and caused an anchor and a boat to be taken and brought to his own vessel. When, however, the Lord de Hely and his companions became aware of this they murmured and were displeased, and Messer Rasse de Renty went to them, and told them that the Lord de Hely did not at all approve of their taking either the boat or the anchor.

Bethencourt answered that it was done with the sanction of the Earl of Crauford, and that they would not restore them. When the Lord de Hely heard this answer, he came to Monseigneur de Bethencourt, and told him that he must bring back, or cause to be brought back, what he had taken from the ship, but he still replied that he had done it by leave of the earl, and many high words ensued. Whereupon, Monsieur de Bethencourt said to the Lord de Hely, "Take your boat and anchor in God's name, and be off." Nay, so please you, answered the Lord de Hely, I shall do nothing of the sort, but I insist on their being brought back to-day, or I shall take other steps. Bethencourt and Gadifer replied, "Take them if you will,

le Comte luy octroya, et Bethencourt s'en alla en la nef, et fit prendre vne ancre et vn batel, et les fit amener à sa nef. Mais quand le Seigneur de Hely et ses compagnons le sceurent, ils n'en furent mie contens, et leur en despleut; et vint Messire Rasse de Renty vers eux, et leur dit qu'il ne plaisoit mie au Sire de Hely qu'ils eussent le batel, ne l'ancre. Bethencourt leur respondit que c'estoit par la volonté du Comte de Craforde, et qu'ils ne le rendroyent point : ouye leur response, le Sire de Hely vint vers Monseigneur de Bethencourt, et luy dit qu'il ramenast, ou fist ramener ce qu'il auoit prins de leur nef, et il luy respondit qu'il auoit fait par le congé du Comte. Si y eut de grosses paroles assez. Quand Monsieur de Bethencourt vid cela, il dit au Sieur de Hely, prenez batel et ancre de par Dieu, et vous en allez. Puis qu'il vous plaist, respondit le Sire de Hely, ce ne feray-je mie, ainchois les y feray mener aujourd'huy, ou i'y pouruoiray autrement : respondit ledit Bethencourt et

for we have something else to do." As he said this, Bethencourt was on the point of sailing, and was about to lift his anchors and leave the port. In fact immediately afterwards he set sail.

When they saw this, they manned a boat and followed after Bethencourt, but came only within speaking distance, and much was said which would be tedious to relate.

However, they received no other answer than what was given at the first, and so they were fain to return.

CHAPTER III.—How Monsieur de Bethencourt was accused by the Genoese, Placentian, and English merchants.

Monsieur de Bethencourt and his company then proceeded on their voyage, and after rounding Cape Finisterre, followed the coast of Portugal as far as Cape St. Vincent, and then changed their course and made for Seville. At Cadiz, which is near the strait of Marocco, they remained a

---

Gadifer, prenez les si vous voulez, car nous auons autre chose à faire. Ledit Bethencourt estoit sur son partir et vouloit leuer les ancres et soy tirer hors du port, et incontinent se partit.

Qvant ils virent cela, ils armerent vne galiotte et vindrent apres ledit Bethencourt, mais ils n'approcherêt point plus prés, fors qu'on parla à eux, et y eut assez de paroles qui trop longues seroyent à raconter. Ils n'eurent onc autre chose, ne autre response, que ainsi la premiere estoit, et s'en retournerent à tant.

[CHAPITRE III.]—*Comme Monsieur de Bethencourt fut accusé par les marchands Genevois, Plesantins, et Anglois.*

Et Monsieur de Bethencourt et sa compagnie prindrent leur chemin, et quand ils eurent doublé le Cap de Fine-terre, ils suiuirent la costiere de Portugal, iusques au Cap de S. Vincent, puis reployerent, et tindrent le chemin de Siuille, et arriuerent au port de Calix, qui est assez prés du destroit de Marroc, et ils

long time. Here de Bethencourt was detained; for the
Genoese, Placentian, and English merchants resident at
Seville, who had lost their goods at sea, although by
whose hands they knew not, brought accusations against
him and his before the King's Council, to the effect that
they could recover none of their goods, for they said that
he and his crew were robbers, and had sunk three ships,
and taken and pillaged all the contents.

Bethencourt landed and went to Port St. Mary's, to
learn what had happened, and was there made prisoner
and taken to Seville; but when the King's Council had
spoken to him, and he had made his reply, they begged
him to let the matter rest, and that no more should be said
about it at present, and so they set him at liberty. Whilst he
was at Seville, some of the sailors, actuated by evil motives, so
discouraged all the company, by saying that they had too
little food, and that they were being brought out to die,
that, out of eighty people only fifty-three remained.
Bethencourt returned to the ship, and with this small

---

y sejournerêt longuemèt. Et fut ledit de Bethencourt empesché;
car les marchands demourans en Seuille, qui auoient perdu le
leur sur la mer, que l'on ne sçauoit parqui, c'est à scauoir les
Janevois, Plesantins, et les Anglois, les accuserent tellement
devers le Conseil du Roy, qu'ils ne peuvent rien recouurer, en
disant qu'ils estoient robeurs, et qu'ils auoient affondré trois
nauires, et prins et pillé ce qui estoit dedans.

Si descendit Bethencourt à terre, et alla à S. Marie du Port,
pour scauoir que c'estoit, si fut prins et mené en Siuille : mais
quand le Conseil du Roy eut parlé à luy, et il leur eut fait
response, ils luy prierent que la chose demourast ainsi, et qu'il
n'en fust plus parlé quant à present, et le deliurerent tout au
plain, et luy estant en Siuille, les mariniers meus de mauuais
courages descouragerent tellement toute la côpagnie, en disant
qu'ils auoiët peu de viures, et qu'on les menoit mourir, que de
quatre vingt personnes n'en demoura que cinquante trois. Bethencourt s'en revint en la nef, et auec ainsi peu de gens qui leur en

residue continued his voyage, in which those who remained with him and had not consented to the evil doings of Berthin de Berneual[1] suffered much poverty, trouble, and labour in a variety of ways, as you will hereafter hear.

CHAPTER IV.—How they left Spain and arrived at the island of Lancerote.

So they left the port of Cadiz and put out to sea. For three days they were becalmed and made no progress. The weather then cleared, and in five days they came to the island of Graciosa. They embarked at the island of Lancerote, and Monsieur de Bethencourt went inland and made great efforts to capture some of the people of Canary, but without success, for as yet he did not know the country: so he returned to Port Joyeuse without doing anything more.

---

demourerent prindrent leur voyage, auquel ceux qui sont demourez auec Bethencourt, et n'ont mie voulu consentir aux mauuais faicts de Berthin de Berneual, ont souffert moult de pauureté, de peine, et de trauail en plusieurs manieres, ainsi que vous orrez cy apres.

[CHAPITRE IV.]—*Comme ils se partirent d'Espagne, et arriuerent en lille Lancelot.*

Et apres se partirent du Port de Calix, et se mirent en haute mer, et furent trois iours en bonasse, sans auancer leur chemin se peu non, et puis s'addressa le temps, et furent en cinq iours au port de l'Isle Gratieuse, et descendirent en l'Isle Lancelot, et entra Monsieur de Bethencourt par le pays, et mit grande diligence de prendre des gens de Canare, mais il ne peût, car il ne sçauoit mie encore le pays; si retourna au port de Ioyeuse sans autre chose faire. Et lors Monsieur de Bethencourt de-

---

[1] The author's thoughts seem so full of this man's villainy that he imagines him already presented to the reader, who will, however, become better acquainted with him further on.

M. de Bethencourt then asked Messer Gadifer de la Sale
and the other nobles what they recommended to be done;
and it was determined that they should form themselves
into companies and spread themselves over the country, and
not leave until they had found some of the natives. Presently some were perceived coming down from the mountains. These came forward, and made an arrangement with
M. de Bethencourt that the King of the country should
hold a conference with him in the presence of Gadifer and
several other nobles. The King accordingly came and did
homage to Bethencourt and his company, as a friend, not as
a subject, and they promised to him and his protection from
all those who might seek to harm them. But this promise
was not kept, as you shall more fully hear hereafter.

The Saracen King and M. de Bethencourt continued on
friendly terms, and the Sieur de Bethencourt had a castle
built there named Rubicon. There M. de Bethencourt left
a part of his company, and as it appeared to him that one
named Berthin de Berneual was a man of energy, he en-

---

manda à Messire Gadifer de la Sale, et aux autres gētilhommes,
qu'il leur estoit aduis de faire; fut aduisé qu'ils prendroient des
compagnons, et se remettroient au pays, et n'en partiroient
iusques à tant qu'ils eussent trouué des gens; et tantost en fut
trouué qui descendirent des montagnes, et vindrent par deuer
eux, et appointerent que le Roy du pays viendroit parler à M. de
Bethencourt, en la presence de Gadifer et plusieurs autres
Gentilhommes, et se vint ledit Roy en l'obeissance dudit Bethencourt et de la compagnie, comme amis, non mie comme subiets,
et leur promit-on qu'on les garderoit à l'encontre de tout ceux
qui leur voudroient mal faire. Mais on ne leur à mie bien tem
conuenant, ainsi comme vous orrez plus à plain cy apres declaré.
Et demourerent ledit Roy Sarrasin et M. de Bethencourt d'accord,
et fit faire le dit Sieur de Bethencourt vn chastel, qui s'appelle
Rubicon. Et laissa M. de Bethencourt vne partie de sa compagnie semblant audit de Bethencourt qu'un nommé Berthin de
Berneual estoit homme de bonne diligence, et luy bailla tout le

trusted to him the government of his people and of the country ; while he himself and Gadifer de la Salle, with the rest of the company, passed over to the island of Erbanie called Forteventura.

CHAPTER V.—How Monsieur de Bethencourt, by the advice of Gadifer de la Salle, left the island of Lancerote to go to the island of Erbanie called Forteventura.

Soon afterwards Monsieur de Bethencourt advised with Gadifer that an expedition should go to the island of Forteventura by night, and accordingly it was done. Gadifer and Remouet de Levedan, with a company, pushed on as far as they could until they came to a mountain where was a fresh running spring. Here they made great efforts to find their enemies, and were much vexed that they could not fall in with them. These latter, however, had withdrawn to the further end of the country, as soon as they had seen the ships arrive in the port. Gadifer and

gouuernement de ses gens et du pays : puis passa ledit de Bethencourt et Gadifer de la Sale auec le surplus de sadite compagnie, en l'Isle d'Albainie nommée Forte-Aduanture.

CHAPITRE V.—*Comment Monsieur de Bethencourt se partit de l'Isle Lancelot, pour aller en l'Isle d'Erbane, nommée Forte Auanture, par le conseil de Gadifer de la Salle.*

Et tantost apres Monsieur de Bethencourt print conseil de Gadifer qu'on iroit de nuict en ladite Isle de Forte-Aduanture, et ainsi fut fait, le dit Gadifer et Remouet de Leuedan à tout vne partie des compagnons y allerent tout le plus auant qu'ils peuvent, et iusques à vne montagne, là où est vne fontaine viue et courante et mirent grande peine et grande diligence d'encontrer leurs ennemis, bien marris qu'ils ne les peuvent trouuer ; mais s'estoient lesdits ennemis retraits en l'autre bout du pays, des adonc qu'ils virent arriuer la nauires au port, et demeura

his company stayed there eight days, and were then
obliged to return for want of bread to the port of Lobos.

The knights then held a council, and determined that
they would go by land along the shore to a river called the
Vien de Palme, and encamp at its mouth; that the ship
should haul in as close as possible, and send them their
provisions on shore, and that they would fortify themselves
at that point, and not leave until the country should be
conquered and the inhabitants brought to the Catholic faith.

CHAPTER VI.—How the mariners refused Gadifer admission on board of
his own ship.

Robin le Brument, master mariner of a ship which Gadifer
affirmed to be his, would neither tarry nor receive either
Gadifer or his companions on board, but agreed, on condition of receiving hostages, to pass them over to the island
of Lancerote; otherwise they would be left behind without

ledit Gadifer, et la compagnie huict iours, tant qu'il leur conuint
retourner, par faute de pain, au port de Louppes, et puis prindrent lesdits Cheualiers conseil ensemble, et ordonnerent qu'ils
s'en iroient par terre au long du pays iusques à vne riuiere
nommée la Vien de Palme, et se logerent sur le bout d'icelle
riuiere; et que la nef se retrairoit tout le plus pres qu'elle
pourroit, et leur descendroient leurs viures à terre, et là se
fortifieroient, et n'en partiroient iusques a tant que le pays
seroit conquis, et mis les habitans à la foy Catholique.

CHAPITRE VI.—*Comme les maronniers refuserent Gadifer de la
nef mesmes.*

Robin le Brument maistre marinier d'vne nef que ledit Gadifer
disoit auoir, ne vouloit plus demeurer ne recueillir Gadifer et ses
compagnons, et conuint qu'ils eussent ostages pour les repasser
en l'isle Lancelot, ou autrement ils fussent demourez par dela

HOW THE MARINERS REFUSED GADIFER ADMISSION ON
BOARD OF HIS OWN SHIP.

any provisions; and Robin Brument and Vincent Cerent sent word by Colin Brument, a brother of the former, to say that Gadifer and his companions should not come on board with more men than they had in the ship; and so they took Gadifer and his bastard son Hannibal as hostages on board the ship's boat, the former being in great heaviness of heart at finding himself in such a state of subjection that he was debarred from the use of his own property.

CHAPTER VII.—How Monsieur de Bethencourt went away to Spain, and left Messire Gadifer in charge of the islands.

Then Monsieur de Bethencourt and Gadifer returned to the castle of Rubicon, and while they were there many of the seamen who were very evilly inclined showed impatience to get away. Therefore the Sieur de Bethencourt, by the advice of Gadifer and many other nobles, resolved to go with the said seamen to satisfy their requirements, and to return as soon as might be possible with fresh men and victuals.

---

sans viures nuls, et firent dire Robin Brument, et Vincent Cerent, par Colin Brument son frere à Gadifer, que luy et ses compagnõs n'entroiët point plus forts qu'eux en la nef, et les rapasserent au bastel de la nef en laquelle il entra luy et Hannibal son bastard en grād douleur de cœur de ce qu'il estoit en telle subiection, qu'il ne se pouuoit aider du sien propre.

CHAPITRE VII.—*Comment Monsieur de Bethencourt s'en alla en Espagne, et laissa Messire Gadifer, à qu' il donna le charge des Isles.*

Adonc Monsieur de Bethencourt, et Gadifer reuindrent au chastel de Rubicon, et quand il furent là, les maronniers pensans grand mauuaistié se hasterent moult d'eux en aller. Si ordonne ledit Sieur de Bethencourt par le conseil dudit Gadifer, et de plusieurs autres gentilshommes, qu'il s'en iroit auec lesdits maronniers, pour les venir secourir à leurs necessitez, et que le plutost qu'il pourroit reuiendroit, et ameneroit aucuns refraichissements de

They then desired the seamen to put on shore all the provisions that were in the ship except those necessary for their homeward voyage. And they did so, but not without doing as much damage as they could both to the artillery and other things which would afterwards have been of great service.

Monsieur de Bethencourt now left the port of Rubicon with the seamen, and came to the other end of the island of Lancerote, and there remained. He then sent to Rubicon for Messire Jean le Verrier the priest, who was his chaplain, to whom he said many things in confidence, as well as to one Jean le Courtois, to whose charge he committed all matters which might affect his honour and profit, and he enjoined on them to look well to everything that had to be done, and that they two should be united as brothers, and always maintain peace and harmony among the rest; for his own part he assured them that he should make every effort to return as soon as possible. Bethencourt then took

---

gens et de viures. Puis parlerent aux maronniers, que les viures qui sont au nauire fussent descendus à terre, excepté ceux qui leur auoit besoin pour leur retour. Et ainsi fut fait, iaçoit que lesdits maronniers en demusserent le plus qu'ils peuuent, et d'artillerie et d'autres choses qui leur eust esté depuis bon besoin. Et se partit Monsieur de Bethencourt du port de Rubicon, auec les maronniers en son nauire, et s'en vindrent en l'autre bout de l'Isle Lancelot, et là demourerent. Ledit Sieur de Bethencourt enuoya querir a Rubicon Messire Jean le Verrier Prestre, et chapellain du dit Seigneur a qui il dit plusieurs choses de segret, et à vn nommé Jean le Courtois, auquel il bailla aucunes charges, qui pouuoient toucher son honneur et profit, et luy enchargea qu'il print bien garde en toutes choses qu'ils verroient qu'il seroit de faire, et qu'ils fussent eux deux comme freres, en gardant touiours paix et vnion en la compagnie, et que le plutost qu'il pourroit il feroit diligence de retourner. Et adonc ledit Bethencourt print congé de Messire Gadifer et de

leave of Messire Gadifer and of all the company, and departed and returned to Spain.

And here we will digress, in order to speak of the doings of Berthin de Berneval, a native of Caux in Normandy and a nobleman of name and renown in arms, in whom the said lord had placed great confidence, and who, as I said before, had been selected by him and Messer Gadifer as lieutenant and governor of the island of Lancerote and of the company. This Berthin did all the harm that he could, and acted very treasonably, as you shall hear more fully set forth.

CHAPTER VIII.—How Berthin de Berneval began his malicious doings against Gadifer.

It may be judged what evil designs Berthin de Berneval had conceived in his heart, from the fact that when he joined Monseigneur de Bethencourt at la Rochelle, he began to attach to himself partizans, and to make allies of a great

toute sa compagnie, et se partit ledit Sieur et cinglerent tant qu'ils vindrēt en Espagne. Cy laissons à parler de ceste matière, et parlerons du fait de Berthin de Berneual, natif de Caux en Normandie, et gentil-homme de nom et d'armes, auquel ledit Sieur se fioit fort, et auoit este eslue de luy et de Messire Gadifer, comme i'ay deuant dit, lieutenant et gouuerneur de l'isle Lācelot et de la compagnie ; et ledit Berthin tout le pis qu'il peut faire, il le fit, et des grandes trahisons, comme vous orrez plus a plain declaré.

[CHAPITRE VIII.]—*Comment Berthin de Berneual commença ses malices à l'encontre de Gadifer.*

Afin qu'on sçache que Berthin de Berneual auoit pieça manuaistié machinée en son courage, il est vray que quand il fut venu deuers Monsieur de Bethencourt à la Rochelle, il commença a soy rallier des compagnons, il fit les alliances auec plusieurs

number of people; and shortly after, through him, there arose in the ship a great dissension between the Gascons and the Normans, and truth to say, this Berthin did not at all like Messire Gadifer, and sought to do him despite by every means in his power. And it went so far that, while Gadifer was putting on his armour in his cabin, with the intention of going to appease the disorder among the seamen, who had retreated to the ship's forecastle, they hurled at him two darts, one of which passed between him and Hannibal, who was helping him on with his armour, and stuck into a chest. Some of the seamen had gone up into the top and had darts and iron bars all ready to throw at us, and it was only with much trouble that the tumult was appeased. From that time commenced plots and dissensions amongst the crews, which grew to such an extent that, before the ship left Spain to sail to the Canary Islands, they had lost a good two hundred of their ablest men. This subsequently proved a great mischief in many ways, for if they only had remained loyal, Bethencourt would already

---

gents; et vn peu apres par luy fut commencée vne grande dissension en la nef entre les Gascons et Normands, et de vray ledit Berthin n'aimoit point Messire Gadifer, et cherchoit à luy faire tout le plus de desplaisir qu'il pouuoit. Et tant aduint que Gadifer s'armoit en la chambre pour vouloir appaiser le debat d'entre eux mariniers qui s'estoyent retrais au chastel de deuant en ladite nef, ils ietterent audit Gadifer deux dardes, dont l'vne passa par entre luy et Hannibal, qui luy aidoit à soy armer en sa chambre, et s'attacha en vn coffre, et estoient aucuns des maronniers montez au chastel du mast, et auoient dardes et barres de fer toutes prestes pour ietter sur nous, et en moult grand peine fut rapaisée ceste noise, et de là en auant commencerent bendes et dissensions les vns contre les autres. En telle manière, que deuant que la nef partist d'Espagne, pour trauerser és Isles de Canare, ils perdirent bien deux cents hommes des mieux aparliez qui y fussent, dequoy on a eu depuis grand souffrette par plusieurs fois. Car s'ils eussent esté loyaulx,

have been lord of the Canary Islands, or of the greater part of them.

CHAPTER IX.—How Gadifer, who had confidence in Berthin, sent him to speak to the captain of a ship.

Shortly after the departure of Monsieur de Bethencourt from Rubicon, although he had laid his injunctions on Berthin de Berneval to do his duty in all things reasonable, and, like the rest, to obey Messire Gadifer, whom Monsieur de Bethencourt had made his associate, looking upon him as a good knight and a man of judgment, there arose great quarrels and dissensions between these two, as you shall presently hear. Monsieur de Bethencourt was now gone to Spain, and Gadifer, who put more trust in Berthin de Berneval than in any other, sent him across to a ship which had recently arrived at the port of Lobos. Berthin thought that it was the ship Tajamar, with whose captain, Fer-

---

ledit Bethencourt fust ores Seigneur des isles de Canare, ou de la plus grande partie d'elles.

CHAPITRE IX.—*Comment Gadifer qui auoit fiance à Bertin, l'enuoya parler à vn patron d'vne nef.*

Et apres que Monsieur de Bethencourt fut party de Rubicon, et qu'il eut commandé à Berthin de Berneual qu'il fist son deuoir en tout ce qu'il est de raison de faire, et qu'il obeist à Messire Gadifer, et tous les gents dudit Sieur de Bethencourt; car Monsieur de Bethencourt tenoit Messire Gadifer pour vn bon cheualier et sage; et estoit du bien de Messire Gadifer qu'il s'estoit boutté en la compagnie de Monseigneur de Bethencourt; jaçoit que dedans vn pou de temps apres il y eust de grands dissensions et de grands noises entre eux deux, comme vous orrez cy-apres; or est parti Monsieur de Bethencourt de Rubicon, et est allé en Espagne, et Gadifer qui auoit plus de fiance à Berthin de Berneual qu'en nul autre, le transmit vers une nef qui estoit

C

nando d'Ordoñez, he was intimately acquainted. It proved not
to be that ship, but another, named Morella, of which Francisco Calvo had command. To him Berthin proposed,
through one of the crew, named Ximenes, and in the presence of some others, that they should take him and thirty
of the ship's company with them, and so they would capture
forty of the best of the natives of the island of Lancerote.
But they would not consent to such great wickedness;
and Francisco Calvo said that it did not beseem Berthin
to propose such a thing, and that, please God, they would
never be so disloyal to good knights like Monsieur de
Bethencourt and Messire Gadifer as to deprive them of the few
men who remained to them, or to take by force those whom
Bethencourt and all his people had assured of security and
placed under their protection, in good hopes of seeing them
baptized and brought into our faith.

---

arriuée au port de l'isle de Loupes, et cuidoit que ce fut la nef
Tranchemar, de laquelle Ferrant d'Ordongnes en estoit maistre,
auquel il cuidoit auoir grande accointance ; mais ce n'estoit elle
mie, ains estoit vne autre nef qui s'appelloit la nef Morelle, de
laquelle Francisque Calue auoit le gouvernement, et parla Berthin,
ou fit parler à vn des compagnons de la nef, qui s'appelloit
Simene, en la presence d'aucuns autres qu'ils l'ēmenasserent
auec eux ; et trente des compagnons de la nef, et qu'il prendroit
quarāte hommes des meilleurs qui fussent en l'isle Lancelot.
Mais ils ne se voulurent mye consentir à celle grande mauuaistié ;
et leur dit Francisque Calue qu'il n'appartenoit mye à Berthin,
et que ja à Dieu ne pleust qu'ils fissent vne telle desloyauté à
tels et si bons cheualiers comme estoient Monsieur de Bethencourt
et Messire Gadifer, de les desgarnir ainsi d'vn pou de gens que
demeuré leur estoit ; et aussi de prendre et rauir ceux que ledit
Bethencourt et toutes ses gens auoient asseurez et mis en leur
sauuegarde, lesquels auoient bonne esperance d'estre baptisez et
mis en nostre foy.

CHAPTER X.—How Berthin deceived his own confederates.

Soon after this, Berthin, still cherishing treachery in his heart, sounded all those whom he thought to be as evilly disposed as himself, by holding out vague hopes of something that should be for their own welfare, advancement, and honour. He then suggested to them, under an oath of secrecy, that Bethencourt and Gadifer ought to send Remonnet de Leneden and himself with a certain sum of money in the first ship that sailed for France, and that meanwhile their companions should be portioned out amongst the islands till their return. He thus won over certain Gascons; to wit, Pierre de Liens, Augerot de Montignac, Siort de Lartigue, Bernard de Chastelvary, Guillaume de Nau, Bernard de Mauleon called the Cock, William de Salerne called Labat, Morelet de Couroge, Jean de Bidouville, Bidaut de Hournau, Bernard de Montauban, and one

---

CHAPITRE X.—*Comment Berthin donna faulx à entendre a ceux de son alliance.*

Apres vn peu de temps Berthin qui touiours auoit mauuaise voulenté et trahison en sa pensée, parla à tous ceux qu'il pensa qu'ils fussent du mauuais courage qu'il estoit, et les enhorta et dit, qu'il leur diroit telle chose que ce seroit le bien, l'exaucement et l'honneur de leurs personnes, et à tous ceux que auec luy s'accorderent, il leur fit iurer qu'ils ne le descouuriroient point, puis leur donna à entendre comment Bethencourt et Gadifer leur deuoient donner, a Remonnet de Leneden, et à luy, certaine somme d'argent, et qu'ils s'en iroient au premier nauire qui venroit en France, et que les compagnons seroient departis parmy les isles, et là demourroient iusques à leur retour, et auec ledit Berthin aucuns Gascons s'accorderent, desquels les noms s'ensuiuent, Pierre de Liens, Ogerot de Montignac, Siort de Lartigue, Bernard de Chastelvary, Guillaume de Nau, Bernard

from the country of Aunis, named Jean l'Alieu. All these agreed with Berthin, as well as several from other places, of whom mention shall be made hereafter.

CHAPTER XI.—How Gadifer went to the island of Lobos, where he found himself deprived both of men and provisions.

Meanwhile Gadifer, in no wise suspecting that Berthin de Berneval, who was of noble lineage, would be guilty of any baseness, set sail with Remonnet de Leneden and several others in his boat from Rubicon and passed to the island of Lobos to procure some seal skins, to make shoes for the crew ; and there they remained for some days, till at last their provisions failed them (for the island was barren, and there was no fresh water). Gadifer therefore sent back Remonnet de Leneden in the boat to the castle of Rubicon to procure some food, desiring him to return on the morrow, for he had only provisions for two days. When Remonnet

de Mauleon dit le Coq, Guillaume de Salerne dit Labat, Morelet de Couroge, Jean de Bidouuille, Bidaut de Hournau, Bernard de Montauban, et vn du pays d'Aunys, nommé Jehan l'Alieu ; et tous iceux s'accorderent auec ledit Berthin et plusieurs autres d'autre pays, desquels mention sera faite cy-apres, ainsi qu'il escherra en leur endroit.

CHAPITRE XI.—*Comme Gadiffer alla en lille de Louppes la ou il se trouva desgarny des gens et de vitailles.*

Depuis Gadifer non doubtant rien en aucune maniere que Berthin de Berneual qui estoit de noble ligne deust faire nulle mauuaistié, se partit luy et Remonnet de Leneden, et plusieurs autres, auec son Bastel, de Rubicon, et passerent en l'Isle de Loupes, pour auoir des peaux de Loups marins, pour la necessité de chausseure qui failloit aux compagnons, et là demourerent par aucuns iours tant que viures leur faillirent : (car c'est vne isle deserte et sans

arrived at the port of Rubicon, he found that as soon as
Gadifer and his party had gone to the island of Lobos,
Berthin had taken his confederates to a port in the island of
Graciosa, where the ship Tajamar had arrived. To the master
of this ship Berthin told a number of lies, promising that he
would capture forty of the best men in the island of Lancerote,
who would be worth two thousand francs, and deliver them
to the said master, if he would receive himself and his companions into his ship, and so effectual were his falsehoods
that the master, yielding to his cupidity, assented. This
happened on the fifteenth day after Michaelmas, Oct. 14,
1402, and Berthin at once returned, persevering in his malice
and in his evil intentions.

---

eauë douce ;) si renuoya Gadifer Remonnet de Leneden auec le
bastel au chastel de Rubicon pour querir des viures, et qu'il
retournast le lendemain ; car il n'auoit viures que pour deux
iours. Quand Remonnet et le bastel furēt arriuez au port de
Rubicon, ils trouuerent que tantost que Gadifer et les dessusdits
furent passez en l'Isle de Loupes, Berthin s'en estoit allé auec
ses aliez à vn port nommé l'isle Gratieuse, où estoit arriuée la
nef *Tranchemare*, et donna ledit Berthin au maistre de la nef
assez de mensonges, et luy dit qu'il prendroit quarante hommes
des meilleurs qui fussent en l'Isle Lancelot, qui valloient deux
mil frans, afin que ledit maistre le vousit receuoir en la nef luy
et ses compagnons, et tant fit par ses fausses paroles, que le
maistre meu de grande conuoitise luy octroya ; et ceste chose
aduint le quinzieme iour apres la sainct Michel, mil quatre cens
deux, et s'en retourna incontinent ; Berthin perseuerant en sa
malice et en sa tres-mauuaise intention.

CHAPTER XII.—How the traitor Berthin, with plausible pretences, induced the King of the Island of Lancerote and his people to come to him, that he might take them.

While Gadifer was yet at the island of Lobos, and shortly after the return of Berthin from the island of Graciosa to the castle of Rubicon in the island of Lancerote, two Canarians came to him, saying that the Spaniards had landed in order to capture them. Berthin told them to hold out till he came, and, promising to bring speedy assistance, dismissed them. Berthin then, holding a lance in his hand, said with a blasphemous oath, "I will go and speak to these Spaniards, and if they interfere, either I will kill them, or they shall kill me, and I pray God that if I do not effect my purpose I may never return." Whereupon some of the bystanders said, "That is ill spoken, Berthin;" but he again said, "On my life I pray it of the God of Heaven." He then left the castle of Rubicon, accompanied by several of his partisans—namely, Pierre de

---

CHAPITRE XII.—*Comment [le traitre Berthin soubs beau semblant fit venir le roy de Lancelot auec les siens pour les prendre.]*

Gadifer qui estoit en l'isle de Loupes et Berthin en l'isle Lancelot au chastel de Rubicon, tantost apres qu'il fut retourné de l'isle Gracieuse, la vint deux Canares vers luy, disant comment les Espagnols estoient descendus à terre pour eux prendre, ausquels Berthin respondit qu'ils s'en allassent et se tinssent ensemble; car ils seroient tantost secourus, et ainsi s'en allerét les deux Canares, et là dit Berthin qui tenoit vne lance à sa main, je renye Dieu! J'iray parler aux Espagnols et si ils y mettét la main ie les tueray, ou ils me tuëront, car ie prie à Dieu que iamais ie n'en puisse retourner, dequoy aucuns de ceux qui là estoient luy dirent, Berthin c'est mal dit, et de rechief ma vye je emprie à Dieu de Paradis. Et cependāt se partit du chastel de Rubicon, accompagné de plusieurs ses alliez, c'est à sçauoir

Liens, Bernard de Montauban, Olivier de Barré, Guillaume the Bastard de Blessi, Phelipot de Baslieu, Michelet the cook, Jacquet the baker, Peruet the blacksmith, with divers others, whose names are not here mentioned; and the rest of his accomplices remained at the castle of Rubicon. Thus accompanied, Berthin went to a certain village named the Great Aldea, where he found some of the Canarian chiefs; and he, with his mind full of treacherous intentions, said to them, "Go and fetch hither your king and his retinue, and I will protect them completely against the Spaniards." The Canarians believed in him, by reason of the confidence which they had in the Sieur de Bethencourt and his company; and they came, four and twenty in number, to the said Aldea as to a place of safety and retreat. Berthin gave them welcome, and made them a supper, at which he had present two Canarians, one named Alphonse, and a woman named Isabelle, whom the Sieur de Bethencourt had brought to be their interpreters in the island of Lancerote.

Pierre de Liens, Bernard de Montauban, Oliuier de Barré, Guillaume le Bastart de Blecy, Phelipot de Baslieu, Michelet le Cuisinier, Jacquet le Boulanger, Pernet le Mareschal, auec plusieurs que ne sont mye icy nomméz; et les autres ses complices demeurerent au chastel de Rubicon. Berthin ainsi accompagné, s'en alla à un certain village nommé la Grād' Aldee, où il trouua aucuns des grands Canares; et luy ayant grand trahison en pensée, leur fit dire: allez, et me faites le Roy venir et ceux qui auec luy sont, et ie les garderay bien contre les Espagnols, et les Canares le creurent parmy la seureté et affiance que eux auoient du Sieur de Bethencourt et de sa compagnie, et vindrent à ladite Aldée comme à sauueté et retraict iusques au nombre de vingt-quatre, ausquels Berthin fit bonne chere, et les fit souper, et auec ce detenoit deux Canares, vn nommé Alphonce, et vne femme nommée Isabel, lesquels ledit Bethencourt auoit amenez pour estre leur truchement en l'isle Lancelot.

CHAPTER XIII.—How that after Berthin had captured the king and his people, he took them to the ship Tajamar, and handed them over to the robbers.

When the Canarians had supped, Berthin sent to them to say, " Sleep in peace and fear nothing, for I will protect you." Accordingly most of them went to rest ; and when Berthin saw that it was time, he placed himself before their doors with his drawn sword in his hand, and had them all taken and bound. One only, named Avago, escaped. When Berthin now plainly saw that he was discovered, and could capture no more, he took his departure, still cherishing his evil intentions, and went straight to the port of the island of Graciosa, where was the vessel from Spain named Tajamar, and took the prisoners with him.

CHAPITRE XIII.—*Comment apres que Berthin eut prins le Roy, et ses gens, il les mena à la nef Tranchemare, et les bailla aux larrons.*

Quand les Canares eurent soupé, Berthin leur fit dire: dormez vous seurement et ne vous doutez de riens ; car ie vous garderay bien. Et cependant les vns s'endormirent et les autres non, et quand Berthin vit qu'il estoit temps, il se mit deuant leur huis l'espée en la main toute nuë, et les fit touts prendre et lier ; et ainsi fut il fait, fors que vn nommé Auago qui en eschapa, et quand il les eut prins et liez, et il vit bien qu'il estoit descouuert, et qu'il n'en pouuet plus auoir, il se partit de là perseuerant en sa grande malice, et s'en alla droit au port de l'isle Gratieuse où estoit la nef d'Espagne nommé Tranchemare, et amena les prisonniers auec luy.

CHAPTER XIV.—How the king escaped from those into whose charge Berthin had delivered him.

When the king found himself in this position, and became aware of the treachery of Berthin and his companions and the outrage that they had done to him, being a brave and powerful man, he burst his bonds, and broke away from three men who had him in their charge. One of them, who was a Gascon, pursued him; but the king turned most fiercely round upon him, and dealt him such a blow, that none of the rest dared to approach him. This was the sixth time that he had delivered himself from the hands of the Christians by his own prowess. There now remained only twenty-two prisoners, whom Berthin handed over to the Spaniards of the ship Tajamar, after the example of the traitor Judas Iscariot, who betrayed our Saviour Jesus Christ and delivered Him into the hands of the Jews to crucify Him, and put Him to death. So did Berthin, who delivered up these poor innocent people into the hands of robbers, who sold them into perpetual slavery in foreign lands.

CHAPITRE XIV.—*Comment le Roy se deliura des larrons à qui Berthin les auoit livrés.*

Quand le Roy se vit en tel poinct et cognut la trahison de Berthin et de ses compagnons, et l'outrage qu'ils leur faisoient, comme homme hardy, fort et puissant rompit ses liens, et se deliura de trois hommes qui en garde l'auoient, desquels estoit vn Gascon qui le poursuiuit; mais le roy retourna moult aigrement sur luy, et luy donna vn tel coup, que nul ne l'osa plus aprocher; et c'est la sixiesme fois qu'il s'est deliuré des mains des Chrestiens par son apertise; et n'en demeura que vingt et deux, lesquels Berthin bailla et deliura aux Espagnols de la nef *Tranchemare*, à l'exemple du traistre Judas Iscariot qui trahit nostre Sauueur Jesus-Christ et le livra en la main des Juifs pour le crucifier et mettre à mort; ainsi fit Berthin qui bailla et liura ces pauures gens innocents en la main des larrons qui les menerent vendre en estranges terres en perpetual seruage.

CHAPTER XV.—How Berthin's companions took the boat which Gadifer
had sent for provisions.

Berthin meanwhile being in the ship, sent the Bastard de
Blessi and some of his allies to the castle of Rubicon. They
there found Gadifer's boat, which, as already stated, he had
sent to fetch provisions for himself and his companions who
were in the island of Lobos, and being bent on accomplish-
ing their wicked designs, they went in search of certain
Gascons their sworn confederates, and together they took
possession of the boat and went on board of it. When
Remonnet de Leneden ran forward to recover it, the bastard
de Blessi fell upon him with his drawn sword and would
have slain him. The conspirators, however, pushed the
boat off to sea, leaving the others on shore, and cried
out—"If any one of Gadifer's men dares to lay hands on the
boat we will put him to death, for, in any case, Berthin
and all his people shall be received on board the ship even

CHAPITRE XV.—*Comment les compagnons de Berthin prindrent
le batel que Gadifer auoit transmis pour viures.*

Cependant Berthin estant en la nef enuoya le Bastart de
Blessi et aucuns autres de ses allies au chastel de Rubicon, et
trouuerent le bastel qui estoit à Gadifer, lequel il auois transmis
pour querir viures pour luy et ses compagnons qui estoient demourez en l'isle de Loupes comme dessus est dit; et adonc les
compagnons Berthin pensans du tout à accomplir leur entreprinse, se retirerent deuers aucuns Gascons leurs compagnons de
serment, lesquels à l'aide les vns des autres se saisirent du
bastel et entrerent dedans; mais Remonnet de Leneden y courut
pour le recouvre. Là estoit le bastard de Blessi qui courut sus a
Remonnet l'espée tout nuë en la main et le cuida tuer. Si
eslargirent le bastel en la mer bien auant et les autres demeurerent
hors, disans, s'il y a si hardy des gens de Gadifer de mettre la
main au bastel nous le tuerons sans remede: car qui poise et qui
non, Berthin sera recueilly en la nef et toutes ses gens, et ain-

though Gadifer and his men should never eat another mouthful." Some of Gadifer's men who were at the castle of Rubicon then spoke thus: "Fair sirs, you are well aware that Gadifer is gone yonder to the island of Lobos on account of the need of shoes for the crew, and that he has with him neither bread nor flour, nor fresh water, nor can he receive any except by means of the boat; pray, then, let us have it, that we may send him some victuals for himself and his people, or otherwise they will die of starvation." To which they replied: "Spare your breath; for, once for all, we will do nothing of the sort until Berthin and all his people are safe in the ship Tajamar.

CHAPTER XVI.—How Berthin sent the boat of the Tajamar to fetch Gadifer's provisions.

The next day, at the hour of nones [3 p.m.], the boat of the ship Tajamar arrived at the port of Rubicon with

chois que Gadifer ne ses gens mengeussent iamais. Aucuns de Gadifer estans au chastel de Rubicon dirent ainsi, beaux Seigneurs, vous sçauez bien que Gadifer est passé par delà en l'isle de Loupes pour la necessité de chausseure qui estoit entre nous, et n'a deuers luy ne pain, ne farine, ne eau douce, et si n'en peut point auoir de ne recouurer se n'est par le bastel, plaise vous que nous l'ayons pour luy transmettre aucunes vitailles pour luy et pour ses gens, ou autrement nous les tenons pour morts. Et ils respondirent: ne nous en parlez plus; car nous n'en serons rien, c'est à bref parler, ainchois sera Berthin et toutes ses gens du tout retraits en la nef Tranchemare.

CHAPITRE XVI.—Comment Berthin transmit le bastel de Tranchemare querir les viures de Gadifer.

Lendemain heure de nonne arriua le bastel de la nef Tranchemare au port de Rubicon auec sept compagnons dedans: le

seven men in her. Gadifer's people asked them : " Fair
sirs, what do you seek?" and they in the boat answered,
" Berthin sent us here, and he told us when we left the
ship that he would be here as soon as we." Meanwhile,
Berthin's confederates inside the castle made great waste
and destruction of the stores belonging to Monsieur de
Bethencourt, which he had left for Gadifer and his companions, such as wine, biscuit, salt meat, and other
victuals, although Gadifer himself had divided the provisions with perfect impartiality, allotting as much to
the least as to the greatest, and had only kept for his
own use his rightful portion, with the exception of one cask
of wine which had not been yet served out.

CHAPTER XVII.—How Berthin delivered up the women of the castle
to the Spaniards, who violated them.

The following evening Berthin came by land to the castle

gens de Gadifer leur demanderent, beaux Seigneurs que querez
vous, et respondirent dudit bastel, Berthin nous a enuoyez icy et
nous dit au partir de la nef qu'il seroit icy aussitost comme
nous : et les alliez dudit Berthin cependāt estans au chastel de
Rubicon firent grand degast et grand destruction de viures qui
là estoient appartenans à Monsieur de Bethencourt, lesquels
viures il auoit laissé audit Gadifer et à ses gens de la compagnie,
comme de vins, de biscuit, de chair salée, et autres vitailles, nonobstant qu'il auoit departy les viures tout esgallement autant au
petit comme au grand, et ne luy estoit demouré tant seulement
que sa droite portion, excepté vn tonneau de vin qui n'estoit mie
encore desparty entre eux.

CHAPITRE XVII.—*Comment Berthin liura les femmes du chastel
aux Espagnols, et les prindrent à force.*

Et au vespre ensur, vint Berthin par terre au chastel de

of Rubicon, followed by thirty men of the company of the ship Tajamar, to whom he said : "Take bread and wine, and whatever there is ; and may he be hanged who spares anything, for it has cost me more than any of them ; and cursed be he who leaves anything which he can take away." Such and many other expressions did Berthin address to them, which it would be tedious here to write down ; he even took away by force, and against their will, some women who had come from France, and delivered them up to the Spaniards, who dragged them from the castle down to the beach, and violated them in spite of their loud cries and shrieks of distress. Furthermore, while at the same place, Berthin used the following expression—" I wish that Gadifer de la Salle should know that if he were as young as I am, I would certainly kill him, but as he is not, I may perhaps forego that wish ; yet if it takes my fancy, I will go and drown him off the island of Lobos, and let him fish for seals there." A very affectionate expression this to use with regard to one who had never shown anything but love and kindness to him.

Rubicon accompagné de trente hommes des compagnons de la nef Tranchemare, luy disant ainsi, prenez pain, et vin et ce qui y sera, pendu soit-il qui riens en espargnera : car il m'a plus cousté que à nul d'eux, et maudit soit il qui riens y laissera qu'il puisse, et ce disoit Berthin et moult d'autres paroles qui longues seroient à escrire ; et mesmement aucunes femmes, lesquelles estoit du pays de France les bailla et liura parforce, et outre leur gré aux Espagnols ; et les trainerent d'amont le chastel iusques en bas sur la marine, et furent auec elles, et les efforcerent, nonobstant les grands cris et les grands griefs qu'elles faisoient, et ledit Berthin estant audit lieu disant ainsi : ie veux bien que Gadifer de la Salle sçache qui si fust aussi ieune que moy, ie l'allasse tuer, mais pour ce qu'il ne l'est mie, par auanture ie m'en deporteray ; s'y me monte vn pou à la teste ie l'iray faire noyer en l'isle de Loupes, s'y peschera aux Loups-Marins ; c'estoit bien affectueusement parlé contre celuy qui oncques ne luy auoit fait fors que amour et plaisir.

CHAPTER XVIII.—How Berthin caused the two boats to be laden
with provisions and other things.

The next morning Berthin de Berneval had Gadifer's
boat and that of the Tajamar laden with a variety of things,
such as bags of flour in great quantity, armour of different
kinds, and the only cask of wine which was there. They
filled a small cask which they had brought with them, and
drunk and wasted the rest. They also took several trunks,
boxes, and packages of all sorts, with their contents,
which will be spoken of at the proper time and place, as
well as a good many cross-bows, and all the bows that there
were, excepting those which Gadifer had with him at the
island of Lobos. They carried off two hundred bowstrings and
great quantities of line for making cross-bow strings. From
the artillery,[1] of which there was a large quantity both fair

CHAPITRE XVIII.—*Comment Berthin fit charger les deux batiaux
de viures et d'autres choses.*

Et lendemain au matin fit charger Berthin de Berneval le
bastel Gadifer et celuy de la nef Tranchemare de plusieurs
choses, comme de sacs de farine à grande quantité, et du harnas
de plusieurs guises, et vn tonneau de vin qui y estoit, et plus
non y auoit; eux emplirent vne queuë qu'ils amenerent auec eux,
et le demourant beurent et gasterent, et plusieurs coffres, malles
et bouges de plusieurs manieres auec toutes les choses qui
dedãs estoient, lesquelles seront declarees quand temps et lieu
sera ; et plusieurs arbalestres, et tous les arcs qui y estoient, excepté ceux que Gadifer auoit auec luy en l'isle de Loupes : et de
deux cens cordes d'arcs qui y deuoient estre n'en demeura nulle,
et de grand foison de fil pour faire cordes d'arbalestres, tout emporterent auec eux ; et de toute l'artillerie, dequoy il y auoit

---

[1] At that period the word "artillerie" was used very vaguely, including even bows and cross-bows, which indeed seem to be meant in
this very passage.

and good, they took whatever they pleased, and we were obliged to unlay an old cable which was left us to make strings for our bows and arblasts; and had it not been for this small remainder left to us, we had all been in danger of being utterly destroyed; for the Canarians are more afraid of bows than anything else. Besides all these, the Spaniards carried away four dozen darts, and two coffers belonging to Gadifer, with their contents.

CHAPTER XIX.—How Francisco Calvo sent in search of Gadifer in the island of Lobos.

While the boats were going to the ship, Gadifer's people, taking into consideration the destitute condition of their captain, who was entirely deprived of provisions, despatched the two chaplains and two squires of the castle of Rubicon to beg assistance from the captain of the ship Morella,

grand foison de belle et bonne; ont prins et emporté à leur plaisir, et nous à conuenu despesser vn vieux cable qui nous estoit demeure pour faire cordes pour arcs et pour arbalestres: et ce ne fust ce pou de trait que nous auions, nous estions en auanture d'estre tous perdus et destruits: car ilz craignent les arcs sur toutes riens; et auec ce quatre douzaines de dardes que les Espagnols emporterent en leurs mains, et prindrent deux coffres à Gadifer, et ce qui estoit dedans.

CHAPITRE XIX.—*Comment Francisque Calue enuoya querir Gadifer en l'isle de Loupes.*

Ce temps pendant que les batiaux s'en allerent en la nef, les gens de Gadifer considerans que le capitaine auoit telle necessité de viures, comme celuy qui point n'en auoit, lors se partirent les deux chappellains, et deux escuyers du chastel de Rubicon, et s'en allerent deuers le maistre de la nef Morelle, qui estoit au

which, like the Tajamar, was lying in the port of Graciosa.
They prayed the captain, of his charity, to carry succour
to Gadifer de la Salle, who, with eleven companions,
was in the island of Lobos in peril of death, having
been eight days without provisions. The master, moved
with pity on hearing of Berthin's great treachery to Gadifer,
sent one of his comrades, named Ximenes, who came to
Rubicon and set out with four of the Sieur de Bethencourt's
company, namely, Guillaume the Monk, Jean the Chevalier,
Thomas Richard, and Jean the Mason. They crossed
to the island of Lobos in a little cockboat, which had
been left there; but although Berthin had left the cockboat, he had taken away all the oars. Ximenes took
what little provision he could carry, for although the distance is only four leagues, it is the most horrible passage
to be found in these seas, according to the account of all
those who have tried it.

---

port de l'isle Gratieuse, là où estoit la nef Tranchemare, lesquels
prierent le maistre d'icelle comme il luy pleust de sa grace secourir Gadifer de la Salle, lequel estoit en l'isle de Loupes luy
vnzieme en peril de mort sans viures nuls passé auoit huict
iours, et ledit maistre meu de pitié regardant le grand' trahison
que Berthin luy auoit faite, luy enuoya l'vn de ses compagnons
nommé Simene; e luy venu à Rubicon, se mit à l'aduanture
auec quatre compagnons de la compagnie dudit Sieur de Bethencourt, c'est à sçauoir Guillaume le Moyne, Jean le Cheualier,
Thomas Richard, et Jean le Masson; et passerent en l'isle de
Loupes en vn petit coquet qui là estoit demouré : car combien
que Berthin eust laissé le coquet, il emporta tous les auirons, et
print ledit Simene tant pou de viures qu'il peût porter : c'est le
plus horrible passage que nuls sçachent tenir de tous ceux qui en
la mer là endroit conuersent, et ne dure que quatre lieuës.

CHAPTER XX.—How Gadifer returned in the little cockboat to the island of Lancerote.

Meanwhile Gadifer was at the island of Lobos in great distress from hunger and thirst, and looking to our Lord for mercy. Every night he spread out a linen cloth to catch the dew of heaven, then wrung it, and drank the drops to quench his thirst. He knew nothing of what Berthin had done, and was greatly astonished when he came to hear of it. Gadifer alone went into the cockboat, which was steered by Ximenes and his comrades, and they came to Rubicon. "I am much grieved," he said, "at the wickedness and great treachery which have been shewn to these poor people, to whom we had given our assurance of friendship. But we must needs let it pass, for it is beyond our power to remedy the mischief. Praised be God in all his works: He is the judge of this quarrel." Gadifer further said : "Neither M. de Bethencourt nor myself could ever have supposed that this man would have dared to do or to imagine

---

CHAPITRE XX.—Comment Gadifer repassa en vn petit coquet en l'isle Lancerote.

Gadifer estant en l'isle de Loupes en grand' destresse de faim et de soif attendant la mercy de nostre Seigneur, toutes les nuits mettoit vn drap de linge dehors à la rosée du ciel, puis le tordoit, et buuoit les goutes pour estancher la soif, non sçachant riens de tout le fait dudit Berthin : dequoy ledit Gadifer fut fort esmerueillé quand il en ouït parler. Adõc se mit tout seul dedans le coquet, auec le gouuernement dudit Simene et les compagnons dessusdits ; et vindrent à Rubicon, Gadifer disant ainsi: il me poise moult de la grand' mauuaistié et grande trahison qui a esté faite sur ces pauures gẽs que nous auions asseurex. Mais de tout ce nous faut passer, nous n'y pouuons mettre remede, loué soit Dieu en tous ses œuures, lequel est iuge en ceste querelle : et disoit ainsi ledit Gadifer, que Monsieur de Bethen-court et luy n'eussent iamais pensé qu'il eust ozé faire ne

D

what he has done; for both the Sieur de Bethencourt and I chose him as being in our opinion one of the most serviceable men in the company, but we were grievously mistaken."

CHAPTER XXI.—How the two chaplains, Brother Pierre Bontier and Messire Jean le Verrier, went to the ship Tajamar.

Some days afterwards, the two chaplains being in the ship Morella, saw (Berthin's) two boats leaving Rubicon, and carrying off the provisions intended for the support of the garrison, with many other things. They therefore begged the master of the ship to accompany them to the other vessel called Tajamar, which he did, and with them went two nobles, named Pierre du Plessis and Guillaume d'Allemagne. Then said Berthin, "Do not suppose that any of these things are Bethencourt's or Gadifer's; they are mine, as these two chaplains can bear witness." But they, in the presence of

machiner ce qu'il a fait: car ledit Bethencourt et moy, nous l'esleumes en nostre auis comme vn des plus suffisans de la compagnie, et le bon Seigneur et moy fusmes bien mal auisés.

CHAPITRE XXI.—Comment les deux chapelains, l'un nommé Frere Pierre Bontier, et l'autre Messire Jean le Verrier, alerent en la nef Tranchemare.

Les deux chapellains estans à la nef Morelle, aucuns iours apres virent les deux bastiaux venir de Rubicon, qui estoit chargez de vitailles, dequoy nous deuions viure, et de moult d'autres choses. Adonc prierēt le maistre de la nef qu'il luy plut aller auec eux en l'autre nef, dite Tranchemare, lesquels y allerent tous ensemble et deux gentils hommes qui là estoient, l'vn nommé Pierre du Plessis, et l'autre Guillaume d'Alemaigne. Là disoit Berthin, ne cuidez point que nulles de ces choses soient à Bethencourt ne à Gadifer, ils sont miēnes, tesmoings ces deux chapellains-cy, lesquels luy dirent en la presence de tous,

all, replied : " Berthin, what we do know perfectly well is, that when you first came out with M. de Bethencourt, you brought little or nothing with you. And in fact, M. de Bethencourt at the beginning handed over to you in Paris a hundred francs in furtherance of our common enterprise, which please God shall issue to his honour and profit; but these things here present are his property and Gadifer's, as may be seen by the arms and device of the Sieur de Bethencourt." Berthin replied, "If it please God, I shall go straight to Spain, where M. de Bethencourt now is, and if I have anything belonging to him I will restore it to him; but do not you meddle in this matter, and be quite sure that M. de Bethencourt will put to rights certain matters which may easily be guessed without my mentioning them."

Berthin did not like Messire Gadifer, because he held a higher position and was in greater authority than himself, and his idea was that his master M. de Bethencourt would not be so much displeased with him as the others imagined, or at any rate that if he were to fall under his displeasure, it

Berthin nous sçauons bien que quand vous vintes premieremēt auec Monsieur de Bethencourt vous n'auiez qui votre fust, se pou non ou neant, ainchois bailla mōsieur de Bethencourt pour entre nous cent francs à Paris quand il entreprint l'emprise, que se Dieu plaist acheuera et viendra à son hoñeur et proufit, mais ce qui est cy à present est audit Seigneur et à Monsieur Gadifer, et peut bien apparoir par les liurees et deuise dudit Seigneur de Bethencourt. Ledit Berthin respond et dit, se Dieu plaist, i'iray tout droit en Espagne là où est Monsieur de Bethencourt, et se i'ay aucune chose de sien ie luy rendré bien, et de ce ne vous meslez, et ne doutez que ledit Sieur de Bethencourt mettra remede en aucunes choses dequoy on se peut bien douter, et de- quoy ie me peux bien taire ; ledit Berthin n'aimoit point Messire Gadifer pour ce qu'il estoit plus grand maistre que luy et de plus grāde autorité, et ledit Berthin pensoit que ledit Seigneur de Bethencourt son maistre ne luy sçauroit pas si malgré, qu'il estoit aduis aus autres, et que s'il auoit quelque chose qui des-

would not be to them that he should look to make his peace. As they left the ship, they said to Berthin: "Since you are taking away those poor people, leave us at least Isabelle the Canarian, for without her we shall be unable to speak with the inhabitants of the island. Leave us also the boat which you have brought, for we cannot well find means of living without it." Berthin answered, "It is not mine, but belongs to my comrades; they can do as they please." Then the two chaplains and the two squires who accompanied them took possession of the boat. Upon which Berthin's comrades took Isabelle the Canarian and threw her into the sea through the ship's porthole, and she would have been drowned had it not been for the chaplains and squires, who drew her out of the water into the boat; and so the two parties separated, and soon afterwards the ship made ready to put out to sea. This is how things occurred in the matter of Berthin, as above stated, and as you will hereafter hear.

---

pleut à son dit Seigneur qu'il ne les appelleroit pas à en faire la paix, et à tant issirent de la nef, disans ainsi: Berthin puis que vous amenez ces pauures gens, laissez nous Isabel la Canare, car nous ne sçaurions parler aux habitãs qui demeurent en cette isle; et aussi laissez-nous vostre bastel que vous auez amené, car nous ne pouuons pas bonnement viure sans luy; respond Berthin, ce n'est point à moy, mais à mes compagnons, ils en feront leur voulenté, et lors se saisirent les deux chapellains et les deux escuiers qui estoient, dudit bastel. Adonc les compagnons de Berthin prindrent Isabel la Canare et par le sabort de la nef la jetterent en la mer, et elle eut esté noyée ce ne fussent les dessus-dits chapelains et escuiers, lesquels la tirerent hors de la mer, et la mirent au bastel: et à tant partirent les vns des autres, et assez-tost apres s'aparlierent ceux de la nef pour eux en aller, et ainsi se porta le fait de Berthin comme dessus est dit et comme vous orrez cy apres.

CHAPTER XXII.—How Berthin left his comrades on shore and went off with his booty.

And now that Berthin had all his companions with him on board the ship, he, having made up his mind to go all lengths in wickedness, so contrived as to get his more immediate accomplices on shore again, even those by whose help he had carried out all the treachery that has been described; for if they had not been leagued with him, he never could have ventured on his treasonable practices. But now this miscreant said to them, " Shift for yourselves as best you can, for you shall not come with me." Berthin's reason for doing this was that he feared that they might do the same to him, and he also intended to tell his own tale to M. de Bethencourt when he arrived in Spain, and make his peace with him. And so in fact he did, by putting a good face upon his story, and making certain statements, which Monsieur de Bethencourt found to be partly true, as you shall hear further on. Nevertheless, M. de Bethencourt became

CHAPITRE XXII.—*Comment Berthin laissa ses compagnons à terre, et s'en alla à tout sa proye.*

Et combien que Berthin et ses compagnons fussent en la nef en sa compagnie, luy ayant voulonté de tout mal accomplir fit tant que ses compagnons qui estoient de sa bende furent mis à terre ; par lesquels il auoit fait tout l'exploit deuant dit de sa trahison ; car s'ils n'eussent esté auec luy et de son alliance, il n'eust ozé faire ne entreprendre la trahison et la mauuaistié qu'il fit, et leur dit le tres-mauuais homme, donnés vous le meilleur conseil que vous pourrez : car auec moy ne vous en vendrés point, et pour ce le faisoit ledit Berthin qu'il auoit peur que iceux ne luy fissent au cas pareil, et aussi ledit Berthin auoit intention de parler à Monsieur de Bethencourt quand il viendroit en Espagne et de faire sa paix enuers luy, laquelle il fit le mieux qu'il peût, en luy donnant entendre aucunes choses dont vne partie ledit Seigneur de Bethencourt trouua verité, comme vn

fully aware of what had taken place, and that Berthin had
done it all from avarice.

CHAPTER XXIII.—How the followers of Berthin, whom he had left on
shore in despair, made their way straight to the land of the Saracen.

Berthin's accomplices whom he had left on shore were in
great dismay, for they dreaded the anger not only of M. de
Bethencourt and of Gadifer, but of their companions. They
poured out their complaints to the chaplains and squires,
and said—" Berthin is a convicted traitor, for he has betrayed not only his captain but us. Then some of them
confessed to Messire Jean le Verrier, Monseigneur de
Bethencourt's chaplain, and said, " If our captain Gadifer
would pardon the wickedness we have committed against
him, we would bind ourselves to serve him all our lives ;"
and they commissioned Guillaume d'Allemagne to lay their
request before him, and to let them know the answer.

---

temps aduenir vous orrez, iaçoit que ledit Seigneur fust bien aduerty de son fait, et qu'il auoit tout ce fait par son auarice.

CHAPITRE XXIII.—*Comment les compagnons que Berthin laissa à
terre desesperez, prindrent leur chemin droit à la terre des
Sarrasins.*

Iceux compagnons à terre tout desconfortez doutans l'ire de
Monsieur de Bethencourt, et de Gadifer, et aussi des compagnons
qui y estoyent, se compleignerent aux chapellains et escuyers
dessusdits, disans aussi-bien est Berthin approuué traistre ; car
il a trahy son capitaine aussi a-il nous-mesmes, et là se confes-
serent aucuns d'eux à Messire Jean le Verrier, chapelain de
Monseigneur de Bethencourt, et disoient ainsi ; se nostre capitaine Gadifer nous vouloit pardonner la mauuaistié que nous
auons faite contre luy, nous serions tenus à le seruir toute nostre
vie ; et chargerent Guillaume d'Alemaigne de luy requerir au
nom d'eux, et de leur faire asçauoir la responce ; et se partit in-

Guillaume went off immediately on his message, but they soon afterwards, having misgivings about his return, and fearing the wrath of their captain whom they had so grievously offended, took the boat and put out to sea, steering straight for the country of the Moors, half way between the Canary islands and Spain. They were upset on the coast of Barbary near Morocco, and ten out of the twelve were drowned. The other two were made slaves. One is since dead, and the other, whose name is Siot de Lartigue, is still alive in the hands of the infidels.

CHAPTER XXIV.—How, after M. de Bethencourt had reached Spain, Gadifer's ship was lost.[1]

We will return to M. de Bethencourt, who, on reaching Spain, anchored the ship (which is said to have belonged to

continent ledit Guillaume pour aller deuers luy. Mais assez-tost apres, eux doutans sa venue, se saisirent du bastel et se mirent dedans, et s'eslargirent bien auant en la mer, eux considerans le mal et le peché enquoy ils auoient offensé deuers vn tel cheualier et leur capitaine, eux craignans l'ire et le courroux d'iceluy comme gens desesperez prindrēt leur chemin à tout le bastel droit en terre des Mores, car les Mores peuuent bien estre myvoy de là et d'Espagne, et de leur gouuernemēt. Ils s'allerent noyer en la coste de Barbarie prés de Maroc, et de douze qu'ils estoient les dix furent noyez, et les deux furent esclaues : dequoy l'vn est depuis mort, et l'autre qui s'appelle Siot de Lartigue est demouré vif en la main des Payens.

CHAPITRE XXIV.—*Comment la nef de Messire Gadifer fut perie.*

Si retournerons à parler de Monsieur de Bethencourt, et dirons que la nef où il estoit arriué en Espagne, laquelle on disoit

[1] In order to place the narrative clearly before the reader, it has been found necessary to transpose the order of events in this chapter.

Gadifer) in the harbour of Cadiz. And knowing that the
crew was mutinous and badly disposed, he lost no time in
throwing the ringleaders into prison, and so secured the
vessel to himself. As he could now leave the ship with
safety, he set off to Seville, where was the King of Castile,
and while there he encountered Francisco Calvo, who had
just arrived from the Canaries, and who offered, if Bethencourt saw fit, to return thither and revictual Gadifer.
Bethencourt replied that he would give the matter his
earliest consideration, but that at present he must seek an
audience of the King. This he did, as we shall hear more
fully, and received a most gracious welcome. Several
merchants made him offers for the purchase of the ship,
but he refused them all, intending to take it and many
others back with him to the Canaries laden with provisions,
for he had risen high in the favour of the King of Castile.
Accordingly he sent word for it to come from Cadiz to
Seville, but on her road she was unfortunately wrecked and

---

qu'elle estoit à Gadifer, et arriua au port de Calix, ledit sieur
sçachāt bien que les maroniers de ladicte nef estoient mauuais et
malicieux, fit grand' diligence encontre eux; et en fit mettre en
prison aucuns des plus principaux et print la nef en sa main. Il
vint aucuns marchands pour l'achepter, mais ledit sieur ne le
vouloit pas; car son intention estoit de retourner dedans la nef
et d'autres auec, esdites Isles de Canare, et y porter et enuoyer
de la vitaille: car il estoit fort entré en grace du Roy de Castille.
Il fit ladite nef partir du port de Calix pour la mener en Siuille
cuidant bien faire, et en allant elle fut perduë et perie, dont fut
vn grand dommage, et fut au port de Basremede, et ainsi qu'ō
dit, il y auoit des bagues qui valoiēt de l'argent qui appartenoient
à Messire Gadifer de la Salle, et ce qui en fut recueilly valoit
bien cinq cens doubles, ainsi qu'on dit, qui ne vint point au profit ne à la cognoissance dudit Gadifer. Et aucun pou deuant que
la nef fut perie, s'en estoit allé Monsieur de Bethencourt de
Calix en Siuille là où estoit le Roy de Castille; et là vint Francisque Calue qui promptement estoit arriué des Isles de Canare,

lost on the bar of San Lucar de Barrameda, whither he immediately hastened. It is said that several rings belonging
to Messire Gadifer de la Salle were found, to the value of
five hundred ducats, which the owner never saw or heard
of again.

CHAPTER XXV.—How the ship Tajamar arrived at the port of Cadiz
with the prisoners.

Some days afterwards the ship Tajamar arrived at the
port of Cadiz with Berthin on board and some of his partizans, the rest having in their desperation made their way
to the Moorish coast and been drowned. With Berthin
were the poor Canarians from Lancerote, who, under a
semblance of good faith, had been treacherously captured,
to be sold as slaves in foreign lands. But with him also
came one Courtille, Gadifer's trumpeter, who forthwith had
Berthin arrested, with all his accomplices, proceeded against

---

et se presenta de retourner deuers Gadifer s'il luy plaisoit de
l'auitailler; et il luy dit qu'il en ordonneroit le plus tost qu'il
pourroit; mais il falloit qu'il allast deuers le Roy de Castille qui
adonc estoit en Siuille, et ainsi fit-il, comme vous orrez plus à
plain; et la grand' chere et la bien-venüe que ledit Roy luy fit.

CHAPITRE XXV.—*La nef Tranchemare arriue au port de Calix auec
les prisonniers.*

En aucuns iours apres arriua la nef Tranchemare au port de
Calix; là où estoit Berthin et vne partie de ceux qui auoient esté
consentans auecques luy; car les autres qui estoient de son alliance par desespoir s'estoient allez noyer en la costiere de la terre
des Mores. Et auoit Berthin auec luy les poures Canares
habitans de l'Isle Lancelot, que soubz ombre de bonne foy ils
auoient pris par trahison pour les mener vendre en estranges
terres comme esclaues au perpetuel seruage; et là estoit Courtille,
trompette de Gadifer, qui incontinent fit prendre Berthin et tous
ses compagnons; et fit faire le procez contre eux, et par main de

them at law, and had them put in chains and cast into the king's prison at Cadiz. At the same time he sent information to Monsieur de Bethencourt, who was then at Seville, of all that had occurred, and intimated that if he would come, he could rescue all the poor Canarians. Monsieur de Bethencourt was much amazed to hear such news; and sent to say that he would put all these matters to rights as soon as he was able, but that he could not leave Seville at once, as he was about to have an audience of the King of Castile to speak of that and other matters. But whilst Monsieur de Bethencourt was transacting his business with the King of Castile, Fernando d'Ordoñez took the ship to Aragon with all her cargo and the prisoners and sold them.

CHAPTER XXVI.—How M. de Bethencourt did homage to the King of Spain.

Before Monsieur de Bethencourt took his departure from the island of Lancerote and the Canaries, he had put every-

---

Justice les fit enchaisner et mettre és prisōs du Roy en Calix, et fit sçauoir à Monsieur de Bethencourt qui estoit en Siuille, tout le faict, et que s'il vouloit là venir il recouureroit tous les pauures Canares. Ledit sieur fut bien esbahy d'ouyr telles nouuelles, et leur māda que le plus tost qu'il pourroit il y mettroit remede. Mais il ne se pouuoit partir pour ceste heure, car il estoit sur le poinct de parler au Roy de Castille pour cela et pour autre chose. Et tandis que ledit Seigneur de Bethencourt fit ses besongnes deuers le Roy de Castille, vn nommé Ferrant d'Ordongnes ammena la nef en Arragon et tout le fardage et les prisonniers, et les vendit.

CHAPITRE XXVI.—*Comment Monsieur de Bethencourt fit hommage au Roy d'Espagne.*

Et comme il soit ainsi que auant que Monsieur de Bethencourt se partit de l'Isle Lancelot et des Isles de Canare, ledit Seigneur

thing in order to the best of his power, and had left Messire
Gadifer the entire command, promising to return as soon as
he could with reinforcements both of men and provisions, and
never contemplating such disorder as afterwards ensued.
Still, as one may readily understand, it is not easy to
obtain an early audience of so great a prince as the King
of Castile upon such a matter as this. When he had made
his reverence to the King, who received him very graciously,
and inquired what he wanted, Bethencourt said, "I come,
Sire, to pray you to be pleased to grant me permission to
conquer and bring to the Christian faith certain islands
called the Islands of Canary, in which I have been, and
have so far made a commencement, that I have left some of
my people there, who are daily looking for my return. I
have also left a good knight named Master Gadifer de la
Salle, who was pleased to join me in the expedition. And,
inasmuch, Sire, as you are king and lord of all the country
adjacent to these islands, and the nearest Christian sovereign,
I am come to ask that you will be graciously pleased to

ordonna au mieux qu'il peût de ses besongnes, et laissa à Messire
Gadiffer tout le gouuernement, luy promettant que le plus tost
qu'il pourroit il reuiendroit le secourir, et rafraischir de gens et
de viures, non pensant qu'il y eust vn tel defroy qu'il y a eu.
Mais comme on peut sçauoir que auoir à besongner à vn tel
Prince, comme le Roy de Castille, on ne peut pas auoir si tost
fait, et pour vne telle matiere que c'est. Ledit Seigneur de
Bethencourt vint faire la reuerêce audit Roy, lequel le receut
bien benignemêt, et luy demanda qu'il vouloit, et ledit Bethencourt luy dit: Sire, ie viens à secours à vous. C'est qu'il vous
plaise me donner congé de cõquerir et mettre à la foy Chrestiêne
vnes isles qui s'appellent les Isles de Canare, esquelles i'ay esté,
et commencé tant que i'y ay laissé de ma compagnie, qui tous
les iours m'attendent, et y ay laissé vn bõ cheualier nommé
Messire Gadifer de la Salle, lequel il luy a pleu me tenir compagnie. Et pour ce, tres-cher Sire, que vous estes Roy et Seigneur de tout le pays à l'enuirõ, et le plus prez Roy Chrestiê : Je
suis venu requerãt vostre grace, qu'il vous plaise me receuoir à

permit me to do you homage for them." On hearing this, the king was very pleased, gave him welcome, and commended him highly for having conceived so good and honourable a project as to come from such a distance as the kingdom of France with the view of making conquests and winning honour. The king further said, " It shows a very good intention on his part to come to do me homage for a country which, as I understand, is at two hundred leagues distance, and of which I never heard before." The king then spoke encouragingly to De Bethencourt, and told him that he was pleased with his proposition and accepted his homage, and in so far as it was possible, gave him the lordship of those Canary islands. He also granted him the fifth of the merchandise, which should come from those islands to Spain; which fifth Monsieur de Bethencourt received for a long time. The king further made him an immediate grant of twenty thousand maravedies,[1] to be received in Seville, for the purchase of provisions for Gadifer and those who were left with him. This money was made payable by

---

vous en faire hommage. Le Roy que l'ouyt parler fut fort ioyeux, et dit qu'il fust le bien venu, et le prisa fort d'auoir si bon et honneste vouloir de venir de si loin, comme du Royaume de France, conquerir et acquerir honneur. Et disoit ainsi le Roy: "Il luy vient d'vn bon courage, de vouloir venir me faire hōmage d'vne chose qui est, ainsi que ie peux entendre, plus de deux cens lieues d'icy, et dequoy ie n'ouys oncques parler." Le Roy luy dit qu'il fist bonne chere, et qu'il estoit content de tout ce qu'il voudroit, et le receut à l'hommage, et luy donna la Seigneurie, tout autant qu'il estoit possible, des dictes Isles de Canare; et en outre luy donna le quint des marchandises qui des dites isles iroyent en Espagne; lequel quint ledit sieur de Bethencourt leua vne grand' saison; et encore donna le Roy, pour auitailler Gadiffer et ceux qui estoyent demourez auec luy, vingt mille marauesins à les prendre en Siuille. Lequel argent fut

---

[1] This coin was so named from the Moorish tribe of Almoravides, who introduced it into Spain. The smallness of its value may be judged by twenty thousand being given for the purpose here mentioned.

order of Monsieur de Bethencourt to Enguerrant de la Boissière, who seems not to have done his duty with respect to it, for it is said that he went off to France with all, or at any rate a part of it. However, Monsieur de Bethencourt soon supplied the loss by sending stores of provisions, and himself returned to the islands as soon as he could, as will be seen presently. The king also gave him leave to coin money in the Canaries, which he did, when he came into peaceful possession of those islands.

CHAPTER XXVII.—How Enguerrand de la Boissière sold the boat belonging to the lost ship.

As Enguerrand de la Boissière had sold the boat of the wrecked ship, had taken the money, and written letters in which he pretended to be about to send provisions, Gadifer and his party were in great want of necessaries till M. de Bethencourt sent to supply them; they even passed a whole Lent with nothing but flesh-meat.[1] There is no one, how-

baillé par le commandement de Monsieur de Bethencourt à Enguerrant de la Boissiere, lequel n'en fit pas fort son deuoir; et dit on que ledit de la Boissiere s'en alla en France à tout, ou vne partie. Mais pourtant ledit sieur de Bethencourt y remedia bien bref, et tant qu'ils eurent des viures, et y retourna luy mesme tout le plus bref qu'il peut, comme vous y orrez cy aprés. Le Roy luy donna congé de faire monnoye au pays de Canare, et aussi fit-il, quand il fut vestu et saisi paisiblement desdites isles.

CHAPITRE XXVII.—*Comment Anguerrand de la Boissiere vendit le bastel de la nef perie.*

Comme Enguerrāt de la Boissiere le bastel de la nef qui fut perie il vendit, et en print l'argent, et feignit lettres qu'il leur vouloit transmettre vitailles; pour laquelle chose ils eurent grande deffaulte iusques à tant que Monsieur de Bethencourt y eust remedié: car ils vescurent vn caresme qui falut qu'ils mangeassent

---

[1] The meaning seems to be that they were destitute of all food except such meat—probably goat's flesh—as they could get.

ever powerful, who is not liable to deceit and treachery, and
M. de Bethencourt, in entrusting the money of the King of
Castile to the said Enguerrand, had full faith in his
probity. A certain Jean de Lesecases informed him of
Enguerrand's dishonesty, and he immediately applied to the
King for a ship and men to go to the relief of his people in
the islands. Accordingly the King gave him a well mounted
vessel, with eighty active men, besides four tuns of wine,
seventeen sacks of corn, and other useful things in the
shape of arms and other provisions. And M. de Bethencourt wrote to Master Gadifer bidding him to manage
matters as well as he could, and to keep the men he was
sending well employed, promising to come himself as soon
as possible. He also sent him word that he had done
homage for the islands to the King of Castile and had been
welcomed very graciously, and moreover had received a sum
of money and many promises of future benefits, and that he

---

de la chair; et comme on peut sçauoir nully tant soit grand ne
se peut garder de faulseté et de trahison. Ledit Seigneur auoit
fait bailler l'argent que le Roy de Castille luy auoit donné, audit
Enguerrant, cuidāt qu'il en fist son deuoir. Vn nommé Jean de
Lesecases encusa audit Bethencourt ledit Enguerrant, et qu'il ne
faisoit pas son deuoir de l'argent que le Roy luy auoit fait bailler.
Adonc ledit Sieur de Bethencourt vint deuers le Roy, et luy
pria qu'il luy pleust luy faire auoir vne nef et des gens pour
secourir ceux des isles: laquelle chose luy fit bailler vne nef bien
artillée, et en celle nef y auoit bien quatre vingt hommes de fait :
et si luy fit bailler quatre tonneaux de vin, et dix-sept sacs de
farine, et plusieurs choses necessaires qui leur falloit, feust artillerie et autres prouisions; et rescrit Monsieur de Bethencourt a
Messire Gadifer, qu'il entretinst les choses tout le mieux qu'il
peust, et qu'il seroit és isles tout le plus bref qu'il se pourra
faire, et qu'il mist les gens qu'il luy enuoye en besōgne et qu'ils
besongnassent tousiours fermement : et si luy rescrit qu'il auoit
fait hommage au Roy de Castille des Isles de Canare, et que le
Roy luy a fait grād' chere et plus d'honneur qu'à luy n'appartient,
et si lui avoit donné de l'argent et promis de faire beaucoup de

did not doubt to rejoin Gadifer very shortly. "The vessel," he wrote, "will be under your orders to make a tour of the islands, as I should counsel you to do, that you may better judge of your future line of conduct. I have been amazed at the treachery of Berthin de Berneval, who is sure to suffer for it sooner or later. He had given me no cause to suspect him; though I was told subsequently that he had no great affection for you, and wrote to warn you against him. My very dear brother and friend, one must suffer many things in this world; it is best to forget what is past, and to do our duty to the best of our ability."

Gadifer was very pleased at the arrival of the vessel and the contents of the letter, except at the announcement of the homage to the King of Castile, for he had expected to share in the possession and profits of the islands, which was not the intention of M. de Bethencourt, as will be seen. Consequently there arose disputes and quarrels between the two gentlemen, which very probably prevented the con-

---

biens, et qu'il ne doutast point qu'il ne feust pas deuers luy bien bref, et tout le plustost qu'il se pourra faire, la barque ira là où vous voudrez requerir d'aller autour des isles, laquelle chose ie conseille que faciez; pour tousiours sçauoir, comme on s'y deuera gouuerner. I'ay esté bien esbahy des grands faulsetés que Berthin de Berneual a fait, et ly en mesprendra quelle qui tarde: il ne m'a pas donné à entēdre ainsi, que ie l'ay sçeu depuis, ie vous auois rescrit que on prinst garde à luy: car on m'auoit biē dit qu'il ne vous aimoit point de grand' amour; mon tres-cher frere et amy, il faut souffrir beaucoup de choses; ce qui est passé il le faut oublier, en faisant tousiours le mieux qu'ō pourra. Le-dit Gadifer fut tout iouieux de tout, de la venuë de la barque et de ce qu'il luy auoit rescrit, sinon de ce que il lui rescrisoit qu'il fait hommage au Roy de Castille: car il en pensoit auoir part et portion desdites isles de Canares, laquelle chose n'est pour l'in-tention dudit sieur de Bethencourt, comme il apperra de fait; iaçoit qu'il y aura de grosses paroles et des noises entre les deux cheualiers; et peut bien estre que les dites isles eussent esté piessa conquises, ce ne fust esté aucunes ennies. Car la com-

quest of the islands; for the crew would obey none but
M. de Bethencourt, as was natural, since he was the proper
head and leader, and the promoter of the expedition.
Meanwhile M. de Bethencourt was making his preparations
with all possible speed, for his one only object was to
accomplish the conquest of the Canaries. When M. de
Bethencourt left Lancerote, it had been his intention to go
to France, and bring back Madame de Bethencourt; and
he did in fact bring her as far as Cadiz, but no farther
(for reasons which do not appear). And as soon as he
had done homage to the King, he sent back Madame
de Bethencourt with great honour to his house of Grainville la Teinturière in Normandy, under the care of Enguerrand de la Boissière. Soon afterwards M. de Bethencourt left Seville with a small escort which the King had
given him, together with all sorts of arms, with which he
was much gratified. Meanwhile, Mme. de Bethencourt
arrived safely at Grainville, where she was joyfully wel-

pagnie ne vouloit obeyr qu'à Monsieur de Bethencourt; aussi
c'estoit bien raison, car il estoit le droit chef et meneur, et
premier mouuemēt de la conqueste desdites isles: ledit de Bethencourt fait ses apprestes tant le plutost qu'il peut, car tout le
desir qu'il a, c'est de venir parfaire la conqueste des isles de
Canare. Quand ledit sieur de Bethencourt partit de l'isle Lancelot, c'estoit son intention d'aller iusques en France et ramener
Madame de Bethencourt, car il l'auoit fait venir auec luy iusques
au port de Calix, et elle ne passa point ledit port de Calix et incontinent qu'il eust fait hommage au Roy, il fit ramener madite
Dame sa femme en Normandie iusques à son Hostel de Grainuille de Tanturiere, et Enguerrant de la Boissiere fut en sa compagnie, ledit Seigneur la fit mener bien honnestement: et tantost
apres ledit Seigneur se partit de Siuille, à toute vne belle petite
compagnie que le Roy de Castille luy fit auoir; et si luy donna
le Roy de Castille de l'artillerie de toute maniere tant qu'il fut et
deuoit bien estre content. Or s'en va Madame de Bethencourt
en son pays de Normandie, en sondit Hostel de Grainuille, au

comed by her people, and where she remained till her husband returned from the Canaries, as you will hear in the sequel.

CHAPTER XXVIII.—The names of those who were treacherous to Gadifer, the natives of Lancerote, and their own comrades.

The following are the names of those who were accomplices in Berthin's treachery. After Berthin, Pierre des[1] Liens, Augerot de Montignac, Ciot[2] de Lartigue, Bernard de Castellenau,[3] Guillaume de Nau, Bernard de Mauléon called the Cock, Guillaume de Salerne called Labat, Maurelet de Conrengé,[4] Jean de Bidouville, Bidaut de Hornay,[5] Bernard de Montauban, Jean de l'Aleu,[6] the Bastard de Blessi, Philippot de Baslieu, Olivier de la Barre, big Perrin, Gillet de la Bordeniere, Jean le Brun, Jean, Bethencourt's seamster,

---

pays de Caux, là où ceux du pays luy firent grand' chere, et fut là iusques à tant que mondit Seigneur reuinst de Canare comme vous orrez cy-apres.

CHAPITRE XXVIII.—*Les noms de ceux qui trahirent Gadifer, et ceux de l'isle Lancelot et leurs propres compagnons.*

Ce sont les noms tous ensemble de ceux qui ont esté traistres auec Berthin; et premierement ledit Berthin et Pierre des Liens, Ogerot de Montignac, Ciot de Lartigue, Bernard de Castellenau, Guillaume de Nau, Bernard de Mauleon, dit le Coq, Guillaume de Salerne, dit Labat, Maurelet de Conrengé, Jean de Bidouille, Bidaut de Hornay, Bernard de Montauban, Jean de l'Aleu, le Bastart de Blessi, Phlippot de Baslieu, Oliuier de la Barre, le grand Perrin, Gillet de la Bordeniere, Jean le Brun, Jean le

---

[1] In chapter 10, " de."
[2] In chapter 10, " Siort."
[3] In chapter 10, " Chastelvary."
[4] In chap. 10, " Morelet de Couroge."
[5] In chapter 10, " Hournau."
[6] In chapter 10, " Alieu."

E

Pernet the blacksmith, Jacques the baker, Michelet the
cook. All these were the cause of much mischief. Most
of them were from Gascony, Anjou, and Poitou. Three
were from Normandy. But we will leave speaking of
this matter, and return to Messire Gadifer and those who
were with him.

CHAPTER XXIX.—How the natives of Lancerote became alienated
from the followers of Bethencourt after the treachery of Berthin.

The people of Lancerote were much aggrieved at being
thus betrayed and captured, and imagined that our faith
and law could not be as good as we represented, since we
betrayed each other, and were not consistent in our actions.
At last their rage and terror became so extreme, that they
turned against us and killed our people. And because

Cousturier de Bethencourt, Pernet le Mareschal, Jacquet le
Boulanger, Michelet le Cuisinier; tous iceux deuant dits ont esté
cause de beaucoup de mal, et la plupart estoient du pays de
Gascongne, d'Anjou, de Poitou et trois de Normandie. Nous
laissons à parler de celle maniere, et parlerons de Messire et de
la compagnie.

CHAPITRE XXIX.—*Comme ceux de l'isle Lancerote s'estrangerent
des gens de Monsieur de Bethencourt apres la trahison que
Berthin leur auoit faite.*

Les gens de l'isle Lancerote furent tres mal contens de ce
qu'ils furent prins et trahis, tant qu'ils disoient que nostre foy et
nostre loy n'estoit point si bonne que nous disions quãd nous
traissons l'vn l'autre, et que nous faisions si terrible chose l'vn
contre l'autre, et que nous n'estions point fermes à nos faits : et
furent iceux Payens de Lancerote tous meus contre nous, et
s'estrangeoient fort, tant qu'ils se rebellerent et tuerent de nos
gens, dont ce fut pitié et dommage : et pour ce que Gadiffer ne

Gadifer had it not then in his power to pursue the matter himself, he appealed to all the authorities in France and elsewhere to bring to justice the authors of all this mischief, if they should fall into their hands.

CHAPTER XXX.—How Asche, one of the principal men in Lancerote, proposed to betray the King.

Matters being brought to this pass, that our religion was despised, ourselves evil spoken of, and above all our companions killed and wounded, Gadifer threatened to kill all upon whom he could lay hands unless those who had slain our companions were given up. About this time a certain native named Asche, who aspired to the throne of Lancerote, held much consultation with Messire Gadifer: presently he went away, and a few days after sent his nephew (whom M.

peut, quant à present, le fait bonnement poursuiure, ainsi qu'il desire, il requert tous iusticiers du Royaume de France et d'ailleurs en ayde de droit, et que en cecy, ils accomplissent iustice, se aucuns des malfacteurs peuuent estre attains et cheoir à leurs mains, ainsi comme à tel cas appartient.

CHAPITRE XXX.—*Comme Ache, vn des plus grands de lille Lancerote, fit traiter de prendre le Roy.*

Or est ainsi que apres que ceste chose est aduenuë, dequoy nous sommes fort diffamez par deçà, et nostre foy desprisée, laquelle ils tenoient à bonne, et maintenant tiennent le contraire, et en outre ont tué nos compagnons; et blessé plusieurs. Si leur manda Gadiffer qu'ils luy rendissent ceux qui ce auoient fait, ou qu'il feroit mourir tous ceux qu'il pourroit attaindre des leurs. Durant ces choses vint deuers luy vn nomme Asche payen de ladite isle qui vouloit estre Roy de l'isle Lancerote, et parlerent Messire Gadiffer et luy moult longuement sur celle matiere. Et tant s'en alla Asche, et aucuns iours apres il transmit son neveu;

de Bethencourt had sent from France as interpreter) to say
that the King hated the Christians, so that during his life
they would have little success; that he had caused the
death of our companions, but that Asche would find means
to deliver him and all the other culprits into our hands.
At this Gadifer rejoiced greatly, and sent word to him to
take his measures well and to let him know the place and
the hour, which was done.

CHAPTER XXXI.—How Asche betrayed his master in the hope of en-
        trapping Gadifer and his companions.

Now this was a double treachery, for by betraying the
King his master, he hoped, with the help of his nephew
Alphonse, who was constantly with them, to entrap Gadifer
and his men, thinking that their small numbers would ren-

lequel Monsieur de Bethencourt auoit amené de France pour estre
son truchement, et luy manda que le Roy le hayoit, et que tant
qu'il vesquist nous n'aurions riens d'eux sinon à grand' peine; et
qu'il estoit du tout coulpable de la mort de ses gens; et s'il vouloit qu'il trouueroit bien maniere qu'il luy fairoit bien prendre le
Roy et tous ceux qui furent à la mort de ses compagnons; dont
Gadiffer fut moult ioyeux, et luy manda qu'il appoinctast bien la
besongne, et que il luy fit sçauoir le temps et l'heure, et ainsi fut
fait.

CHAPITRE XXXI.—*Comme Ache trahit son Seigneur en esperance
        de trahir Gadifer et sa compagnie.*

Or estoit ceste traïson double, car il vouloit trayr le Roy son
Seigneur et estoit son propos et son intention de traïr apres
Gadiffer et toutes ses gens, par l'enhortement de son neveu
nommé Alphonce, lequel demeuroit continuellement auec nous;
et sçauoit que nous estions si peu de gens, qui luy sembloit bien
qu'il n'y auoit gueres affaire à nous destruire, car nous n'estions

der them an easy prey. But we shall see in the sequel how he succeeded. When Asche judged that the opportunity was come, he sent to summon Gadifer, telling him that the King was in one of his castles, in a village near Acatif, with fifty of his people. This was on the eve of St. Catharine, 1402. Gadifer immediately took nineteen men, and, marching all night, arrived at the spot before daybreak, and found them in a house taking counsel against the Christians. He thought to have entered without difficulty, but they had set a guard round the house, who made a desperate defence, and wounded several of our men. Five of those who killed our companions came out, three of whom received fearful wounds, one with the sword and the others with arrows. At last the Christians succeeded in forcing the house, but as Gadifer had found that the men in it were not guilty of the death of his men, he set them free at the instance of Asche. He only retained the King and another named Alby, and having chained them round the neck, led them straight to the

---

demeurez en vie qu'vn bien peu de gens de deffence. Or orrez qu'il en aduint ; quand Asche vit son poinct pour faire prendre le Roy, il manda à Gadifer qu'il vinst et que le Roy estoit en vn de ces chastiaux en vn village pres de l'Acatif, et auoit cinquante de ses gens auec luy, et fut la veille Saincte Catherine, mil quatre cens et deux, et s'en alla toute nuit et arriua sur eux ainchois qu'il fust iour, là où ils estoiët tous en vne maison, et auoient leur conseil contre nous. Si cuida entrer sur eux, mais ils garderent l'entrée de la maison, et mirent grand' deffence en eux, et blesserent plusieurs de nos gens, et s'en yssirent cinq de ceux qui auoient esté à tuer nos compagnons, dont les trois furent mallement blessés, l'vn d'vne espée parmy le corps, les autres de flesches ; si entrerent nos gens sur eux à force et les prindrent ; mais pource que Gadifer ne les trouua point coulpables de la mort de ses gens, il les deliura à la requeste dudit Asche ; et fut retenu le Roy et vn autre nommé Alby, lesquels il fit enchesner par les cols, et les mena tout droit en la place où ses gens

place where his men had been killed. When he reached
this spot, where the bodies had been covered over with
earth, his anger overcame him, and seizing Alby, he would
have struck off his head, but the King assured him that he
had not been guilty of the death of the men, and offered
his own head to the axe if he should be found either guilty
or conniving at the slaughter. Gadifer warned him that
what he said would be at his own peril, for he should in-
form himself thoroughly on the matter. The King further
promised Gadifer to. give up all those who were concerned
in the death of his men. They then returned all together
to Rubicon, where the King was put into two sets of irons.
After a few days he freed himself from one pair of fetters,
which were too wide. When Gadifer saw this, he had him
put in chains, and removed the other pair of fetters, which
galled him badly.

---

auoient este tuez, et les trouua où il les auoient couuers de terre,
et moult courcé print ledit Alby, et luy vouloit faire trencher la
teste ; mais le Roy luy dit enverité qu'il n'auoit point esté à la
mort des compagnons ; et s'il trouuoit qu'il en eust oncques esté
consentant ne coulpable, qu'il obligeoit sa teste à coupper. Lors
dit Gadiffer que bien se gardât, et que ce seroit à son peril, car il
s'informeroit tout à plain, et en outre le Roy luy promit qu'il luy
bailleroit tous ceux qui furent à tuer ses gens, et atant s'en
allerent tous ensemble au chastel de Rubicon, là fut mis le Roy
en deux peres de fers. Aucuns iours apres se deliura par faute
de fers mal acoustrés qui estoient trop larges ; quand Gadifer vit
cela, il fit enchainer ledit Roy, et luy fit oster vn pere de fers qui
moult le blessoient.

CHAPTER XXXII.—How Asche stipulated with Gadifer that he should
be made King.

A few days after Asche came to the castle of Rubicon, and
it was arranged that he should be made King on condition
that he and his partisans should receive baptism. When
the King saw him, he looked at him with indignation, exclaim-
ing: "*Fore troncqueuay*," which means "Wicked traitor."
Asche, however, took leave of Gadifer, and invested himself
with the royal robes. A few days after, Gadifer sent
seven men in quest of barley, for the store of bread was
almost out. They collected a great quantity, and placed it
in an old castle, which was said to have been built by
Lancelot Maloisel,[1] and then set out to fetch men from

CHAPITRE XXXII.—*Comme Asche appointa à Gadifer qu'il seroit
Roy.*

En aucuns iours apres vint Asche au chastel de Rubicon: et
parlerent qu'il seroit Roy par condition qu'il feroit baptiser luy
et tous ceux de sa part, et quand le Roy le vit venir, il le regarda
moult despitement en disant: "*Fore troncqueuay*," c'est à dire,
Traistre mauuais. Et ainsi se partit Asche de Gadifer, et se
vestit comme Roy; et aucuns iours apres transmit Gadifer de
ses gens pour querir de l'orge: car nous n'auions plus de pain si
peu non. Si assemblerent grande quantité d'orge, et le mirent
en vn vieil chastel que Lancerote Maloisel auoit jadis fait faire,

---

[1] This important reference to an earlier occupation of the island is
connected with the naming of the island of Lancerote, and also carries
us back to a fact in the history of Atlantic exploration which has been
only recently developed. M. d'Avezac, with his usual untiring research,
has shewn that the discoverer of this island was of the ancient, but now
extinct, Genoese family of Malocello. In a Genoese map of the date of
1455, made by Bartolommeo Pareto, are inserted against the island the
words "Lansaroto Maroxello Januensis;" and a passage in Petrarch
(born in 1304), to the effect that an armed Genoese fleet had penetrated
as far as the Fortunate Islands a generation back (a patrum memoriâ),

Rubicon to carry the barley. On their road they met the
new King Asche with twenty-three men, who greeted them
with great appearance of friendship, and joined company
with them. But Jean le Courtois and his companions began
to mistrust him, and kept close together, except Guillaume

---

selon que lon dit, et de là se partirent et se mirent en chemin
sept compagncns pour venir à Rubicon querir des gens pour y
porter l'orge, et quand ils furent sur le chemin, ledit Asche qui
estoit fait nouueau Roy, soy vingt-quatriesme, vint allencontre
d'eux en semblance d'amitié et allerent longuement ensemble :
mais Jean le Courtois et ses compagnons se commenceret à
douter vn peu, et se tenoient tous ensemble, et ne vouloient
point qu'ils assemblassent fors que Guillaume d'Andrac qui

---

makes the voyage, which in all probability was that in which Lancelote
Malocello sailed, to take place at latest in the close of the thirteenth
century. In this fact we find the reason why Genoese map-makers of
the fourteenth century affixed the arms of Genoa to this island by way
of reserving a claim to it. But from this very reservation by the
Genoese of a claim to the island of Lançarote we are led to another
most important fact, to which the present writer called especial attention in his *Life of Prince Henry the Navigator and its Results*, London,
1868, viz., that the Canaries in the year 1341, the Madeira group and
the Azores at periods anterior to 1351, were discovered for the crown
of Portugal by Portuguese vessels commanded by Genoese captains.
These facts are based upon a Genoese map of the latter date in the
Laurentian library at Florence, in which all these groups are laid down,
but with the sole claim of Lancerote for Genoa, a sufficient proof that
they had not been discovered by the Genoese on their own account. By a
treaty concluded in 1317, Denis the Labourer, King of Portugal, had
secured the services of the Genoese Emmanuele Pezagno as hereditary admiral of his fleet, on the condition that he and his successors should supply
annually twenty experienced Genoese captains to command the King's
galleys. The re-discovery of the Canaries in 1341 is shewn by a document in the handwriting of Boccaccio, discovered in 1827 by Sebastiano
Ciampi, which informs us that in that year two Portuguese vessels,
commanded by Genoese captains, but manned with Italians, Spaniards
of Castile and other Spaniards (Hispani, including Portuguese), made
that re-discovery.—R. H. M.

d'Andrac, who rode with the natives, and suspected nothing. When the latter saw their opportunity, they fell upon the said Guillaume, and dragging him down gave him thirteen wounds, and would have killed him; but Jean le Courtois and his companions hearing the noise, turned vigorously upon them, rescued him with great difficulty, and carried him back to the castle of Rubicon.

CHAPTER XXXIII.—How the King escaped from Gadifer's custody, and how he had Asche put to death.

Now it happened that in the night of this same day the rightful King escaped from his prison at Rubicon, carrying with him the fetters and chains with which he was bound; and as soon as he reached his own dwelling, he seized Asche (who had betrayed him, and made himself King), and had him stoned and afterwards burned. The next day but one, the garrison of the old castle, on learning how Asche

cheminoit auec eux, et ne se doutoient de riens. Quand ils eurent cheminé vne piece, et ils virent leur poinct, ils chargerent sur ledit Guillaume, et l'abatirent à terre, et le blesserent de treize playes, et l'eussent paracheué, mais ledit Jean et les compagnons ouyrent le bruit et retournerent vigoureusement sur eux, et le recoüirent à grand peine, et le ramenerent au chastel de Rubicon.

CHAPITRE XXXIII.—Comment le Roy eschapa des prisons de Gadiffer, et comment il fit mourir Asche.

Or aduint que ce iour proprement par nuit le premier Roy eschapa de la prison de Rubicon, et emporta les fers et la chaine dont il estoit lié, et tantost qu'il fut à son hostel, il fit prendre ledit Asche qui s'estoit fait Roy, et aussi il l'auoit trahy, et le fit lapider de pierres, et puis le fit ardoyer. Le second iour apres, les compagnons, lesquels estoient au vieil chastel sceurent com-

had fallen upon Jean le Courtois, d'Andrac and their companions took one of their Canarian prisoners to a high mountain, and having cut off his head, stuck it on a high pole, so that everyone might see it, and opened war upon the natives. They captured great numbers of men, women, and children, and the remnant betook themselves for refuge to the caverns, not daring to wait for the approach of the Christians, the greater number of whom scoured the country, while the rest remained at home to guard the castle and the prisoners. They used all their efforts to make captives, for it was their only solace till the arrival of M. de Bethencourt, who, as you will hear, soon sent them relief. Berthin had caused them many troubles and difficulties, and had occasioned the loss of many lives.

---

ment le nouueau Roy auoit couru sus à Jean le Courtois et à d'Andrac et aux compagnons. Si prindrent vn Canare qu'ils auoient et luy allerent trencher la teste sur vne haute montagne, et la mirent sur vn pal bien hault, afin que chacun le peût bien voir, et de là en auant commencerent guerre à l'encontre de ceux du pays. On print grand foison de leurs gens et femmes et enfans, et le surplus sont en tel poinct, qu'ils se vont tapissans par les cauernes; et n'osent nulluy attendre; et sont tousiours sur les champs la plus grand' partie d'eux, et les autres demeurent à l'hostel pour garder le chastel et les prisonniers et mettent toute diligence qu'ils peuuent de prendre gens; car c'est tout leur reconfort, quant à present, en attendāt Monsieur de Bethencourt, lequel enuoyra de bref reconfort comme vous orrez. Berthin leur a fait vn grand mal et destoubier, et est cause de mainte mort donnée.

CHAPTER XXXIV.—How Gadifer proposed to kill all the fighting men in the island of Lancerote.

Gadifer and his companions resolved, if they saw no other course open to them, to kill all the men of the country who bore arms, and to save the women and children, and have them baptised; and to remain there till God should provide otherwise for them. At Pentecost, in this year, more than eighty persons, men, women, and children, were baptised, with a good hope that God would confirm them in the faith, and make them a means of edification to all the country round about. There is no reason to doubt that if M. de Bethencourt had been able to return sooner to the Canaries, and if a few princes had given him their assistance, he might have conquered not only the Canaries, but many other great countries then very little known, but as profitable as any in the world, and full of misbelievers of divers laws and languages. If Gadifer and his companions

---

CHAPITRE XXXIV.—*Comment Gadifer eut propos de tuer tous les hommes de deffence de lisle Lancerote.*

Si est le propos Gadiffer et aux compagnons tel que si ne trouuent autre remede, ils tueront tous les hommes de deffence du pays; et retendront les fēmes et les enfans, et les feront baptiser, et viuront comme eux iusques à tant que Dieu y ait autrement pourueu, et s'y ont esté à ceste Pentecoste que hommes et femmes et enfans plus de quatre vingts baptisez : et Dieu par sa grace leur vueille tellement confermer en nostre foy, que se soit bonne exemple à tout le pays de par deçà. Il ne faut point faire de doute que si Monsieur de Bethencourt peut venir, et qu'il eust vn peu d'ayde de quelque Prince, on ne conquerroit pas seulement les isles de Canare, on conquerroit beaucoup de plus grands pays dequoy il est bien peu de mention, et de bon, d'aussi bon s'il soit gueres au monde, et de bien peuplé de gens mescreans, et de diuerses loix, et de diuers langages. Se ledit Gadifer eust

would have put their prisoners to ransom, they would soon
have recovered the expenses of the expedition. But God
forbid that they should have done so, for most of them received baptism. And God forbid that they should ever be
forced to sell them! But they were amazed at receiving no
tidings from M. de Bethencourt, and at seeing no ships
arrive from Spain or elsewhere which were wont to frequent
those parts, for they stood in great need of refreshment and
comfort, and prayed God of His mercy to send them relief.

CHAPTER XXXV.—How M. de Bethencourt's vessel arrived with
vouchers.

God's work is not long a-doing, and things are soon
changed when it pleases Him ; for He sees and knows the
thoughts and imaginations of the heart, and never forgets
them who trust in Him, but brings them speedy comfort.

voulu et ses compagnons prendre les prisonniers à renson, ils
eussent bien recouuert les frais qui leur ont cousté en ce voyage.
Mais ja Dieu ne plaise, car la plupart se font baptizer, et ja
Dieu ne plaise que necessité les contraigne qu'il conuinst qu'ils
fussent vendus ; mais ils sont esbahies que Monsieur de Bethencourt n'enuoye quelques nouuelles, ou qu'il ne vient quelque
nauire d'Espagne ou d'ailleurs, qui ont accoustumé de venir et
frequenter en ces marches ; car ils ont grande necessité d'estre
rafraichis et reconfortez, que Dieu par sa grace y veuille re-
medier.

CHAPITRE XXXV.—*Comment la barge de Monsieur de Bethencourt
arriua bien authorisee.*

En peu d'heure Dieu labeure, les choses sont biē tost muees
quand il plaist à Dieu, car il voit et cognoist les pensees et
volonté des cœurs, et n'oublie iamais ceux qui ont en luy bonne
esperance, et sont à ceste heure reconfortez. Il arriua vne

There arrived at the port of Graciosa a vessel from M. de Bethencourt, which cheered their hearts, and supplied them with victuals and other necessities. There were in the vessel more than eighty men, although more than forty-four of them were almost laid up. The King of Castile had given them to M. de Bethencourt, with a store of arms and provisions. And, as has before been said, M. de Bethencourt sent letters to Messire Gadifer de la Salle, in which, among other things, he informed him of his having done homage to the King of Castile for the Canary Islands. This vexed Gadifer, and made him less cheerful than usual in his manner, which astonished his companions who were ignorant of the cause, and only knew of the reasons he had for rejoicing. Every one knew that M. de Bethencourt had done homage for the islands, but did not suspect that that was the cause of Gadifer's displeasure, and he enlightened none of them, but calmed himself and shewed his vexation as

---

barque au port de l'Isle Gracieuse, que Monsieur de Bethencourt leur a transmis, dequoy ils furent tous ioyeux et en furent rafraischis et rauitaillez. Il y auoit bien en la barque plus de quatrevingts hommes, dont il y en auoit plus de quarante-quatre en poinct de se trouuer sur les rens ; car le Roy de Castille les auoit baillez à Monsieur de Bethencourt, et si y auoit de plusieurs artilleries et de viures assez : et comme i'ay deuant dit, le sieur de Bethencourt a rescrit à Messire Gadiffer de la Salle vnes lettres ; ausquelles il lui rescriuoit plusieurs chozes, entre lesquelles il luy mandoit qu'il auoit fait hommage au Roy de Castille des Isles de Canare de laquelle chose il n'en estoit pas ioyeux, et ne faisoit point si bonne chere qu'il vouloit faire. Les gentils-hommes et les compagnons s'en emerueilloient, car il sembloit qu'il deuoit faire bonne chere, et qu'il n'auoit pas autre cause, mais nul ne peut sçauoir que c'estoit. Les nouuelles estoient par tout que Monsieur de Bethencourt auoit fait hommage au Roy de Castille, des Isles de Canare. Mais iamais personne n'eust pensé que ce fut esté à cette cause, et ledit Gadifer ne s'en fust descouuert en nulluy : Il s'appaisa, et en fit le moins

little as possible. Also, the master of the ship and of the
bark told them of the fate of the traitors who had injured
them whose names are mentioned above, on whom God had
worked His Will and punished them for their sins; for
some were drowned off the coast of Barbary, and some were
in their own country in punishment and disgrace. And
now occurred a great marvel; for one of the boats of
Gadifer's ship—that one which the Gascons had taken in
the month of October of 1402, when they were drowned off
the coast of Barbary—returned safe and sound from the
place where they had perished, a distance of five hundred
leagues,[1] and arrived at the port of Graciosa in the August
of 1403, at the same place whence they had taken it when
the traitor Berthin deserted them and set them on shore.
This was hailed as a great boon, for they needed the boat
greatly; and now that the bark was come with the men and
provisions, Gadifer gave them the best welcome he could,
though with a heavy heart. He asked what news they

semblant qu'il peut : Item le maistre de la nef et barque leur dit
au vray qu'estoient deuenus les traistres qui tant leur ont fait de
mal, desquels les noms sont cy deuant declarez ; ausquels Dieu y
a monstré son bon plaisir, et en a prins vengeãce du mal qu'ils
leur ont fait. Car les vns sont en Barbarie noyez, et les autres
sont à leur pays à honte et à des-honneur, et est aduenu vne
grande merueille : car l'vn des bateaux de la nef Gadiffer, que les
Gascons qui là estoient amenerent au mois d'Octobre mil quatre
cens et deux, auquel ils sont noyez et peris en la coste de Barbarie, est reuenu sain et entier de plus de cinq cens lieuës d'icy,
là où ils furent noyez, et arriua au port de l'isle Gratieuse au
mois d'Aoust, mil quatre cens et trois, en la propre place où ils
auoient prins, quand le traistre Berthin les eut trahis, et fait
bouter hors de la nef la où ils estoient et mettre à terre ; et ce
tenoient-ils à moult grand chose : car c'est vn grand reconfort
pour eux. Or est la barque recueillie et les gens et les viures, et
leur fit ledit Gadifer la meilleure chere qu'il peût, prenez qu'il ne

---

[1] An exaggeration, more likely two hundred miles at the most.

brought from Castile, and the master of the vessel replied : "I know of none but that the King had welcomed M. de Bethencourt, who will soon be here; but he had sent Mme. de Bethencourt back to Normandy, where I believe she now is. It is now some time since I left the country, and even then he was making every preparation for his return hither, for which he is very anxious; and we must not fail to do the best we can till he arrives." To which Gadifer replied : " We shall not fail, nor cease to labour, though he be absent, as we have hitherto done."

CHAPTER XXXVI.—How Gadifer left Lancerote in the barge to inspect all the other islands.

After M. de Bethencourt's vessel had arrived at Rubicon and unloaded her cargo of provisions (wine, corn, etc.), Messire Gadifer went on board of her with the greater part

fut pas trop ioyeux; il leur demanda des nouuelles de Castille, et le maistre de la nef luy respondit qu'il n'en sçauoit nulles, fors que le Roy fait bonne chere à Monsieur de Bethencourt, et sera de bref par deçà, mais qu'il ait fait mener Madame de Bethencourt en Normandie ; et ie cuide de ceste heure qu'elle y est ; Il y a ja grand' piece que ie suis party du pays, et il se hastoit fort dès à donc de l'enuoyer, à celle fin qu'il retournast par deça: car il luy ennuye tres-fort qu'il n'est par deça, et seurement il y sera de bref, il ne faut pas laisser à faire du mieux que l'on pourra tant qu'il soit venu. Si respondit Gadiffer, aussi fera non dea, on ne lairra pas à besongner si n'y est, nyent plus qu'on à fait.

CHAPITRE XXXVI.—*Comme celle barge partit de l'Isle Lanzerote pour visiter toutes les autres isles.*

Et apres que la barge de Monsieur de Bethencourt fut arriuée au port de Rubicon, et ils eurent recueillis tous les viures qui y estoient, vins, et farines, et autres choses ; Messire Gadifer se

of his company, and put to sea to visit the other islands on
behalf of M. de Bethencourt with a view to their future
conquest. The master and crew of the bark were moreover
very anxious to secure some of the produce of these parts,
which would bring them great profit in Castile, such as
skins, fat, orchil,[1] (which is very valuable, and is used for
dyeing), dates, dragon's blood, and many other things. For

---

partit et se mit en la mer dedans la barque auec la pluspart de la
compagnie, pour aller visiter les autres isles, pour Monsieur de
Bethencourt, et pour la conqueste qui, se Dieu plaist, se fera à
bonne fin. Aussi le maistre de barque et les compagnons
auoient grand desir de gaigner, pour remporter des besongnes de
par deçà, pour y gaigner en Castille, car ils peuuent emporter
plusieurs manieres de marchandises, comme cuirs, gresses, our·
solle, qui vaut beaucoup d'argent qui sert à tainture, dattes, sang
dragō, et plusieurs autres choses qui sont au pays : car lesdites

---

[1] Orchil ; *Ital.* orciglia, *Span.* orchilla. This lichen yielding a beautiful
purple dye was for centuries imported largely, and still is imported,
from the Canaries and the other Atlantic islands, especially the Cape
Verde Islands, though by far the largest quantity has in recent times
been brought from the east coast of Africa. Some have supposed, from
the passage now under the reader's notice, that this plant was first
found in the Canary Islands, but it was known and in use as a dye long
before the time of Bethencourt. We learn from the *Istoria Genealogica
delle famiglie nobili Toscane* of Eugenio Gamurrini, Fiorenza, 1668,
vol. i, p. 274, that the noble Florentine family of the Rucellai derived
their name from the secret of dyeing with orciglia, introduced for the
first time into Italy from the Levant by one of their ancestors. The
date of this event is placed by the *Giornale de' Letterati d'Italia*, tom.
33, part 1, art. 6, p. 231, about the year 1300. Hence the family were
named Oricellari, frequently mentioned in the archives of Florence.
This name by corruption became Rucellari and Rucellai, and from it
comes the modern botanical name of the lichen " Roccella tinctoria."
The dye itself is called " oricello," and I venture to surmise that this
word is derived from the Latin " oricella" or " auricella" (the diminutive
of auricula), the lower fleshy part of the ear, an idea which the con-
sistency and feel of the plant when growing may have suggested.—
R. H. M.

these islands were under the protection and dominion of M. de Bethencourt, who had made a proclamation on the part of the King of Castile that none should visit them but by his permission, he having gained that privilege from the King, of which fact Gadifer, when he went to the islands, was ignorant. They arrived at the island of Erbanie, where Gadifer disembarked with Remonnet de Leneden, Hannequin d'Auberbosc, Pierre de Revil (or Reuil), Jamet de Barège, and others of the company, together with their prisoners and two Canarian guides.

CHAPTER XXXVII.—How Gadifer landed on the island of Erbanie.

A few days after the landing of Gadifer in the island of Erbanie, he and Remonnet de Leneden, with thirty-five companions, started for the river Vien de Palmes to see if they could come upon any of the natives, and nearly reached

---

isles estoient et sont en la protection et seigneurie de Monsieur de Bethencourt et auoit-on crié de par le Roy de Castille que nul n'y allast sinon par son congé, car ainsi auoit il impetré du Roy ; lequel Gadiffer quand il vint és isles il ne sçauoit mie que c'estoit. Et arriuerent en l'isle d'Albanye, et descendit ledit Gadifer, Remonnet de Leneden, Hannequin d'Auberbosc, Pierre de Reuil, Iamet de Barege, auec autres de ceux de la compagnie, et du nauire et des prisonniers qu'ils auoient, et deux Canariens pour les conduire.

CHAPITRE XXXVII.—*Gadifer part de la barge pour aller en l'Isle d'Erbanie.*

Qvand Gadifer fut passé auec la barque en l'isle d'Albanie, aucuns iours apres se partit luy et Remonnet de Leneden, et les compagnons de la barque iusques au nombre de trente cinq hommes pour aller à Ruissel de Palmes veoir s'ils pourroient rencontrer aucuns de leurs ennemis : et arriuerent prés de là

it by nightfall. They came upon a fountain, by which they rested a while, and then began to climb a high mountain whence they could overlook a great part of the country; and when they were halfway up the mountain, the Spaniards would go no farther, but twenty-one of them turned back, most of them cross-bow men. Gadifer was much displeased, but kept on his road with his twelve remaining men, only two of whom were archers. After reaching the summit, he took six companions and went to the place where the river falls into the sea, to ascertain whether there were any harbour; and then returning up the stream, found Remonnet de Leneden and his companions waiting for him at the entrance of the Palm Grove, which is wonderfully difficult of access, and is only two stones' throw in length and two or three lances broad. They found it necessary to take off their shoes to pass over the slabs of marble, which were so smooth and slippery that they could only cross them on hands and feet, and even those who were behind had to hold the ends of

---

par nuict, et trouuerent vne fontaine là ou ils se reposerēt vn peu, puis cōmencerent à mōter vne haute mōtaigne ; dequoy l'on peut biē aduiser vne grand' partie du pays ; et quand ils furent bien my-voye de la montaigne, les Espagnols ne voulurent aller non plus auant, et s'en retournerent vingt et vn qu'ils estoient Arballestriers la plus grand' partie d'eux, et quand Gadifer vit cela il n'en fut pas ioyeux, et s'en alla son chemin luy treizieme, et n'y auoit que deux archers. Quand ils furent à mont, il print six compagnons, et s'en alla là où le ruisseau chet en la mer, pour sçauoir s'il y auoit aucun port : et puis s'en retourna contremont le ruisseau, et trouua Remonnet de Leneden et les compagnons qui l'attendoient à l'entrée des palmiers ; là est l'entrée si forte que c'est vne merueille, et ne dure pas plus de deux iets de pierre, et de deux ou trois lances de large ; et leur conuint deschausser leurs soulliers pour passer sur les pierres de marbres et estoient si honnies et si glissantes qu'on ne s'y pouuoit tenir fors à quatre pieds, et encor conuenoit-il que les derniers ap-

their lances for the foremost to push their feet against, and they, when safely over, in their turn pulled the hindmost after them; beyond, the valley was lovely and unbroken, and very pleasant: it was shaded by about eight hundred palm trees in groups of a hundred and twenty-six, with streams running between them; they were more than twenty fathoms high, like the masts of a ship, and were so green and leafy and full of fruit that they were a goodly sight to behold. There they dined in the shade on the turf, near the running brooks, and rested awhile, for they were very weary.

CHAPTER XXXVIII.—How they came upon their enemies.

They then resumed their journey, and climbed the side of a great hill, and sent forward three of their number, who,

---

puyassent les pieds à ceux des autres de deuant auec les bouts des lances, et puis tiroient les derniers apres eux: et quand on est outre, l'on trouue le val bel et honny, et moult delectable, et y peut bien auoir huict cens palmiers qui ombroient la vallée, et les ruisseaux des fontaines qui courent parmy, et sont par troupeaux cent et six vingts ensemble, aussi longs comme mats de nef, de plus de vingt brasses de hault, si verds et si feüillus, et tant chargéz de dattes que c'est vne moult belle chose à regarder. Et la se disnerent sous le bel ombre sur l'herbe verte, prés des ruisseaux courans, et là se reposerent vn petit, car ils estoient moult lassez.

CHAPITRE XXXVIII.—*Comme ils s'entr'encontrerent sur leurs ennemis.*

Apres se mirent au chemin et monterent vne grand coste, et ordoña trois compagnons pour aller deuant assez longuet; et quand ces trois compagnons furēt vn peu eslongnez, ils encon-

when they had gone some distance, came upon their enemies, whom they attacked and put to flight. Pierre the Canarian captured a woman, and caught two others in a cavern, one of whom had a little child at the breast, which she strangled, it is supposed from fear of its crying. Meanwhile Gadifer and the others knew nothing of all this, but suspecting that in so fruitful a country as the plain before them there must be inhabitants, he arranged his men wide apart, so as to cover as much ground as possible, for there were only eleven left.

CHAPTER XXXIX.—How those whom they encountered in the fruitful country attacked the Castilians.

It happened that the Castilians who remained with them came upon a band of about fifty natives, who ran at them and held them in check till their wives and children were out of reach. Their companions, who were scattered

trerent leurs ennemis et leur coururent sus, et les mirent en chasse, et leur tollit Pierre le Canare vne femme, et en prit deux autres en vne cauerne, dont l'vne auoit vn petit enfant allaitant qu'elle estrangla : en pense bien que ce fust pour doute qu'il ne criast. Mais Gadifer ne les autres ne sçauoient de tout ce fait, sinon qu'ils se douterent bien qu'en vn fort pays qui estoit là deuāt en la plaine auoit des gens. Si ordonna Gadifer de si peu de gens qu'il auoit à comprendre tout ce mauuais pays ; et se rengerent assez loing l'vn de l'autre : car ils n'estoient demeurez derriere que onze.

CHAPITRE XXXIX.—Comment ceux qu'ils encontrerent au fort Pays coururent sus aux Castillans.

Si aduint que les Castillans qui estoient demourez auec eux, si arriuerent sur vne compagnie de gens qui estoient enuiron cinquante personnes ; lesquels coururent aux Castillans, et les enchanterent, tant que leurs femmes et leurs enfans furent

in different directions, hastened to their help with all speed, the first who arrived being Remonnet de Leneden all alone, who threw himself upon the natives, but was surrounded, and but for Hannequin d'Auberbosc, who attacked them vigorously, and made them give way, would have been in peril of his life. Then in the moment of need came Geoffroy d'Auzonville, armed with a bow, and completed the discomfiture of the natives. Gadifer, who was near the scene of the encounter with three companions, came up as quickly as he could and made straight for the mountains, whither the Canarians had fled; but before they could meet, the night overtook them, and though they came within speaking distance, they could hardly see one another. It was so dark that with great difficulty he collected his men together; and when, after walking all night, they reached the vessel, they had only taken four women, though the chase had lasted from vespers till midnight, and they were so tired that they could hardly drag one step before the other. But for the sudden nightfall which surprised

---

esloignez. Les autres compagnons qui estoient de bien loin espartis se trayrēt vers le cry le plus tost qu'ils purent, et arriua premier Remonnet de Leneden tout seul, qui leur courut sus, mais ils l'encloïrēt entre eux : et ne se fust Hannequin d'Auberbosc, qui là serrément vint ferir entre eux, et apertement fit guerpir la place; Remonnet estoit en peril de mort. Aussi il survint Geoffroy d'Auzonuille atout un arc en sa main, et bien leur estoit besoin, et les mit du tout en fuite. Mais Gadifer qui estoit bien auant au fort pays venoit tant qu'il pouuoit, soy quatriesme, et print le chemin droit aux montagnes, là où ils tiroient leur en aller; et venoit au deuant quand la nuict le surprint, et en fut si pres qu'il parla à eux, et à grand' peine s'entre trouuerent entre eux, tant faisoit obscur, et s'en reuindrent tout nuict à la barque, et ne peurent riens prindre fors que quatre femmes, et dura la chasse de haute-heure de vespre iusques à la nuit, et furent si lassez d'vne part et d'autre que à peine peurent ils haster leurs pas, et se n'eust esté l'obscurité de la nuict qui

Gadifer and his companions, not one of the Canarians would have escaped them, though the Castilians had hung back from the beginning and had not joined in the chase. After this, Gadifer would not trust them throughout the voyage, which lasted for about three months, till M. de Bethencourt came to the country with an entirely fresh crew.

CHAPTER XL.—How Gadifer passed over into the Great Canary, and spoke with the people of the country.

They then quitted Erbanie, and arriving at the Great Canary at the hour of prime, they entered a large harbour, between Feldes and Argonnez, where about five hundred Canarians came out to speak with them, two-and-twenty of whom were persuaded to come on to the vessel and exchange figs and dragon's blood for fishing hooks, old iron, and little knives. The dragon's blood was well worth two

---

surprint Gadifer et ses cōpagnons, il n'en fust ia eschape nulluy, et dès le commencement les Castillans s'arresterent, et ne furent point à la chasse. Et oncques puis Gadifer ne s'y voulut fier en tout le voyage, trois mois ou enuiron, iusques à tant que Monsieur de Bethencourt vinst au pays à tout vne autre compagnie.

CHAPITRE XL.—*Comment Gadifer passa à la grand' Canare et parla aux gens du pays.*

Et lors se partirent d'Erbanie et arriuerent en la grand Canare à heure de Prime, entrerent en vn grand port, qui est entre Feldes et Argonnez, et là sur le port vindrent des Canares enuiron cinq cens, et parlerent à eux, et venoient à la barque vingt et deux tous ensemble, apres qu'ils les auoient asseurez, et leur apportoient des figues et du sang du dragon, qu'ils changeoiēt pour hains à pescher, et pour vieille ferraille de fer, et pour petits cousteaux, et eurent du sang du dragon, qui valloit bien

hundred ducats, while what was given in exchange was hardly worth two francs. When they had gone away and their boat was near the shore, they began quarrelling, and the commotion lasted for a long while. When it was over, they put out to sea again, and came to the bark as before, bringing their articles of traffic, and this lasted all through the two days that the ship remained there. Gadifer also sent Pierre the Canarian to speak with the King, who was five leagues distant, and as he did not return exactly at the appointed time, the Spaniards who were masters of the vessel, would not wait, but set sail, and went four leagues off to take in water, but were prevented from landing by the Canarians, who never fail to attack any small force which seeks to enter their country, for there are a great number of nobles amongst them, according to their condition and manner of life. In this place we found the testament of the thirteen Christian brothers who had been killed by the natives twelve years before. The Canarians killed them,

---

deux cens doubles d'or, et tout tant qu'ils leur baillerent ne valloit mie deux francs. Et puis quand ils estoient retraits, et le bastel s'accoustoit à terre, ils couroient sus l'vn à l'autre, et duroit l'escarmouche vne grand' piece. Quand cela estoit passé, ils se remettoient en la mer, et venoient en la barque comme deuant, et apportoient de leurs choses, et dura ce fait deux iours qu'ils furent là ; et transmit Gadifer Pierre de Canare parler au Roy, qui estoit à cinq lieues de là. Et pource qu'il ne retourna mie à la droite heure qu'il deuoit retourner, les Espagnols qui estoient maistres de la barque ne vouloient plus attendre, ains firent voile, et s'en allerent à quatre lieuës de là, et cuiderent prendre eau, mais les Canares ne les laisserent prendre terre, et sans faute ils combattront qui y entrera à peu de gens, car ils font grand quantité de nobles gens selon leur estat et leur maniere; et nous auons trouué le testament des Freres Chrestiens qu'ils tuerent ores a douze ans qui estoient treize personnes ; pour ce les tuerent selon que dient les Canares, car ils auoient

according to their own account, for having sent into Christian countries a bad account of these people, among whom they had lived seven years promulgating the articles of the faith. The testament warned all who might read it to beware of trusting the natives, in spite of their fair seeming, for that they were traitors by nature, although six thousand of them were of gentle blood. Nevertheless, Gadifer resolved, if he could get a hundred archers and as many fighting men, to enter the country, take up a strong position, and there remain till by God's help he had subjugated the people and converted them to the faith of our Lord Jesus Christ.

CHAPTER XLI.—How the company left the Great Canary, and, passing by Ferro, came to Gomera.

The company then departed and resumed their journey to the other islands, and when they came to Ferro, they coasted along it without landing, and passed straight on to Gomera, where they arrived in the night, and found the

---

transmis lettres en terre des Chrestiens alencontre d'eux auec lesquels ils auoient demouré sept ans, qui de iour en iour leur annoncerent les articles de la foy ; lequel testament dit ainsi, que nul ne se doit fier à eux pour beau semblant qu'ils facent, car ils sont traistres de nature, et se disent entre eux six mille gentils-hommes. Si est le propos Gadifer que s'il peut finer de cent archers ; et autant d'autres gens, d'entrer au pays, et soy fortifier et demourer iusques à tant que à l'aide de Dieu il soy mis en nostre subiection et à la foy de nostre Seigneur Iesus Christ.

CHAPITRE XLI.—*Comment la compagnie se partit de la Grand' Canare, et passa l'isle de Fer, iusques à l'isle de Gomere.*

Et lors se partirent la compagnie, et prindrent le chemin pour aller visiter toutes les autres isles ; et vindrent à l'isle de Fer, et les costierent tout du long sans prendre terre, et passerent tout droit en l'isle de Gomere, et arriuerent par nuit, et ceux de l'isle

natives making fires on the shore. They accordingly sent
some of the crew in a boat in the direction of the fires, who,
finding a man and three women, captured them and brought
them back to the vessel. There they remained till daybreak, when some of them landed to take in water, but the
people of the country assembled and attacked them, so that,
the position of the ground being against them, they were
forced to return to the ship without taking in water.

CHAPTER XLII.—How Gadifer and his company left Gomera and
came to Ferro, where they remained twenty-two days.

Soon afterwards they departed and took the road to the
island of Palma, but a great storm and a contrary wind
drove them towards Ferro, where they arrived in the day-
time and landed. There they remained at least twenty-two
days, and took four women and a child. They found great

faisoient du feu en aucuns lieux sur le riuage de la mer, si se
mirent les compagnons en vn coquet, et descendirent au feu, et
trouuerent vn homme et trois femmes qu'ils prindrent et les
amenerent a la barque, et la demeurerent iusques au iour, et puis
descendirent aucuns pour prendre eau ; mais les gens du pays
s'assemblerent, et leur coururent sus, et tant qu'ils furent con-
traincts eux en retourner à la barque sans prendre eau ; car la
place estoit en trop grand desauantage pour nos gens.

CHAPITRE XLII.—Comment Gadifer et la compagnie se partirent de
la Gomere, et vindrent en l'isle de Fer, là où ils demourent
vingt deux iours.

Apres se partirent de là, et prindrent leur chemin en l'isle de
Palmes, mais ils eurent vent contraire et grand tourment ; et
leur conuint tenir le chemin de l'isle de Fer, et y arriuerent de
iour et prindrent terre : et là demourerent bonne piece vingt
deux iours: et prindrent quatre femmes et vn enfant, et trouuerent

numbers of pigs, goats, and sheep, though the country is
very barren all round for a league from the shore; but in
the centre of the island, which is very high, the country is
fertile and pleasant, and full of large groves, which are
green in all seasons; it contains more than a hundred
thousand pine trees, most of which are so thick that two
men can hardly make their arms meet round them; the
water is good and plentiful, for it often rains in those parts;
and quails abound in astonishing quantities. There are now
very few inhabitants in this place, for every year some of
them are carried off captive, and in 1402, it is said that
no less than four hundred of them were taken; still, those
who were then in the island would have spoken with the
Christians if they had had an interpreter.

CHAPTER XLIII.—How they passed over into Palma and returned
from the other group, coasting along the islands.

Having found means to secure an interpreter, who knew

porcs, chieures, brebis grand plante, et est le pays tres mauuais,
vne lieue tout en tout par deuers la mer; mais sur le milieu du
pays qui est moult haut, est beau pays et delectable, et y sont les
boccages grands, et sont vers en toutes saisons, et y a des pins
plus de cent mille, dequoy la plus grande partie sont si gros que
deux hommes ne les sçauroient embrasser, et y sont les eaux
bones a grand plante, et tant de cailles que merueilles, et y pleut
souuent; et ne sont or endroit que peu des gens, car chacun an
on les prend: et encor l'an mil quatre cens et deux, il fut prins,
selon ce que lon dit, quatre cens personnes; mais ceux qui y sont
a present feussent venus s'il y eust eu quelque truchement.

CHAPITRE XLIII.—Comment ils passerent en l'isle de Palmes, puis
retournerent de l'autre Bende, costeant les Isles.

Si a depuis trouue maniere d'auoir vn truchement qui scache

the country and spoke the language of this island and the others, they departed and went straight on to Palma, where they anchored to the right of a river which fell into the sea, and having supplied themselves with water for their return, again set sail. When they had passed the island of Palma, they had so good a wind that in two days and nights they reached the port of Rubicon, a distance of five hundred miles, having coasted along the other group of islands without landing anywhere. After an absence of about three months, they found their companions like themselves well and hearty, and more than a hundred prisoners in the castle of Rubicon. They had killed many natives, and reduced the others to such extremity that they knew no longer what to do, but came from day to day to throw themselves upon their mercy, so that hardly any who remained alive were unbaptised, especially of those who might have given trouble and been too much for them. The island of Lancerote, in which there were only three hundred men when they first

---

le pays, et parler le langage pour entrer en icelle isle et es autres; puis se partirent, et s'en allerent tout entour par dela droit en l'isle de Palmes, et print port au droit d'vne riuiere qui chet en la mer, et la se fournirent d'eau pour leur retour, et se partirent de la : et quand ils eurent double l'isle de Palmes, ils eurent si bon vent qu'ils furent en deux iours et deux nuits au port de Rubicon, la ou il y a cinq cens mil entre deux; et s'en vindrent costeant de l'autre bende toutes les isles iusques audit port sans predre port nulle part; et auoient demeure trois mois ou enuiron, et reuindrent sains et haitiez, et trouuerent les compagnons en bon poinct, qui auoient plus de cent prisonniers en chastel de Rubicon ; et y en auoit en grand foison de morts, et tenoient leurs ennemis en telle necessite qu'ils ne sçauoient plus que faire, et se venoient de iour en iour rendre en leur mercy; puis les vns, puis les autres ; tant qu'ils sont demourez peu de gens en vie qu'ils ne soient baptizes ; et specialement des gens qui les puissent greuer et sont au dessus de leur fait. Quant a l'isle de Lancerote en laquelle auoit plus de deulx cens hommes, quad ils

arrived, is a pleasant little island, twelve leagues in length
by four in breadth, and here M. de Bethencourt landed in
July 1402.

CHAPTER XLIV.—How Gadifer visited all the other islands, and what
advantages they possessed.

Gadifer also visited all the other islands by the direction
of M. de Bethencourt, in order to discover the best means
of conquering them. Having visited and remained in them
some time, he was able to observe their peculiarities and
the profit to which they might be put. They were very
fruitful and pleasant, with a healthy and agreeable climate,
and he saw no reason to doubt that if they fell into skilful
hands, such as there were in France, they would prove very
profitable, and that if, please God, M. de Bethencourt would
return, the enterprise might be brought to a successful conclusion.

---

y arriuerent; c'est vne bonne petite isle qui ne contient que
douze lieuës de long et quatre de large, et y descendit Monsieur
de Bethencourt au mois de Juillet, mil quatre cens et deux.

CHAPITRE XLIV.—*Comment toutes les autres Isles furent visitées
de Gadifer, et de quelles vertus elles estoient.*

Et quant des autres isles, Monsieur de Bethencourt les a faict
visiter par Messire Gadiffer et autres chargez de ce faire, et tant
qu'ils ont aduisé comment elles seront conquises, et y ont frequenté et demeuré par espace de temps, et ont veu et cogneu de
quelles manieres et de quel profit ils sont ; et sont de grand profit et fort plaisantes, et en bon air et gracieux, et ne faut point
doubter que s'il y auoit des gens comme il y a en France, qui
sceussent faire leur profit, ce seroient vnes fort bonnes isles, et
profitables; et si plaist a Dieu que Monsieur de Bethencourt soit
venu, au plaisir de Dieu on en viendra a chef et bonne intention.

CHAPTER XLV.—How M. de Bethencourt arrived at Rubicon in the island of Lancerote and the welcome he received.

On the same day that the bark arrived at Rubicon, on returning from the islands, she again set sail and anchored in another port, called Aratif, [or Alcatif] and made the natives supply her with meat for her return. Thence she set sail for Spain, carrying with her a gentleman named Geoffroy d'Ausonville, whom Gadifer had sent with letters to M. de Bethencourt acquainting him with the state of things, and of all that had been done in the said bark. But before the vessel reached Spain, M. de Bethencourt had arrived at Rubicon with a small but gallant company, and received such a welcome from Gadifer and his companions as would be difficult to describe. Then came the Canarians who had been baptized, and prostrated themselves upon the ground to do him reverence, according to the custom of their country, signifying by this action that in everything they threw them-

CHAPITRE XLV.—Comment Monsieur de Bethencourt arriua à Rubicon en l'Isle Lancerote, et la chere qu'on luy fit.

Le iour proprement que la barque arriua au port de Rubicon au retour des isles, la barque se partit et s'en alla en vn autre port nommé l'Aratif, là leur fit-on liurer chair pour leur retour, et se partirent de là pour eux en aller en leurs pays en Espagne, et là transmit veoir M. de Bethencourt par Gadiffer vn gentilhomme nõmé Geofray d'Ausonuille, lequel porta lettres à Monsieur de Bethencourt cõme tout se portoit, et tout le demaine que ladite barque auoit faict; mais deuant qu'icelle barque arriuait en Espagne, Monsieur de Bethencourt fut arriué au port de Rubicon à belle petite compagnie, et Messire Gadifer et toute la compagnie vindrent au deuant de luy, on ne sçauroit dire la grand' chere qu'on luy faisoit. Là y vindrent les Canariens qui s'estoient faict baptiser, qui se couchoient à terre en luy cuidant faire reuerence, disant que c'est la coustume du pais, et leur maniere et disent que c'est à dire quand ils se couchent que du tout ils se

selves upon his clemency and mercy; both great and small
might be seen weeping for joy, so that the news reached the
King who had so often been taken and escaped again; and
he and his party were so terrified that before three days
were out, he was taken again, with eighteen companions,
though not without difficulty. When he was taken, they
found plenty of barley and other provisions; and when the
other Canarians saw that their King was taken, and that
they could no longer hold out, they came every day to yield
obeisance to M. de Bethencourt, of whom at last the King
begged an audience. He was led before him in the presence
of Messire Gadifer and several others, and prostrated himself
before him, owning himself conquered, and throwing himself
upon the mercy of M. de Bethencourt, of whom and of Messire
Gadifer he besought pity, and promised to be baptized and
all his house, at which all rejoiced, for they hoped it was a
good opening for taking the other islands and bringing

mettent en la grace et à la mercy de celuy à qui cela se faict;
vous eussiez veu pleurer tous grands et petits de ioye et tant que
les nouuelles vindrent au Roy qui tant de fois auoit esté pris, et
s'est tousiours eschappé, et luy et tous ses alliez eurent si grand
peur que deuät qu'il fust trois iours accomplis ledit Roy fut pris
luy dix-neufiesme, qui leur auoit faict beaucoup de peine: ils
trouuerent à cause de sa prise assez de viures, orges à planté et
plusieurs autres choses; et adonc quand le demeurant des Canares
vid que leur Roy estoit pris, et qu'ils n'y pouuoiët plus resister,
ils se venoient tous les iours rendre à la mercy de Monsieur de
Bethēcourt. Le Roy requerant qu'il parlast a Monsieur de
Bethencourt, et fut mené vers ledit Seigneur en la presence de
Messire Gadifer et plusieurs autres; et adonc ledit Roy se print
à se coucher disant qu'il se tenoit vaincu, et se mettoit en la
mercy de Monsieur de Bethencourt, et luy cria mercy et à
Messire Gadifer, et leur dit qu'il se vouloit faire baptizer et tout
son hostel, dont Monsieur de Bethencourt fut bien ioyeux et
toute sa compagnie; car ils esperoient que c'estoit vn grand commencement pour auoir le demourant des isles, et pour les tirer

them to the Christian faith. M. de Bethencourt and Messire Gadifer then went and spoke together apart, and embraced each other, weeping for joy at having been the means of bringing so many souls into the way of salvation, and then arranged how and when they should be baptized.

CHAPTER XLVI.—How the King of Lancerote besought M. de Bethencourt that he might be baptised.

On Thursday, the 20th of February, 1404, just before Lent, the pagan King of Lancerote begged M. de Bethencourt to have him baptised, and accordingly he and all his house received baptism, at the hands of Messire Jean le Verrier, chaplain to M. de Bethencourt, on the first day of Lent. He shewed every appearance of sincerity and every hope of becoming a good Christian, and received from M. de Bethencourt the name of Louis. After this, all in the island came

---

tous à la foy Chrestienne. Monsieur de Bethencourt et Messire Gadifer se tirerent à part, et parlerent ensemble et s'entre-accollerent et baiserent pleurans l'vn et l'autre de grand ioye qu'ils auoient d'estre cause de mettre en la voye de saluation tant d'ames et de personnes; et conclurent eux deux comment et quand ils seroient baptisez.

CHAPITRE XLVI.—Comme le Roy de Lancerote requit Monsieur de Bethencourt qu'il fust baptisé.

L'an mil quatre cens et quatre, le ieudy xxvᵉ iour de Feurier, deuant Caresme-prenant, le Roy de Lancerote payen, requit Monsieur de Bethencourt qu'il fust baptisé, lequel fut baptisé luy et son mesnage le premier iour de Caresme; et monstroit par semblant qu'il auoit bon vouloir et bonne esperance d'estre bon Chrestien, et le baptisa Messire Jean Verrier chappellain de Mõseigneur de Bethencourt, et fut nommé de par lodit Seigneur Lovys. Adonc tout le pays l'vn apres l'autre se faisoit baptiser

one by one to be baptized, both small and great ; and therefore an instruction was drawn up as simple as possible for
the guidance of those who were already baptized, and for
the preparation of those who by the grace of God should
afterwards receive baptism. Brother Pierre Bontier, and
Messire Jean le Verrier, priest, both learned clerks, compiled it to the best of their ability.

CHAPTER XLVII.—Of the Introduction to the Faith which M. de
Bethencourt gave to the newly baptized Canarians.

Firstly, there is one only Almighty God, who, in the
beginning of the world, made the heaven and the earth, the
sun, moon, and stars, the sea, the fishes, beasts, and birds,
and the man who was named Adam, from one of whose
sides He formed the woman who was named Eve, the
mother of all living, and called her Virago, the wife of my
side. He formed and ordained all things under Heaven,
and created a place of great delight called the terrestrial

et petits et grands; et pour ce, on a ordonné vne instruction
ainsi comme ils ont sçeu faire le plus legerement qu'ils ont peu,
pour introduire ceux qu'ils ont baptisez, et qu'ils pensent qui
seront baptisez d'oresnauant s'il plaist à Dieu, ledit religieux
Messire Pierre Bontier et Messire Jean Verrier estoient assez
bons clercs qui la firent au mieux qu'ils peurent.

CHAPITRE XLVII.—C'est l'introduction que Monsieur de Bethencourt baille aux Canariens Chrestiens baptisez.

Premierement il est vn seul Dieu tout puissant qui au cōmencement du mōde forma la ciel et la terre, les estoilles, la lune et
le soleil, la mer, les poissons, les bestes, les oiseaux, l'homme
nommé Adam, et de l'vne des costes forma la femme nommée
Eue, la mère de tous viuans et la nomma Virago, femme de ma
coste et forma et ordonna toutes les choses qui sont soubs le
Ciel, et fit vn lieu moult delectable nomme Paradis Terrestre, la

Paradise, in which He placed the man and the woman ; and there was in the beginning one only woman united to one only man (and whoever believes otherwise sins), and He gave them to eat of all the fruits which were therein, save only of one, which was expressly forbidden to them, but soon after, through the persuasions of the devil, who disguised himself as a serpent and tempted the woman, she ate of the forbidden fruit, and gave of it to her husband ; and for this sin God drove them from the terrestrial Paradise and its pleasures, and uttered three maledictions against the serpent, two against the woman, and one against the man ; and thenceforward were condemned the souls of all those who should die before the Resurrection of our Lord JESUS CHRIST, who willed to take a human body of the Virgin Mary to redeem us from the pains of Hell to which all had previously been condemned.

---

où il mit l'homme et la femme; et là fut premierement vne seule femme conioincte en vn seul homme ; et qui autrement le croit il peche ; et leur abandonna à manger de tous les fruits qui la estoient, excepté d'vn, lequel il leur deffendit expressément ; mais tantost apres par l'exhortement du diable qui se mit en guise d'vn serpent, et parla à la femme, et luy fit manger du fruict lequel Dieu auoit defendu, laquelle en fit manger à son mary ; et par ce peché les fit Dieu bouter hors du Paradis terrestre et delices, et donna trois maledictions au serpent, et deux à la femme, et l'vne à l'homme ; et de là en auant furent condamnés les ames de tous ceux qui auant la Resurrection de nostre Seigneur IESVS CHRIST trespassoient, lequel voulut prendre chair humaine en la Vierge Marie pour nous tous rachepter des peines d'enfer où tous alloient iusques au temps dessus dit.

CHAPTER XLVIII.—In like manner of Noah's Ark, for the introduction
of the natives of the island to the Faith.

And after men had begun to multiply upon the earth,
they committed many bad and horrible sins, at which the
Lord's wrath was kindled, and He caused it to rain so as to
destroy all flesh which was upon the earth; but Noah, who
was a just man and feared God, found grace in His sight, so
that He warned him that He was about to destroy all flesh
from men down to the birds, and that His Spirit should no
longer abide among men, but that He would send upon
them the waters of the Deluge. And He commanded him
to make an ark of wood squared and polished, and to
smear it within and without with bitumen. Bitumen is a
glue so strong and tenacious that when two pieces are
brought together and joined with it, they cannot be separated
by any means except by the natural blood of women's
flowers. It is found on the water in the great lakes of
India. The ark was to be of a certain length and breadth,

CHAPITRE XLVIII.—*De mesme exemple de l'Arche de Nouel pour
introduire ceulx de lille.*

Et apres que les gens commencerent à multiplier sur terre ils
firent moult de maux et d'horribles pechez, dequoy nostre
Seigneur se corrouça, et dit qu'il pleuueroit tant qu'il destruiroit
toute chair qui estoit dessus terre. Mais Noé qui estoit homme
iuste et Dieu craignant, trouua grace deuant luy, auquel il dit
qu'il vouloit destruire toute chair de l'homme iusques aux
oiseaux, et que son esprit ne demeureroit mye en l'homme per-
manablement, et qu'il ameneroit les eaux du deluge sur eux, et
luy commanda qu'il fist vne arche de bois carré, poly, et qu'il
l'oindroit deuant et dehors de Betun ; Betun est vn glu si fort et
si tenant, que quand deux pieces de fait en sont assemblées et
ioinctes, on ne les peut par nul art des-assembler sinon par sang
naturel de fleurs de femmes ; et le trouue l'on flottant és grands
lacs de Indie sur les aygues ; et qu'elle fust de certaine longueur

so that he might place therein his wife and his three sons
with their three wives, and of all things in which was life
one pair of each with him. Hence do we all proceed.
After the Deluge, when they saw that they were increased
to great numbers, one named Nimrod sought to reign by
force, and gathered every one to him in a plain called the
plain of Sanaar, and they resolved to make a general divi-
sion of the three parts of the world. Those which were
descended from Shem, the eldest son of Noah, should have
Asia. Those who were sprung from Ham, the second son
of Noah, should have Africa; and the descendants of Japhet,
the third son, should have Europe. But before they separated, they commenced a tower so large and so strong that
they intended it to reach to heaven in perpetual memorial
of them. But God, who saw that they did not cease from
their work, confounded their tongues in such a manner
that no one could understand what his neighbour said; and
hence came the languages which we now have. Then God
sent His Angels, who caused so strong a wind to blow that
they overturned the tower even to near the foundations,

---

et largeur, là où il mettroit sa femme et ses trois fils et leurs
trois femmes ; et de toutes choses portant vie mit auec luy vne
paire de chacun ; dequoy nous sommes tous issus. Apres le
deluge quand ils virent qu'ils furent multipliez grand nombre, vn
nommé Nimbrod voulut reguer par force, et s'assemblerent tous
en vn champ nommé le chāp de Sanaar, et ordonnerent a comprendre de commun les trois parties du monde ; et que ceux qui
estoient descēdus de Sem l'aisné fils de Noé tendroient Asie ; et
ceux qui estoient descendus de Cam l'autre fils de Noé tendroient
Afrique. Mais ainchois qu'ils se departissent, ils commencerēt
vne tour si grand' et si forte, laquelle ils vouloient qu'elle vinst
iusque au ciel en perpetuelle memoire d'eux ; mais Dieu qui voit
qu'ils ne cesseroient leur ouurage, leur confondit leur langages en
telle maniere que nul n'entendroit la voix de l'autre, et là furent
les langages qui au iourd'huy sont, et puis ennoya les Anges
qui firent si grand vent venter qu'ils abatirent la tour iusques

which are still visible, as reported by those who have seen them.

CHAPTER XLIX.—Continuation of the Instruction in the Faith.

And after that they wandered out into the three parts of the globe, and the generations descended from them still exist. Of one of their tribes issued Abraham, a perfect man and who feared God, to whom God gave the Promised Land, that is, to his descendants. And God loved them much and made them His holy people, and called them the Children of Israel, and brought them out from the bondage of Egypt and did great wonders for them, exalting them above all the nations of the world, as long as they were good and obedient to Him. But, in defiance of His will and His laws, they took to themselves women of other faiths, and worshipped idols and golden calves which Jeroboam had set up in Samaria, wherefore His anger was kindled against them and He destroyed them and delivered

---

prés des fondemens qui encore y paroissent, ce dient ceux qui les ont veus.

CHAPITRE XLIX.—*Encore pour introduire ceulx des illes.*

Et apres se departirent és trois parties du monde, et encores sont les generations qui d'eux sont descenduës; et de lune de ses generacions yssit Abraham homme parfait et Dieu craignant, à qui Dieu donna la terre de promission, voire à ceux qui de luy yssiront; et Dieu les ayma moult et les fit son sainct peuple, et s'appellerent les fils Israël, et les mit hors du seruage d'Egypte, et fit de grãdes merueilles pour eux, et les exauça sur toutes les gens du monde tant comme il les trouua bons et obeïssans à luy. Mais contre son commandement et sa volonté, ils se prindrent aux femmes d'autres loix, et adorerent les idoles et les viaulx d'or que Jeroboam avait faits en Samarie, pourquoy il se courrouça à eux, les fit destruire et les bailla és mains des payens, et

them into the hands of the heathen, and to the Philistines many times. But as soon as they repented and appealed to His mercy, He delivered them and brought them into great prosperity, and did for them such things as He did for no other people; for He gave them Prophets who spoke by the Mouth of His Holy Spirit, and foretold things to come and the advent of our Lord Jesus Christ, who should be born of a Virgin (that is to say of the Virgin Mary, who was descended from this people, of the race of King David, who was of the line of Judah, the son of Jacob) and that He should redeem all those who had been condemned by the sin of Adam. But they would not believe nor take knowledge of His coming, but crucified Him and put Him to death, notwithstanding the great miracles He had done before them. And therefore they were destroyed as everyone knows, for go where you will, you will find no Jews who are not in subjection to others, and who are not day and night in fear and dread for their lives; this is how they have become so pale, as you now see them.

---

les Philistins par plusieurs fois; mais tātost qu'ils se repentoient, et ils luy crioient mercy il les releuoit, et les mettoit en grande prosperité, et fit telles choses pour eux qu'il ne fit onc pour nul autre peuple, car il leur donna les Prophetes qui parlerent par la bouche du sainct Esprit, et leur annonçoient les choses à aduenir, et l'aduenement de nostre Iesus-Christ, qui deuoit naistre d'vne Vierge, c'est à sçauoir la Vierge Marie, laquelle descendit de ce peuple, de la lignée du Roy Dauid, lequel Roy descendit de la lignée de Iuda fils de Iacob, et qu'il rachepteroit tous ceux qui estoient condamnez par le peché d'Adam. Mais ils ne voulurent croire ne cognoistre son aduenement, ains le crucifierēt et le mirent à mort, nonobstant les grands miracles qu'il faisoit en leur presence, et pour cé sont ils ainsi destruits comme chacun sçait; car allez par tout le monde, vous ne trouuerez Iuifs qui ne soient en suiectiō d'autruy, et qui ne soit iour et nuit en peur et en crainte de sa vie, et pour ce sont ils ainsi descoulourez comme vous vecz.

CHAPTER L.—Of the same matter for the instruction of the Canarians.

Now, at the time that the Jews put our Lord to death, He had many disciples, and specially twelve (one of whom betrayed Him), who were continually with Him and saw His great miracles : wherefore they had a firm faith, and witnessed His death, and, after His Resurrection, He appeared to them several times, and illuminated them with His Holy Spirit, and commanded them to go out into all the world to preach concerning Him the things which they had seen, and told them that whosoever should believe in Him and be baptised should be saved; but that all those who believed not in Him should be condemned. Let us, therefore, believe firmly that He is an Almighty All-knowing GOD, Who came down to earth, and took human flesh in the womb of the Virgin Mary, and lived more than two and thirty years, suffered and died on the tree of the Cross to

CHAPITRE L.—*Encores de celle mesme matiere pour introduire les Canariens.*

Or il est vray que ainchois que les Iuifs mirent à mort nostre Seigneur Iesus, il auoit moult de gens qui estoient ses disciples, et specialement il en auoit douze, dequoy l'vn deux le trahit; lesquels estoient continuellement auec luy, et luy voyoient faire les grands miracles; parquoy ils creurent fermement, et le virent mourir, et apres sa resurrection s'aparut-il à eux par plusieurs fois, et les enlumina de son sainct Esprit, et leur commanda qu'ils allassent par toutes les parties du monde prescher de luy toutes les choses qu'ils avoient veuës, et leur dit que tous ceux qui croiroient en luy et seroient baptisez seroient sauuez, et tous ceux qui en luy ne croyoient seroient condamnez. Or croyons donc fermement qu'il est vn Dieu tout puissant et tout sçachant, qui descendit en terre, et print chair humaine au ventre de la Vierge Marie, et vesquit trente deux ans et plus : et puis print mort et passion en l'arbre de la Croix, pour nous

redeem us from the pains of Hell (into which we were falling through the sin of Adam, our first father), and rose again the third day, and, between the hour of His Death and the hour of His Resurrection, descended into Hell, and drew out thence His friends and those who had been cast therein through the sin of Adam, and thenceforward for that sin none shall be cast therein.

CHAPTER LI.—How we must believe the ten Commandments of the Law.

We must believe the Ten Commandments of the Law, which GOD wrote with His Finger on two tables of stone on Mount Sinai a very long time ago, and gave them to Moses to shew to the people of Israel. There are two chief commandments : First, to believe in, to fear, and to love GOD above all things, and with all one's heart; and second, never to do to others what we would not have them do to ourselves. And whosoever shall keep these Commandments,

---

rachepter des peines d'Enfer, en quoy nous descendions tous pour le peché d'Adam nostre premier pere, et resuscita au tiers iour, et entre l'heure qu'il mourut, et l'heure qu'il resuscita, descendit en enfer; et en tira hors ses amis et ceux qui par le peché d'Adam y estoient tresbuchez et de là en auant par ce peché nul n'y entrera.

[CHAPITRE LI.]—*Comment on doit croire les dix Commandemens de la Loy.*

Novs deuons croire les dix Commandements de la Loy que Dieu escriuit de son doigt en deux tables au Mont de Sinay moult long temps deuant, et les bailla à Moyse pour monstrer au peuple d'Israel, dont il y en a deux des plus principaux; c'est que l'on doit croire, craindre, et aymer Dieu sur toutes choses, et de tout son courage, et l'autre que l'on ne doit faire à autruy ce que l'ō ne voudroit qu'autruy luy fist ; et qui gardera bien ces Commandements et les choses dessusdictes croira fermement,

and believe firmly the above-mentioned things, shall be
saved; and we know of a truth that everything which God
commanded in the Old Law prefigures what He has commanded in the New, as, for instance, the brazen serpent
which Moses set up on a staff in the wilderness to cure the
bite of the serpents, prefigures our LORD JESUS CHRIST, who
was suspended on the tree of the Cross and raised on high
to protect and defend all who should believe on Him from
the teeth of the devil, who before that had power over all
the souls which he had up to that time ruined.

CHAPTER LII.—How we must believe in the Holy Sacrament of the Altar.

In those days the Jews killed a lamb, which they sacrificed
at the Passover, none of whose bones they broke, which
prefigured our LORD JESUS CHRIST, Who was crucified and
put to death on the Cross by the Jews on the day [or
rather at the season] of the Passover, but without breaking
his bones; and they ate this lamb with unleavened bread,

il sera sauué. Et sçachons de vray que toutes les choses que
Dieu commanda en la vieille Loy, sont par figures en celles du
nouueau testament, ainsi que seroit par figure par le serpent
derrain que Moyse fit dresser au desert bien haut sur vn fust
contre la morsure des serpents, qui parfigure nostre Seigneur
Iesus Christ qui fut pendu et leué bien haut en l'arbre de la
Croix, pour garder et deffendre tous ceux qui en luy croyent,
contre la morsure du Diable, qui parauant auoit puissance sur
toutes les ames lesquelles il perdit adoncques.

[CHAPITRE LII.]—Comme on doit croire le Sacrement de l'Austel.

En ce temps les Iuifs tuoient vn aignel dequoy ils faisoient
leurs sacrifices à leurs Pasques, et ne luy brisoient nuls os;
lequel pourfigure nostre Seigneur Jesus Christ qui fut crucifié
et mort en la croix par les Iuifs le iour de leurs Pasques, sans
luy briser nuls os, et mangerent iceluy aignel auec pain azyme,

and with the juice of wild lettuces. This shews that the
wafers for the Sacrament of the Mass should be made without leaven, though the Greek Church holds otherwise, and
that because our LORD, knowing that He should die on the
Friday, anticipated the Passover and kept it on the Thursday, so He probably had leavened bread ; but we, who hold
the law of Rome, maintain that He used unleavened bread
and the juice of wild lettuces, which is bitter and prefigures
the bitterness of the servitude of the children of Israel in
Egypt, from which they were delivered by the direction
and will of GOD. And there are many other things which
He said and did which are full of so great mystery that
none but great scholars can understand them ; and for the
sins which we have committed we must never despair, as
did the traitor Judas, but must seek for pardon with great
contrition of heart, confessing them devoutly, and He will
pardon us; also, we must never be idle, which is a great
danger, for by the state in which He finds us when He
comes we shall be judged. We must also keep ourselves

---

c'est pain sans leuain, et auec ius de laituës champestres ; lequel
pain nous pourfigure que l'on doit faire le Sacrement de la
Messe sans leuain, mais les Grecs ont le contraire ; et pour ce
que nostre Seigneur sçauoit qu'il deuoit mourir le Vendredy
auança-il sa Pasque et la fit le Ieudy ; et peut estre qu'il la fist
de pain leué. Mais nous qui tenons la Loy de Romme, disons
qu'il la fit de pain sans leuain; et le ius des laictues champestres,
qui est amer, qui nous profigure l'amertume en quoy les fils
d'Israel estoient en Egypte en seruage; duquel ils furent de-
liurez par le commandement et volonté de Dieu. Et y a tant
d'autres choses qu'il dit et qu'il fit, qui sont pleines de si grands
mysteres que nul ne les peut entendre, s'il n'est moult grand
clerc; et pour peché que nous facions ne nous desperons mie,
ainsi que fit Iudas le traistre, mais en querons pardon auec
grand' contrition de cœur, et nous en confessons deuotement, et
il nous pardonnera ; et ne soyons mie paresseux, c'est vn trop
grand peril; car selon l'estat où il nous trouuera nous serons

from mortal sin as much as possible, which will be the salvation of us and of our souls, and let us always remember the words which are here written, and shew them and teach them to those who shall be baptised in these parts, for in so doing we may gain much of the love of GOD and obtain the salvation of their souls and ours; and, in order that it may be the better understood, we have drawn up this instruction as simply as we could according to the knowledge which GOD has given us; for we have a good hope in Him that one of these days some good and learned clerks shall come out hither who shall arrange all in good form and order, and shall explain the Articles of the Faith better than we have been able to do, and shall bring forward the miracles which GOD has worked for them and for us in days gone by, and the judgment to come, and the general resurrection, so as to root out the false beliefs which have long existed and still remain among many of the people of these islands.

---

iugéz. Si nous gardons de pecher mortellement le plus que nous pourrons, et ce sera le sauuement de nous et de nos ames, et ayons tousiours memoire des paroles qui icy sont escriptes, et les monstrons et apprenons à ceux que nous faisons baptiser pardeça, car en ce faisant nous pouuons grandement acquerir l'amour de Dieu et le sauuement de nos ames et des leurs. Et afin que mieux le puissent entendre nous auons fait et ordonné ceste introduction le plus legerement que nous auons sceu faire selon le peu d'entēdement que Dieu nous a donné; car nous auons bon esperance en Dieu que aucuns bons clercs preud'hommes venront vn de ces iours pardeça qui addresseront et mettront tout en bonne forme et en bonne ordonnance, et leur feront entendre les articles de la Foy mieux que nous ne scauons faire, et leur appliqueront des miracles que Dieu a faits pour eux et pour nous au temps passé; et du Iugcment aduenir, et de la generale Resurrection, afin d'oster leurs cœurs du tout de la mauuaise creance en quoy ils ont longuement esté et sont encore en la plus grand' partie d'eux.

CHAPTER LIII.—(Of the excellence of the islands, and of the facility of subduing them with the other countries of Africa.)

It must not be wondered at that Monsieur de Bethencourt should have undertaken such a conquest as that of these islands, for many others in times past have undertaken equally strange enterprises in which they have succeeded; and there is no doubt that, if Christian men would give a little support to the undertaking, all the islands, both great and small, would be conquered, from which might accrue so much good that it would rejoice all Christendom. M. de Bethencourt, who, together with Messire Gadifer de la Salle, visited and inspected the islands as well as the coasts of the Moors, from the Straits of Morocco to the approach to the islands, said that if any noble Prince of the Kingdom of France or elsewhere would undertake any considerable conquest on this side, a most feasible and reasonable undertaking, he might do so at little cost; for Portugal, Spain,

[CHAPITRE LIII.]—(De la bonté des isles et facilité de les conquerir avec les autres pays de l'Afrique.)

Nulz ne se doit esmerueiller si Monsieur de Bethencourt a entreprins de faire vne telle conqueste, comme est celle des isles de pardeçà; car maints autres au temps passé ont fait d'aussi estranges entreprises dont ils sont bien venus à chef, et ne doute l'on point que si les Chrestiens vouloient vn peu secourir le fait, toutes les isles et vnes et autres, et grandes et petites, seroient conquises; dont si grand bien pourroit aduenir que toute Chrestienté s'en reiouyroit, et Bethencourt, qui toutes ces Isles Canarianes a veu et visité, et aussi a fait Messire Gadiffer de la Salle bon cheualier et sage, et aussi ont-ils toute la costiere des Mores et du destroit de Maroch en venāt vers les isles, dit ainsi, que si aucun noble Prince du Royaume de France ou d'ailleurs vouloit entreprendre aucune grand' conqueste par deçà, qui seroit vne chose bien faisable et bien raisonable, il le pourroit faire à peu de frais : car Portugal, et Espagne, et Aragon les fourniroiēt pour

and Aragon would supply them for money with victuals of
all sorts, with ships better than any other country, and with
pilots who knew the harbours and these countries. Besides,
there could be no point more favourable for the conquest of
the Saracens, nor from which they could be attacked with
less trouble or cost than from here. The journey thither is
easy and short, and comparatively uncostly; and, as to the
islands themselves, especially the Canary Islands, they have
the most healthy climate of any, and contain no venomous
animals, for during all the long time that Bethencourt and
his company remained there, no one suffered from sick-
ness, which surprised them greatly. Moreover, the islands
may be reached, in favourable weather, from Rochelle in
less than a fortnight, from Seville in five or six days, and
from all other parts in the same proportion. Another argument is that the country is flat, wide, and broad; and
supplied with all good things, with fine rivers and large
towns. Then, again, the infidels have no armour nor any

---

leur argent de toutes vitailles, et de nauires plus que nul autre
pays, et aussi de pilots qui sçauent les ports et les contrécs, et si
on ne sçauroit dire par où ne par quelle part qu'il voudroit faire
conqueste sur les Sarrasins, plus licite ne plus propre, ne qui
plus legerement se peust faire et à mendre peine et mendre
coust qu'elle seroit par deçà. Car la raison y est telle que le
chemin est aisé, bref et court, et peu coustable au regard des
autres chemins. Et quant aux isles de pardeçà, le plus sain pays
est qu'on ne peut trouuer, et n'y habite nul beste qui porte velin,
et specialemēt és isles Canariennes, et si y a demouré ledit de
Bethencourt bien longuement et sa compagnie, que nuls n'y ont
esté malades, dequoy ils ont esté bien esbays. Et si y feroit-on
en temps cōuenable de la Rochelle en moins de quinze iours, et
de Siuille en cinq ou six iours, et de tous les autres ports sem-
blablement. Vne grand' raison y est; que c'est vn plain païs
grand et large et garny de tous biens, de bonnes riuieres et de
grosses villes. Encor y a-il vne autre raison, les mescreans sont
tels qu'ils n'ont nulles armures quelconques, ne sens de faire

knowledge of warfare, and they can receive no help from their neighbours, for the lofty and astonishing Montes Cleros divide them from the people of Barbary, who are also situated at a great distance from them. They are not, therefore, to be dreaded like other nations, for they have no projectile weapons, which are thoroughly proved by Monsieur de Bourbon and many others who were at the siege of Africa in [1390,[1]] to be the best and most important of African weapons. Indeed, every one knows that in battle nothing is more formidable than the bow, especially in these regions, for this people cannot carry so much armour as they do in France on account of the length of the roads

---

batailles. Ils ne sçauent que c'est de guerre, et si ne peuuent auoir secours d'autre gens : car les monts de Clere, qui sont si grands et si merueilleux, sont entre eux et les Barbariens qui leur sont moult lointains ; et si ne sont mie gens qui soient à redouter, ainsi que seroient autres nations ; car ils sont gens sans traict, et l'on le peut bien prouuer par Monsieur de Bourbon, et par maints autres qui furent deuant Afrique, l'an [1390][1], que là est le meilleur et le plus bel de toutes leurs puissances ; et c'est vne chose que chacun sçait qu'en bataille c'est la chose qui est plus crainte que trait, et par special és marches de par deçà ; car on ne peut estre si fort armé comme l'on seroit en France pour la longueur du chemin, et aussi pour le pays qui est vn peu plus

---

[1] This date was left in blank in the MS. Africa was an ancient and very splendid city, the Aphrodisium of Ptolemy, standing on a point of land projecting into the sea, now known as Ras Mehediah, some ninety miles south-east of Tunis. It had been destroyed by the Mahometans when they took Carthage, but was rebuilt and fortified by the Caliph Mehedi, who named it Mehedia. At a later period it fell into the hands of the pirates of Sicily, by whom it was called Africa. Andrea Dorio captured it from the pirate Dragut. Charles V, fearing it might fall again into the hands of the Mahometans, and begrudging the immense expense of maintaining it, razed it to the ground. For the description of the attack on Africa by Louis II, Duke of Bourbon, referred to in the text, see Froissart, tom. iv, p. 211.

and the heat of the climate. Again, here one may easily
learn news of Prester John; and, once in the country, one
may encounter a certain people called Farfus,[1] who are
Christians, and who might afford much valuable information, for they are acquainted with the neighbouring countries
and speak the languages. One of these accompanied Bethencourt and his companions in the conquest of the islands,
and through him they learned many useful things.

CHAPTER LIV.—How M. de Bethencourt rode over the country to
make himself acquainted with its different localities.

Now, it is the intention of M. de Bethencourt to examine

---

chaut : et pourroit on auoir legeremēt des nouuelles du Prestre-
Jean ; et qui seroit entré au pays, on trouueroit assez pres de là
vne maniere de gens qui s'appellent *Farfus*[1] qui sont Chrestiens,
et pourroient addresser de moult de choses qui seroient grandement profitables ; car ils sçauent les pays et les contrées, et
parlent les langages, et en cette compagnie en a-il vn qui tousiours a esté en la conqueste visitant lesdites isles, et par luy s'est
on informé de moult de choses.

[CHAPITRE LIV.]—*Comment Monsieur de Bethencourt chevauche le
pais pour le savoir et congnoistre.*

Or est l'intention de Monsieur de Bethencourt de visiter la

---

[1] Bergeron, in his edition of Bethencourt of 1630, offers in a side-note
the following illustration:—" Chrestiens Africains dits Farfanes à Marroc,
et Rabatins à Tunis"; for the following explanation of which I am
indebted to my learned friend Señor de Gayangos. There is even now
existing in Spain a family of the name of Farfan, deriving its descent
from a band of warriors, fifty in number, who served in the wars in
Morocco, and, returning to Spain in the time of John II of Castile,
received the name of " Caballeros Farfanes." Being Spaniards they
were Christians, and hence the reference to their being found in Morocco.
Bergeron's use of the word " Rabatins" as applying to these knights is
simply in the sense of " warriors," the word being derived from the
fortified city of Rabat, on the west coast of Morocco. It is in no way
connected with Tunis.

the country from Cape Cantin, which is half-way between
the Canaries and Spain, to Cape Bojador, a promontory to
the right of the Canaries, extending on the other side to the
Rio d'Ouro,[1] to see if he can find a good harbour, or any
place which he may fortify and make tenable, when place
and time may serve, so as to obtain a footing in the country, and be able to put it to tribute if he succeeds. And
had he received any assistance from France, there is no
reason to doubt that, either now or later he would succeed
in his attempt, especially with regard to the Canary Islands,
for with God's permission and under the advice of his sovereign lord and master the King of France, his intention was
and still is to carry out his enterprise still farther. But
without aid he could not carry it on to any perfection, to the
honour and advancement of the Christian Faith, which is
not as yet known in those parts, through the fault of those

---

contrée de la terre ferme de Cap de Cantin, qui est mi-voye d'icy
et d'Espagne, iusques au Cap de Bugeder qui fait la pointe de la
terre ferme au droit de nous, et s'estend de l'autre bande iusques
au fleuue de l'or,[1] pour voir s'il pourra trouuer aucun bon port et
lieu qui se peust fortifier et estre tenable quand temps et lieu
sera, pour auoir l'entrée du pays, et pour le mettre en treu s'il
chet à poinct. Et si ledit Seigneur de Bethencourt eust trouué
quelque confort au Royaume de France, il ne faut point douter
que de present, ou bien-tost après, qui ne fust venu à son
attente ; et specialement des Isles Canariennes, comme, se Dieu
plaist, ledit Seigneur y aduiendra et du surplus par le conseil de
son Prince et souuerain Seigneur, le Roy de France, son intention estoit et est encores de bouter le fait plus auant : mais sans
ayde il ne le pourroit mie bien maintenir pour venir en vne
grande perfection, à l'honneur et exaucement de la foy Chrestienne, qui n'est mie deça cognuë par faute de ceux qui telles

---

[1] With reference to this Rio d'Ouro or River of Gold, on which have
been raised questions of great importance in the history of geographical
discovery, see note on page 102.

who ought to have undertaken the task long ago to instruct these people in the knowledge of God, whereby they would have gained great honour in this world, and in the sight of God great glory and merit.

CHAPTER LV.—How M. de Bethencourt took measures for learning the ports and passages of the land of the Saracens.

As M. de Bethencourt had a great desire to learn the true state and government of the land of the Saracens and their sea-ports, which were reported to be good on the main land for twelve leagues towards us to the right of Cape Bojador and the island of Erbanie, where M. de Bethencourt now is, we have here inserted sundry notes on this subject, extracted from a book by a mendicant friar who made the tour of this country and visited all the sea-ports, which he mentions by name. He went through all the countries, Christian, Pagan, and Saracen, of those parts,

---

choses deussent entreprendre, et qui pieça le deussent auoir entreprins, pour monstrer au peuple qui y habite la cognoissance de Dieu, et en ce faisant, il puisse acquerir grand honneur en ce monde et de Dieu grand gloire et grand merite.

[CHAPITRE LV.]—*Comment Monsieur de Bethencourt met peine de savoir les port et passagez des pais des Sarazins.*

Et pour ce que ledit de Bethencourt a grand' voulenté de sçauoir la verité de l'estat et gouuernement du pays des Sarrasins, et des ports de mer, que l'on leur dit estre bons du costé de la terre ferme que marche douze lieuës près de nous au droit du Cap du Bugeder, et de l'Isle d'Erbanye là ou ledit Sieur de Bethencourt est à present; auons cy endroit mis aucunes choses, touchant ces marches, extraits d'vn livre que fit vn Frere mendeāt, qui enuironna iceluy pays, et fut à tous les ports de mer, lesquels il deuise et nomme, et alla par tous les Royaumes Chrestiens, et des Payons, et des Sarrazins qui sont de cette

and names them all. He mentions the names of the pro-
vinces, and the arms of the kings and princes, which it
would be tedious to describe. We therefore have only
selected for the present those portions which bear upon
subjects relating to the projected conquest. Finding his
account correct of the countries they already knew, they
relied on his information with regard to all the other countries; they have therefore inserted in the sequel other ex-
tracts from his book, as they found occasion.

CHAPTER LVI.—How a Mendicant Friar explains the things which
he had seen by a book that he had made about them.

We will begin at the part where, being outside of the
Montes Claros,[1] he came to the city of Marocco, which was conquered by Scipio Africanus, and which formerly used to be

bende, et les nomme tous; et deuise les noms des Prouinces, les
armes des Roys et des Princes; qui seroit longue chose à
descrire. Si n'en prendrons, quant à present, fors ce qui nous
est mestier pour nous addresser de moult de choses au fait de la
conqueste là où il escherra à poinct. Et pour ce qu'il parle si
au vray des contrées et des pays dont nous auons vraye cognoissance, il nous semble que ainsi doit-il faire de tous les autres
païs et pour ce auons nous cy-apres mis aucunes choses qui sont
en son liure, dont nous auons mestier.

[CHAPITRE LVI.]—*Comment un Frere mandeant devise des choses
qu'il a veues par un livre qu'il en fit.*

Et commencerons quand il fut outre les monts de Clere, il vint
en la cité de Maroch, laquelle Scipion l'Africain conquit, qui
jadis souloit estre nommée *Carthago*, et estoit chef de toute

---

[1] The Atlas Mountains, called by Bergeron "Montes Claros" from the
Spanish, and translated "Monts de Clere" in the text. The name, which is
not, I think, traceable to any ancient source, seems arbitrarily given in
the sense of the range being "illustrious" or widely known.

H

called Carthage,[1] and was the capital of all Africa. From
thence he went towards the ocean to Nifet[2] and Samor[3] and to
Saffi, which last place is very near Cape Cantin: he then proceeded to Mogador, which is in another province called
Gasulle,[4] and there commences the chain of the Montes
Claros. Thence he came to the aforesaid Gasulle, which is
an extensive country, well stored with all good things. He
then proceeded towards the coast to a port called Samateue,[5]
and thence to Cape Non, which presents itself in coming
near our islands. Thence he put to sea in a *pensil*,[6] and
came to port Saubrun,[7] and coasted along the country of
the Moors, which is called the Sandy Shores, as far as
Cape Bojador, which is twelve leagues from us. It is in a
great kingdom called Guinea. There they took their way

Afrique, et de là s'en vint vers la mer Oceane à Nifet et Samor
et à Saphi, qui est bien pres du cap de Cantin, et puis vint à
Moguedor, qui est en vne autre Prouince qui s'appelle la Gasulle,
et là commencent les Monts de Clere, et de là s'en vint à la
Gasulle dessusdite, qui est vn grand pays garny de tous biens, et
s'en alla vers la marine à vn port qui se nomme Samateue; et
de là au Cap de Non, qui est en venant vers nos isles; et là se
mit en mer en vn pensil, et vint au port de Saubrun, et toute
la costiere des Mores qui se nomme Les Plaigues Areneuses
iusques au cap de Bugeder, qui marche deux lieues près de nous,
et est en vn grand Royaume qui s'appelle la Guinoye, et là

---

[1] A blunder so manifest as to need no comment.

[2] Anafe or Anf, the ancient name of Dahr-el-beida.

[3] Azamor.

[4] Variously spelt Gozola, Godala, Guzzula, and Gazula, from the
ancient well known form Gætulia.

[5] An irrecognisable name, probably Cape Sim or Tafelane, *alias*
Tefetneh.

[6] I have failed entirely in tracking this word. M. Charton, in his
Voyageurs anciens et modernes, translates it "barque."

[7] Bergeron renders this Port Sabreira, but I find no authority for
either name. Query, Porto Cansado.

and proceeded to see and take cognisance of the islands of this side, and they went in search of many other countries by sea and land of which we make no mention. The Friar then parted from his companions and went eastwards through many countries till he reached a kingdom called Dongalla, in the province of Nubia, inhabited by Christians. The Patriarch of Nubia has for one of his titles the name of Prester John. Nubia extends on one side to the deserts of Egypt, and on the other to the Nile, which comes out of the domains of Prester John; and the kingdom of Dongalla extends to the point where the river Nile divides into two branches,[1] one of which forms the River of Gold, which flows towards us, while the other runs through Egypt and falls into the sea at Damietta. From these countries the Friar went into Egypt as far as Cairo, and at Damietta went on board a vessel manned by Christians and came back to Sarretta,[2] which is opposite Granada, and proceeded thence over land to the city of Marocco; he then crossed the Montes Claros and passed into Gazula: there he found

---

prindrent leur chemin et allerent voir et aduiser les isles de par deçà : et chercherent maints autres pays par mer et par terre, dont nous ne faisons nulle mention ; et se partit le Frere d'eux, et s'en alla contre Orient par maintes contrees iusques a vn Royaume qui s'appelle Dongala, qui est en la prouince de Nubie, habité de Chrestiens, et s'appelle le Prestre-Jean, en vn de ses tiltres, Patriarche de Nubie ; qui marchit d'vn des costes aux deserts d'Egypte, et de l'autre costé à la Riuiere de Nil qui vient des Marches du Prestre Jean, et s'estend le Royaume de Don-gale iusques où la riuiere de Nil fourche en deux parties, dont l'vne fait le fleuve de l'Or qui vient vers nous, et l'autre s'en va en Egypte, et entre en mer à Damiette, et de celles marches s'en alla le Frere en Egypte au Caire ; et a Damyate entra en vne nef de Chrestiens, et depuis reuint à Sarette, qui est front à front de Grenade, et s'en alla arriere par terre à la cité de Maroch, et trauersa les monts de Clere, et passa par la Gasulle ; et la trouua

---

[1] See note on page 102.   Zera?

the Moors, fitting out a vessel to go to the River of Gold, with whom he made terms and put to sea with them. They directed their course to Cape Non and Cape Saubrun, and then to Cape Bojador, and so along the whole coast southwards as far as the River of Gold.[1]

CHAPTER LVII.—Continuation of the same.

According to the Friar's book, when they gained this river, they found on its banks ants of very great size, which drew up the grains of gold[2] from under the ground, and the merchants made wonderfully large profits by this voyage. They then departed from this river and held their course along the sea-shore, until they found a rich and fertile island called Gulpis, where they made large profits. The inhabitants are idolaters. Thence they went on till they

---

Mores qui armoient vne galere pour aller au fleuue de l'or, et se loüa auec eux, et entrerent en mer, et tindrēt le chemin au cap de Non, et au cap de Saubrun, et puis au cap de Bugeder, et toute la costiere deuers Midy iusques au fleuue de l'or.

[CHAPITRE LVII.]—*Encore de mesmes.*

Et selon que dit le livre du Frere, quand ils furent là où ils trouuerent fermis sur la riuage du fleuue, dont les fermis estoient moult grands, qui tiroient grauelle d'or de dessoubs la terre, et gagnerent les marchands merueilleusement en ce voyage ; puis se partirent de là et tindrent le chemin selon le riuage de la mer, et trouuerent vne Insula moult bonne et riche, où ils firent grandement leur proffit, qui s'appelle isle *Gulpis*, là sont les gens idolatres, et de là se partirent et allerent plus auant, et trouuerent

---

[1] See note on page 102.

[2] This is but the old story from Herodotus of the Indian ants, which were smaller than a dog but larger than a fox, and which, in making their subterranean dwellings, pushed up sand charged with gold.

came to another isle called Caable, which they left on the right hand. Then they found on the mainland a mountain called Alboc, very lofty and abounding in natural wealth, in which rises a very large river. Here the Moorish galley turned back, but the Friar remained some time there, and then entered the kingdom of Gotome (Ghoroma?), where the mountains are so high that they are said to be the loftiest in the world, and some call them in their language the Mountains of the Moon, while others call them the Gold Mountains: they are six in number, and from them spring six large rivers, which all fall into the River of Gold and form a great lake. In the midst of this lake is an island named Palloya, peopled with blacks. Thence the Friar proceeded further till he came to a river named Euphrates, which comes from the Terrestrial Paradise. He crossed it and passed through many countries and regions till he came to the city of Melée, which was the residence of Prester John. He remained there several days, for he saw there a considerable number of marvellous

---

vne autre isle qui s'appelle *Caable*, et la laisserent à main dextre. Et puis trouuerent vne montaigne en terre ferme moult haulte et moulte abondante de tous biens, qui s'appelle *Alboc*, de laquelle naist vne riuiere moult grande; et de là s'en retourna la galere des Mores, et le Frere demoura aucun temps illec; puis s'en entra au Royaume de *Gotome*; là sont les montagnes si hautes que l'on dit que ce sont les plus hautes du monde, et aucuns les appellent en leurs langages les monts de la Lune, et les autres les monts de l'or; et sont six, et naissent d'elles six grosses riuieres qui toutes cheent au fleuue de l'or, et y font vn grand lac; et dedans ce lac a vne isle qui s'appelle *Paloye*, qui est peuplée de gens noirs. Et de là s'en alla le frere tousiours auant iusqu'en vne riuiere nommé Eufrate, qui vient du Parradis Terrestre, et la trauersa, et s'en alla par maints païs et par maintes diuerses côtrées iusques a la cité de Melée, là où de-meuroit le Prestre Jean; et la demoura moult de iours, pour ce qu'il y voyoit assez de choses meruelleuses, des quelles nous ne

things, of which at present we make no mention in this book, in order to hasten on to other matters, and for fear the reader might take them for lies. In like manner the season before Monsieur de Bethencourt set out in a boat, with fifteen companions, from one of the islands called Erbania and went to Cape Bojador, which lies in the kingdom of Guinea, about twelve leagues from us, and they took some of the people of the country and returned to the Great Canary, where they found their companions and their vessel awaiting them.

CHAPTER LVIII.—The Mendicant Friar speaks of the River of Gold.

And as the Mendicant Friar asserts in his book that it is only a hundred and fifty French leagues from Cape Bojador to the River of Gold[1]—and so the map has shown it to be—it is

faisons nulle mention, quant à present, en ce liure, pour plus brieuement passer outre, et pour doute que se ne semblast au lisant estre mensonges. Et mesmemēt se partit la saison auant Monsieur de Bethencourt, et vint par deçà vn basteau auec quinze compagnons dedans, d'vne des isles nommées Erbanie, et s'en alla au cap de Bugeder, qui siet au royaume de la Guinoye, à douze lieuës pres de nous ; et là prindrent des gens du pays, et s'en retournerent à la grand' Canare, là où ils trouuerent leurs compagnons et leur nauire qui les attendoient.

[CHAPITRE LVIII.]—*Si parle le frere mandeant du fleuve de l'or.*

Et dict ainsi le frere mandeant en son liure, que l'on ne compte du cap de Bugeder iusques au fleuue de l'or que cent cinquante lieuës Françoises ; et ainsi la monstré la carte, ce n'est singlure

---

[1] This story of the Mendicant Friar is a confused embodiment of the geographical traditions of the period. The Rio d'Oro, or River of Gold, here mentioned, is laid down on three maps anterior to the time of Bethencourt: viz., on the Portulano Mediceo, of the date of 1351, in the Laurentian Library at Florence ; on the map made by the Venetian

only a three days' voyage of ships and sailing boats ; for galleys, that hug the shore, take longer. Therefore, to get

---

que pour trois iours pour naues et pour barges ; car gallees qui vont terre à terre prendrent plus long chemin ; et quand pour

---

brothers Pizzigani in 1367, now in the Library at Parma ; and on the famous Catalan map, or rather atlas, of the date of 1375, in the Paris Imperial Library. On the third sheet of this last is the representation of a boat-load of explorers off the coast to the south of Cape Bojador, accompanied by a legend in Catalan, which, as it bears in a very interesting manner upon the Mendicant Friar's story, as well as upon a very important question in the history of national priority in discovery, I shall here quote and comment upon. The legend runs thus :—

"Partich luxer dñ Jac. Ferer, per anar al riu de l'or, al gorn de Sen Lorens qui es à X de Agost, y fo en l'an MCCCXLVI": "The ship of Jaime Ferrer started to go to the River of Gold on St. Lawrence's day, the 10th of August, 1346." The event here recorded is corroborated by the following legend, which occurs in a collection of papers, presented to the Archives of Genoa in 1660 by M. Federico Federici, and discovered in 1802, by M. Gräberg de Hemsö.

"Recessit de civitate majorisarum Galeatia una Joannis Ferne Catalani in festo Sancti Laurentii, quod est in decima die mensis Augusti, anno Domini 1346, causa eundi ad Rujaura, et de ipsa Galeatia nunquam postea aliquid novum habuerunt. Istud flumen de longitudine vocatur Vedamel et similiter vocatur Ruiauri, quia in eo recolligitur aurum de pajola. Et scire debeatis quod major pars gentium in partibus istis habitantium sunt electi ad colligendum aurum in ipso flumine, qui habet latitudinem unius legue et fondum pro majori nave mundi.

"Istud est caput finis Terrarum Affricæ occidentalis, etc."

"On St. Lawrence's day, viz., the 10th of August, 1346, a galley belonging to the Catalan John Ferne, left the city of the Majorcans with the purpose of going to Rujaura [the River of Gold], but of said galley no news has since been received. On account of its length that river is called Vedamel. It is also called Ruiauri, because the gold of Pajola is collected in it. You must also know that the majority of the inhabitants of these parts are employed in collecting gold in this river, which is a league wide, and deep enough for the largest ship in the world.

"This is the Cape Finisterre of West Africa."

Now I have had occasion, in my *Life of Prince Henry the Navigator*, to demonstrate that Cape Bojador, here stated by the Mendicant Friar to be north of the River of Gold only one hundred and fifty French

from here to there we do not hold to be a difficult matter; and if things in that country are such as they are described in the

---

y aller d'icy nous n'en tenons pas grand' compte; et si les choses de par deçà sont telles commes le liure du frere Espagnol le deuise,

---

leagues, had proved the *nec plus ultra* of Atlantic exploration until rounded by Gileannes in the service of Prince Henry, in 1434. The Dieppese claim to have passed it in the previous century; and M. d'Avezac has drawn the inference from these two legends that this voyage must have been preceded by many others, "because," he argues, "one does not fit out an armament with a fixed destination without knowing, approximately at least, the point one has to arrive at."

I have shewn, and here repeat, that the contrary was the case, and that the expedition was fitted out for the express purpose of finding the *unknown* mouth of a river in which gold was collected, and the existence of which had become known to the mercantile populations in the Mediterranean through the medium of commercial intercourse with the Arabs. The fact of the voyage having been recorded not only in the archives of Genoa, but also on the face of a remarkably handsome map prepared with extreme carefulness and labour, is a proof that the expedition was one of unusual importance and anxiety, such as the purpose I have suggested would involve. Had it been merely an unsuccessful venture to a point already known even approximately, we should not expect to find the expedition recorded on the face of a map at all, but we should reasonably hope to find that point laid down with an approximation at least to accuracy on charts of the period, and especially on the one on which this individual expedition was recorded. As, fortunately, the maps are existing on which the river indicated by the legends is laid down, we have by their help, in conjunction with the wording of the legends themselves, an opportunity of testing how far the geographical information they convey is, either approximately or at all, in accordance with the knowledge which would be derived from even one antecedent maritime exploration.

The two legends manifestly refer to the same event: they both record an expedition which started on the same day *for the purpose of going* (in the Catalan *per anar*, and in the Latin *causâ eundi*) to the same river. This river, the Ruiauri or River of Gold, was so called because gold of Pajola was collected in it, and from its length it was called *Vedamel*. Now, in the Venetian map of the brothers Pizzigani, made in 1367, twenty-one years after the expedition of Jaime Ferrer, we find laid down, *in a latitude a little south of the Canaries*, the river Palolus, rising in a large lake, on which is the following legend in

book of the Spanish Friar, and as those who have explored those parts assert, it is Monsieur de Bethencourt's intention,

---

et aussi ceux qui ont frequenté en ces marches dient et racomptent, à l'ayde de Dieu et des Princes et du peuple Chrestien, l'in-

---

Latin :—"This lake proceeds from the Mountain of the Moon, and passes through sandy deserts." In the middle of its course the river bifurcates, and again joins, forming an island, on which in Latin is the inscription—"The island Palola: here gold is gathered." Into the opposite or eastern extremity of the lake flows the Nile, the eastern branch of which takes its northward course towards the Mediterranean, in its well-known position. We thus find a river exactly corresponding with the description of that for which Jaime Ferrer started on St. Lawrence's day, in the year 1346. Three of the four specialities indicated in the Genoese document are here substantiated by Venetians who, like the Genoese, had commercial relations with the Arabs; and that on a map bearing no reference whatever to the voyage of Jaime Ferrer. We have a river on which gold is collected, and it is the gold of Palola or Paiola, and we also have an explanation of the expression that from *its length* it is called Vedamel. That length may be judged when it is made to extend from the Nile, delineated in its true position as falling into the Mediterranean, to another outlet into the Atlantic a little south of the Canaries. The fourth speciality of the river, as given in the Genoese document, is the name Vedamel itself, which I think I can shew to mean River of Nile, in conformity with the old idea of the Nile having a western outlet into the Atlantic, as referred to in the Mendicant Friar's narrative, see page 98.

The Genoese document in which the name Vedamel occurs is so carelessly spelt that the name of "Jayme Ferrer," a well recognisable Catalan name (see "Ferrer," in Torres Amat's *Escritores Catalanes*), is misspelt "Joannes Ferne"; and the Genoese form for the Rio d'Oro is in the course of two or three lines spelt both "Rujaura" and "Ruiauri." It is not difficult, therefore to suppose that "Vedamel" is a misspelling for "Vedanill," in which we recognise the Arabic words "Ved" or "Wadi," a river, and "Nill," the Nile. Pliny had long ago declared that a branch of the Nile debouched on the west coast of Africa, and an ample description of it is given by the Arab geographer Edrisi in the middle of the twelfth century, who, after speaking of the sources of the eastern Nile, says, "The other arm of the Nile (the Nile of the Blacks) flows into the western districts, and, reaching from the east to the extreme west, empties itself into the sea not far from the island of Ulil, which is a day's sail from its mouth; and on that Nile of the

with the help of God, and of Christian princes and people, to
open the road to the River of Gold; and if he succeeds, it

tention de Monsieur de Bethencourt est d'ouurir le chemin du
fleuue de l'or: car s'il en venoit a bonne fin ce seroit grande-

Negroes, or on another river which mixes its waters with it, are situated
the abodes of the people of Nigritia."
    A reference to the map of Abul-Hassan Ali Ben Omar (1230) shews
us this Western Nile, under the name of Nil Gana, falling into the
Atlantic in about the latitude of the Gambia. The map of Ibn Said
(1274) has it, under the name of Os Nili Ganah, a little more northward. That of Abulfeda (1331) with the same name, yet a little more
northward. The retention of the belief in this river as a branch of the
Nile by the Arab geographers is shewn by an Arabic map, preserved to
us by M. Jomard in his *Monuments de la Géographie*, by a Moor named
Mohammed Ebn-Aly Ebn-Ahmed al Charfy of Sfax, and bearing date
1009 of the Hegira, which corresponds with A.D. 1600. That the river
itself was the Senegal is shewn by Azurara, the chronicler of the conquest of Guinea in the time of Prince Henry, who speaks of it as the
Ryo do Nillo, which they call the Canega. Both in the Pizzigani map
and in the Catalan map which records the voyage of Ferrer, this river,
whose existence was thus learned from Arab sources, is called the
River of Gold.
    But while this notion of a river of gold, debouching on the west
coast of Africa, was thus handed down geographically from ancient
times, the mercantile cities of Italy would have the impression more
immediately brought home to them by the gold brought across the
desert from Guinea into the Mediterranean. We find in the treatise
Della Decima of Balducci Pegolotti, who was a factor in the great
Florentine house of the Bardi, and who wrote in the first half of the
fourteenth century that the malaguette pepper, which was the product
of the Guinea coast, was then among the articles imported into Nismes
and Montpellier; and De Barros expressly states (Dec. I, fol. 33) that
the malaguette imported into Italy before Prince Henry's time was
brought from Guinea by the Moors, who, crossing the vast empire of
Mandingo and the deserts of Libya, reached the Mediterranean at a
port named Mundi Barca, corrupted into Monte da Barca, and as the
Italians were not acquainted with the locality whence it came, they
called it "grains of Paradise." It would be unreasonable to doubt that,
with the malaguette from Guinea, gold was also transported by these
merchants across the desert to their port in the Mediterranean, and
though the Italians were ignorant of the country whence it came, they

will be greatly to the honour and profit of the kingdom of France and of all Christian kingdoms ; inasmuch as access

---

ment l'honneur et le profit du Royaume de France et de tous les Royaumes Chrestiens ; veu que l on approcheroit les marches du

---

would not fail to learn that it lay somewhere on the western coast of Africa. We have therefore but to repeat the poet's apostrophe to the "auri sacra fames," to perceive the motive which would induce an enterprising party of men to encounter extreme danger for the sake of discovering a sea-path to the mouth of such a river.

But these very maps themselves prove how utterly ignorant the bold Majorcan adventurer was of the position of that mouth. The Pizzigani map places it north of Cape Bojador ; the Catalan map itself offers a *suggestion only* of where that mouth *might be*, some short distance south of that cape. But both these indications resolve themselves simply into conjectures, inasmuch as *neither north nor south of Cape Boyador is there any river at all which could by any pretence be made to correspond with the Vedamel or Rujauri till we come to the Senegal, which is at least seven hundred miles south of Cape Bojador.* Whether Ferrer himself passed Cape Bojador or not it is impossible to state and futile to conjecture, for the legend itself tells us that nothing more was heard of the expedition. That which was subsequently named the Rio d'Ouro by the Portuguese could by no possibility have anything to do with the Rio d'Oro which Ferrer went to seek, for the simple reason that the former is no river at all, but only an arm of the sea, the appearance of which deceived the Portuguese, and to which they gave the name of the Rio d'Ouro because there they first received gold in ransom for captives.

For precisely the same reason it is clear that the Rio d'Ouro of the Portuguese can in no sense be identical with the Fleuve d'Or referred to in this and the two preceding chapters and in Chapter LVI, where the Spanish mendicant friar lyingly asserts that he had accompanied some Moors in a galley to that river. How far credence is to be conceded to this narrative may be judged from a perusal of Chap. LVII. That an European should, as there described, cross the continent of Africa and escape to tell the tale is not very probable, and the narrator betrays his misgiving that his story may be taken for lies. But I think I can throw some light on this matter. In speaking of a famous and very large city of the negroes named Kucu, Edrisi says, "Some negroes think that this city lies on the Nile itself, others on a river flowing into the Nile ; but in truth the Nile passes through the city Kucu, and then diffuses itself through sandy plains into the desert, and thence merges into lakes, just as the Euphrates does in Mesopotamia. The reader has

would be obtained to the territories of Prester John, from which comes so great a variety of rich commodities. It cannot be doubted that progress has often been retarded in past times for want of enterprise, and without boasting too much of this undertaking [Monsieur Bethencourt and his people], will do as much as in them lies to vindicate their credit therein; for he will take pains to ascertain whether the thing is feasible, or whether it be utterly impossible to carry it out in any way. And so, by God's help, he will overcome much people, and bring them over to the Christian faith, which is always lost for want of teaching and instruction. And this is a great pity; for in all the world you will no-where meet with a finer or better formed race, both male and female, than the people of these islands. They are very intelligent, and only require instruction; and as the Sieur de Bethencourt is very anxious to know the state of the neighbouring countries, both islands and terra firma, he

---

Prestre Jean dont tant de biens et de richesses viennēt. Et ne doit on point doubter que moult de choses sont demourées au temps passé par default d'entreprise, et si ne se vantent mie de ce faire; mais ils feroient bien tant que l'en deura tenir pour excusez luy et toute sa compaignie; car il mettra peine sçauoir s'il se pourra faire ou non; et s'il ne se peult ores faire en nulle maniere; si conquerra-il à l'aide de Dieu moult de peuple, et le mettra à la foy Chrestienne, qui s'est tousiours perdu par faulte de doctrine et d'enseignement, dequoy c'est grand pitié : car allez par tout le monde uous ne trouuerez nulle part plus belles gens, ne mieux formez qui sont és isles de pardeça, et hommes et femmes, et sont de grand entendement, s'ils eussent qui leur monstrast : et pour ce qu'il a grande voulēté de sçauoir l'estast de tous les autres pays qui leurs sōt prochains, tant isles que

---

only to recognise in the mendicant friar's language, as he easily may do, a *rechauffé* of the confused geography of Edrisi, not losing sight of the good friar's stumble over the reference to the Euphrates, to judge whether the fear of the narrator as to his credit for veracity is a reason-able one. What then becomes of the voyage of the Moors to the Fleuve de l'Or?

will spare neither pains nor exertion in making himself acquainted, as fully as possible, with all these countries.[1]

CHAPTER LIX.—How Monsieur de Bethencourt, Messire Gadifer, and their companions, had a great deal to suffer in many ways.

We must now return to our first subject, and recount the events thereto relating in due order; and we must first state that after the capture of the King of Lancerote, and when the provisions which de Bethencourt and Gadifer had obtained by his capture were exhausted, they experienced much suffering, having been accustomed to good and plentiful fare. For the space of a year they were without bread and wine, and lived upon flesh and fish as well as they could. For a very long time they slept upon the bare ground, without either woollen or linen covering beyond the tattered dress which they wore in the day-time. This was

terres fermes, le dit Seigneur de Bethencourt mettra peine et diligence de foy informer tout à plain de toutes ces marches.

[CHAPITRE LIX.]—*Comme le dit Sieur de Bethencourt, Gadifer et leur compagnie eurent beaucoup à souffrir en plusieurs manieres.*

Or faut il retourner à nostre premiere matiere, et la poursuiure ainsi que les choses escheent dorenauant icy endroit; et dirons apres la prinse du Roy de l'isle Lancelot, et que les viures que le dit Bethencourt et Gadifer eurent recouuers à sa prinse furent despēdus, ils auoient eu moulte à souffrir, eux qui auoient accoustumé de bien viure. Ils ont esté par l'espace d'vn an sans pain et sans vin, et vescu de chair et de poisson, car faire le conuenoit; et ont esté moult long temps couchans à terre plaine sans draps, linge ne langes, fors en la pauure robbe deschiree qu'ils auoient vestue, dont ils sont moult greuez, et en outre

---

[1] No better evidence than this fifty-eighth chapter is needed to shew that the French had not previously passed Cape Bojador. Let the reader specially notice, on page 106, "It is Monsieur de Bethencourt's intention to *open the road* to the River of Gold."

a grievous trial to them, independently of the great exertions which they had to make against their enemies, but which finally resulted in bringing them into subjection. By God's grace, they are baptized and brought into our faith, although, in consequence of the treachery before described, they had rebelled against the French and waged mortal war with them, especially the inhabitants of the island of Lancerote.

CHAPTER LX.—How Monsieur de Bethencourt and Messire Gadifer had words together.

One day, during the year one thousand four hundred and four, Master Gadifer de la Salle appeared very thoughtful, so much so, that Monsieur de Bethencourt asked him what was the matter with him, and why he wore so strange a mien; upon which Gadifer replied that he had been a long time in his company, and had undergone great hardships, and that it would be hard upon him to have had to undergo so much for nothing. He therefore desired that one or

pour le grand trauail qu'il leur a conuenu prendre contre leurs ennemis, lesquels ils ont tous mis à mercy, et par la grace de Dieu ils sont baptisez et mis en nostre foy, qui par la trahison qui leur fut faicte, comme dessus est dict, se rebellerent contre eux, en eux faisant guerre mortelle, et par especial ceux de l'isle Lancelot.

[CHAPITRE LX.]—*Comment Monsieur de Bethencourt et Messire Gadiffer eurent paroles ensemble.*

Vng iour aduint que en l'an mil quatre cens et quatre, Messire Gadifer de la Salle estoit tres-fort pensif; tant que Monsieur de Bethencourt luy demanda qu'il auoit et pourquoy il faisoit si estrange chere : adonc le dit Gadifer luy dit, qu'il auoit esté vn grand espace de temps en sa compagnie, là où il auoit eu de grands travaux, et qu'il luy fairoit bien mal d'auoir perdu sa peine, et qu'il luy vaillast vne ou deux de ses isles, à celle fin

two of the islands should be delivered over to him, that he might improve them and increase their value for himself and his descendants. He further asked de Bethencourt to let him have Erbania, another island called Enfer,[1] and Gomera, all these islands being as yet unconquered and having much remaining to be done to them. When Monsieur de Bethencourt had heard all that he had to say, he replied: " Monsieur de la Salle, my brother and my friend, it is quite certain that when I found you at La Rochelle you were willing to come with me, and we were pleased with one another and had no words. The expedition which I have made thus far was commenced from my house of Grainville in Normandy, and I took out my own people, my own ship, my own provisions, and artillery, and everything that I could provide, to La Rochelle, where I met with you, and finally, by God's help, I arrived here in your company and in that of all the worthy gentlemen and other leaders of my company ; and now let me remind you that

---

qu'il les augmentast et mist en valeur pour luy et les siens ; et outre dict au dit de Bethencourt qu'il luy vaillast l'isle d'Erbanie, et vne autre isle qui s'appelle Enfer et la Gomere, toutefois toutes icelles isles n'estoient pas encor conquises ; et y auoit beaucoup a faire à les auoir. Et quand Monsieur de Bethencourt l'eut assez ouy parler, il luy respondit : Monsieur de la Salle, mon frere et mon amy, il est bien vray que quand il vous trouuay à la Rochelle vous fustes content de venir auec moy et estions fort contens l'vn de l'autre sans quelques paroles : le voyage que i'ay faict iusques icy fut commencés dès mon hostel de Grainuille en Normandie, et ay amené mes gens, mon nauire, viures, et artillerie, et tout ce que i'ay peu faire, iusquez en ycelle ville de la Rochelle, là où il vous trouuay, comme jay dit sidevant, tant qu'à la fin où ie suis venu, à l'ayde de Dieu, de vous, et de tous les bons Gentilshommes et autres bons champions de ma cōpagnie : et pour vous respondre a ce que me demandes,

---

[1] Teneriffe.

the islands and countries which you demand are not yet
conquered, nor brought to that condition to which, please
God, they by and bye will be brought, for I trust they will
all be conquered and the inhabitants be baptized. I entreat
you, therefore, as I am not tired of your company, be not
you tired of mine. It is my intention that your trouble
shall not be thrown away, but you shall receive the reward
which is most justly your due. Let us now, I pray you,
dismiss this subject, and do all in our power to remain as
brothers and good friends." "That is very well," said
Messire Gadifer, "but there is one thing which causes me
dissatisfaction, namely, that you should already have done
homage of the Canary Islands to the King of Castille, and
you call yourself sole lord of them, and even have caused
the said King to proclaim, through the greater part of his
kingdom, and especially at Seville, that you are the Lord of
them, and that none should enter the Canary Islands without your permission; the King has further issued a decree
that you are to have a fifth, either in kind or in money,

---

les isles et pays que demandez ne sont pas encor conquis, ne mis
là, où, se Dieu plaist, ils feront; car i'espere qu'ils seront conquis
et baptisez, ie vous prie qu'il ne vous ennuye point, car il ne
m'ennuye pas d'estre auec vous : mon intention n'est point que
perdiez vostre peine, et que vous ne soyez remuneré, car il vous
appartient bien.   Ie vous prie que nous parachenions et faisions
tant que nous soyons freres et amis.   C'est tres-bien dict, ce
dict Messire Gadiffer de la Salle a Monsieur de Bethencourt, mais
il y a vne chose dont ie ne suis pas content, car vous auez desia
faict l'hommage au Roy de Castille des isles Canariennes, et
vous en dictes du tout Seigneur, et mesmes a faict crier ledict
Roy de Castille par la pluspart de son Royaume, et en especial
en Siuille, que vous en estes Seigneur, et que nuls ne viennent
pardeçà esdictes isles Canariēnes sans vostre congé; et outre a
faict crier, que il veut que de toutes les marchandizes qui seront
prinses esdictes isles, et seront portees au Royaume de Castille,
que vous en ayez le quint de la marchandise ou le quint denier.

of all the commodities exported from these islands into the kingdom of Castille."

" With respect to that," said Bethencourt, " It is indeed true that I have done homage, and that I hold myself to be the true lord of these islands, since such is the pleasure of the King of Castille. But to satisfy you, I hereby promise, if you will only wait for the completion of our undertaking, to leave you that which shall give you perfect satisfaction." Messire Gadifer replied : " I shall not remain long enough in this country, for I must return to France. 1 do not wish to stay here any longer." Monsieur de Bethencourt could not at that time hold any further conference with Gadifer. It was evident that Gadifer was by no means satisfied. Nevertheless he had really lost nothing, but had been a gainer in many ways, as, for instance, in prisoners and other things which he had taken in these islands ; and if he had not lost his vessel, his condition would have been still more improved. However, these two knights made as amicable a settlement as they could for the time being, and, leaving the island of Lancerote, they came to Erbania, named

---

Quant au regard de ce que vous dictes, dict Bethencourt, il est bien vray que i'en ay faict l'hommage, et aussi ie m'en tiens le vray Seigneur, puis qu'il plaist au Roy de Castille. Mais quand pour vous contenter, s'il vous plaist attendre la diffinitiue de nostre affaire, ie vous bailleray et laisseray telle chose dequoy vous serez content. Cedict Messire Gadiffer, ie ne feray pas tant en ce païs, car il faut que ie m'en retourne en France, ie ne veux plus icy estre. Monsieur de Bethencourt ne peut oncques pour l'heure auoir plus paroles de luy, et paroist bien que ledit Gadiffer n'estoit point content, si pourtant n'auoit il riens perdu, mais auoit gagné en plusieurs manieres, comme prisonniers et autres choses qu'il auoit eu et prins esdites isles ; et s'il n'eust perdu la nef, il en eust encores plus amendé. Lesdits Cheualiers pour celle heure s'appaiserent le mieux qu'ils peurent, tant que ils se partirent de l'isle Lancelot, et vindrent en l'isle d'Erbanie

I

Forteventura, and occupied themselves very well, as you
will hereafter hear.

CHAPTER LXI.—How M. de Bethencourt went to Erbanie, and
from thence made a long and profitable journey, for it occupied
his attention more than ever.

Then M. de Bethencourt proceeded to the island of Erbanie,
where he made a great raid upon the enemy, and captured
several, and sent them to the island of Lancerote. Then M.
de Bethencourt began to fortify himself against attacks from
enemies, in order to place the country in subjection, and
also because he had been given to understand that the
King of Fez was making preparations to attack him and
his company, declaring that all the islands belonged to him.
Accordingly, M. de Bethencourt remained in that island
three months, and explored the whole country. He found
the inhabitants to be men of large stature, powerful, and
firmly attached to their forms of government. Monsieur de

nommée Fort' auenture, et besongnerent tres-bien comme vous
orrez cy-apres.

[CHAPITRE LXI.]—*Comment Monsieur de Bethencourt s'en alla
en l'isle d'Erbanie, et là fit vn fort grand voyage, et bon, car il
luy besongna plus que oncques mes.*

Puis apres passa Monsieur de Bethencourt en l'Isle d'Erbanie,
et fit vne grand rese, et ont prins de leurs ennemis, et les ont
passez en l'Isle Lancelot. Et apres a commencé Monsieur de
Bethencourt à se fortifier à l'encontre des ennemis, afin de mettre
le pays en sa subiection ; et aussi pour ce qu'on leur a donné à
entendre que le Roy de Fez se vent armer contre luy et sa compagnie, et dit que toutes les Isles luy doivent appartenir; et a
esté Monsieur de Bethencourt en icelle Isle bien trois mois, et
couru tout le païs ; et a trouué ledit sieur des gens de grand
stature, fors et moult fermes en leur loy. Monsieur de Bethen-

Bethencourt knew very well how to fortify himself, and commenced a fortress on the broad brow of a mountain near a fresh spring at a league's distance from the sea. He called it Richeroque. This fortress the Canarians took after M. de Bethencourt had returned to Spain, and they killed some of the people whom he had left behind to defend it.

CHAPTER LXII.—How Bethencourt and Gadifer again had words together.

After Monsieur de Bethencourt had begun to fortify himself, he and Messire Gadifer had several words together which were not very pleasant. Messire Gadifer was in a place that he had to a certain extent fortified. A correspondence took place between the two; and in Messire Gadifer's letters to Monsieur de Bethencourt there were only these words: "If you come here; if you come here; if you come here," and nothing more. To which M. de

court a fort entendu à soy fortifier, et a commencé vne forteresse en vn grand pendant d'vne montagne, sur vne fontaine vifve à vne lieuë près de la mer, qui s'appelle Richeroque; laquelle les Canares ont prins depuis que Monsieur de Bethencourt retourna en Espagne, et tuerent vne partie des gens que ledit sieur y auoit laissé.

[CHAPITRE LXII.]—*Comment Bethencourt et Gadiffer eurent [encore] parolles ensemble.*

Appres que Monsieur de Bethencourt eust commencé à soy fortifier, ledit sieur et Messire Gadifer eurent plusieurs paroles ensemble, lesquelles n estoient pas fort plaisantes l'vn à l'autre et estoit ledit Messire Gadifer en vne place qu'il auoit aucunement fortifiée; et rescrirent l'vn à l'autre; et y auoit aux lettres que Messire Gadifer rescrit à Monsieur de Bethencourt seulement pour toute escriture, *se vous y venez, se vous y venez, se vous y venez*, et non autre chose. Et à donc Monsieur de Bethencourt

Bethencourt replied, by his poursuivant, named Sejepuis: "If you show yourself here; if you show yourself here; if you show yourself here"; and for a time the two felt great hatred towards each other, and used angry words; till, at the end of a fortnight, Monsieur de Bethencourt sent a fair little company to the Grand Canary, and Messire Gadifer went also. This took place on the twenty-fifth of June, one thousand four hundred and four, and he proceeded to the Grand Canary in Monsieur de Bethencourt's barge, in order to see the country in company with the party which that nobleman had sent out; and accordingly they put out to sea. But a few days afterwards they experienced a dreadful storm, for in one day they were driven a hundred miles by a contrary wind. They subsequently reached the Great Canary near Telde, but they dared not enter the harbour, for the wind was too strong, and it was nightfall; so they proceeded twenty-five miles further to a town called Argygneguy, and there they put into port and remained at anchor eleven days. At this place Peter the Canarian came to speak with them, and afterwards the son of Artamy,

luy rescrit par son poursuiuant, nommé Sejepuis, *se vous y trouuez, se vous y trouuez, se vous y trouuez ;* et furent vne espace de temps en grosse haine et en grosses paroles ; iusque au bout de quinze iours, que Monsieur de Bethencourt enuoya vne belle petite compagnie en la grand' Canare ; adonc Messire Gadifer y alla ; ce fut le vingt-cinquiesme iour de Juillet mil quatre cens et quatre, et passa à la grand' Canare en la barge de Monsieur de Bethencourt, pour voir le pays auec la compagnie que Monsieur de Bethencourt auoit ordonné, et entrerent en mer. Mais en aucuns iours apres ils eurent merueilleuse tourmente, car ils singlerent en vn iour entre deux soleils cent milles auec vent contraire ; et apres arriuerent en la grand' Canare pres de Teldes, mais ils n'orent prendre port, car le vent venoit trop fort, et estoit sur la nuitee ; et passerent vingt cinq mille plus auant, iusques à vne ville nommé Argygneguy, et là prindrent port, et demeurerent onze iours à l'ancre. Illec vint Pietre le Canare parler à eux, et puis y vint le fils d'Artamy le Roy du pays, et

King of the country, and other Canarians, came in great
numbers to the vessel, as they had done on former occasions. But when they saw our party, and how few we were
in number, they determined to entrap us, and Peter the
Canarian told us they would give us fresh water, and they
brought some hogs as a present for us. He then set an
ambush, and when the boat touched the shore in order to
take these things on board, the Canarians seized the end of
the rope which was thrown to them out of the boat, while
the boatmen held the other, and at this moment the ambush sallied out and pelted our people with large stones, so
that they were all wounded. They then seized two oars,
and two barrels full of water, and a cable, and prepared to
rush into the water to capture the boat; but Hannibal,
Gadifer's bastard son, all wounded as he was, seized an oar
and drove the Canarians back, at the same time pushing
the boat well out to sea; for several of the company were
lying in the bottom of the boat and dared not raise their
heads : there were two or three of the gentlemen of Mon-

---

des autres Canares grand foison, et venoient à la barge ainsi
qu'ils auoient fait autre fois. Mais quand ils virent nostre com-
mune, et que nous estions peu de gens, à la fin ils nous cuiderent
trahir; et nous dit Pietre le Canare qu'ils nous donneroient de
l'eau fraiche ; et nous fit venir des pourceaux qu'ils nous deuoient
donner, et mit vne embusche ; et quand le bastel fut abordé près
de la terre pour recueillir les choses, les Canares tenoiēt le bout
d'vne corde en terre et ceux du batel tenoient l'autre ; adōc
saillit l'embuche sur eux et leschargerent de moult grand iet de
pierre; tellement qu'ils furent tous blessez, et leurs tollirent
deux auirons, trois barils plains d'eau, et vn chable, et saillirent
tout à coup en la mer pour cuider prendre le bastel : mais
Hanibal, bastart de Gadifer, tout ainsi blessé qu'il estoit, print vn
auirons en sa main, et les rebouta, et eslargit le bastel bien auant
en la mer, car plusieurs des autres s'estoient laissez choir au
fons de bastel et n'osoient dresser la teste. Il y eut deux ou
trois gentils-hommes de Monsieur de Bethencourt qui auoient

sieur de Bethencourt who did good service, and then the
party returned to the vessel much beaten and hurt, and a
fresh company put off in the boat.   It being now quite
evident that truce was broken, they returned to the skirmish,
but the Canarians came against them with shields emblazoned
with the arms of Castile, which they had taken from the
Spaniards the previous season, and our companions suffered
considerable loss, while they inflicted little on the enemy.
So they returned to the ship, weighed anchor, and proceeded
to the port of Telde, and there they remained two days.

CHAPTER LXIII.—How Gadifer and the master of a vessel held a
conversation, as you will hear.

Then they departed and returned to the island of Erbania,
to Monseigneur de Bethencourt; and when they neared
the coast the wind proved contrary, so Gadifer went by
land, and came upon an ambuscade of Castilians who had

pauois qui y seruirent beaucoup, et puis s'en reuindrent à la
barge bien battus et navrez ; puis mirent des autres compagnons
frais au bastel.   Quand ils virent que tréues estoient rompuës,
ils retournerent pour escarmoucher à eux, mais les Canares
vindrent contre eux auec pauois armoyez des armes de Castille,
quils auoient l'autre saison gagné sur les Espagniols ; et gasterent
nos compagnons assez de bon trait sans porter dommage à leurs
ennemis si peu que non.   Si s'en retournerent à la barge et
leuerent leurs ancres et s'en allerent au port de Teldes, et là
demourerent deux iours.

[CHAPITRE LXIII.]—*Comme Gadiffer et le mestre d'une* [*nef*]
eurent parlement, comme vous orrés.

Puis s'en partirent de là, et s'en retournerent en l'isle d'Erbanie
vers Monseigneur de Bethencourt ; et quand ils furent acostez à
la terre, le vent leur fut contraire; si descendit Gadifer et s'en
vint par terre et arriua sur vne embusche de Castillans qui

arrived in a barge, and had brought a large supply of provisions for Monsieur de Bethencourt, and they said that one day of that week forty-two Canarians had met ten of their companions well accoutred, and had severely routed them ; but perhaps they were well aware that they were new comers, for they never gave way to such violence against their neighbours with whom they were acquainted. And when Gadifer, who was already very down-hearted at witnessing many things which displeased him, reached the company, he perceived plainly, and decided in his own mind, that the longer he remained in the country the less he would gain ; and that Monsieur de Bethencourt was altogether in favour with the King of Castile. Besides which, he learned from the master of the vessel which had brought the provisions for Monsieur de Bethencourt, that the King had sent him thither for the purpose of reinforcing him with provisions ; and many things he said in favour of the said De Bethencourt. Gadifer was very downcast at all this, and could not refrain from telling the master of the

---

estoient venus en vne barge, et estoit arriué la barge à tous grand plante de viures pour Monsieur de Bethencourt ; et disoient qu'vn iour de celle sepmaine quarante deux Canares auoient encontré dix de leurs compagnons tres-bien apparliez, et qu'ils les auoient tres asprement chassez, mais peut estre qu'ils cognoissoient bien que c'estoient gens nouueaux. Car ils ne s'abandonnoient mie ainsi sur leurs voisins qu'il cognoissoient. Et quand Gadifer fut arriué à tout la compagnie luy estant bien fort lassé de voir beaucoup de choses qui luy desplaisoient, et voyoit, et pensoit bien que tant plus il seroit au pays et tant mains acquerroit, et que Monsieur de Bethencourt estoit de tout poinct en la grace du Roy de Castille ; et encor outre ce qu'il ouit dire au maistre de la barge qui auoit amené les viures à Monsieur de Bethencourt, car il disoit que le dit Roy l'auoit enuoyé par deçà pour le constiller et rauitailler ; et des biens beaucoup qu'il rapportoit et disoit du dit Bethencourt, et tant que ledit Gadifer s'en eshabit fort, et ne se peut tenir qu'il ne

vessel that M. de Bethencourt had not done everything by
himself, and if others had not seconded him, matters would
not have advanced so far ; and if he had brought these provisions a year or two earlier, it would have been more to
the purpose, and many angry words passed ; in fact, so
many, that they were repeated by the master to M. de
Bethencourt, who was much hurt and annoyed that Gadifer
should be so jealous of him. So much so, that shortly
afterwards, when they met each other, M. de Bethencourt
said to him : "I am very grieved, my brother, that you
should show so much jealousy of my welfare and of my
honour ; and did not think that you would exhibit so much
animosity against me." Then Gadifer replied, that it was
not fair that his trouble should be unrewarded ; that he had
been long away from his country ; and that he clearly saw
that the longer he stayed where he was, the less it would be
to his advantage.

To which M. de Bethencourt rejoined : "That is ill said
of you, my brother ; for I have no such dishonest wish as

---

dît au maistre de la barge que ledit Sieur Bethencourt n'avoit
pas tout fait de luy, et que se autres gens que luy n'y eussent
dusogné, les choses ne fussent pas si auancées; et que s'il fust
venu à tout les viures qu'il auoit aportés depuis vn an ou deux,
ils feussent venus encor plus à poinct ; et y eust beaucoup de
paroles, et tant que les paroles vindrent par le dit maistre à
Monsieur Bethencourt, dont Monsieur de Bethencourt fut bien
esbahy et bien courcé que le dit Gadifer auoit si grande enuie
sur luy ; et tant que tantost apres ils s'entre rencontrerent : et
luy dit Monsieur de Bethencourt, Je suis bien esbahy, mon
frere, comment vous auez si grand enuie de mon bien et honneur,
et ne cuidons pas que vous eussiez vn tel courage contre moy ;
et adonc respondit Messire Gadifer, qu'il ne deuoit pas auoir
perdu sa peine, et qu'il auoit esté grande espasse de temps hors
de son pays ; et qu'il voyoit bien que tant plus il seroit là et
tant moins gaigneroit. Monsieur de Bethencourt luy respondit,
Mon frere, c'est mal dit à vous ; car ie n'ay pas si des-honneste

to withhold the due recognition of your rights so soon as, by God's grace, things shall have reached a better state of perfection than at present." Gadifer then said : " If you would concede to me the islands of which I formerly spoke to you, I would be content." Monsieur de Bethencourt replied that, having done homage of them to the King of Castile, he could not undo that act. Upon which more hard words passed between them, which would be too long to repeat. So it fell out that within eight days M. de Bethencourt, having got together his people and his supplies, he and Gadifer left the Canaries for Spain, neither of them very well pleased with the other. M. de Bethencourt went in one vessel, and Gadifer in another ; and settled their matters in Spain, in the manner that you will presently learn.

---

vouloir que ie ne le vueille recognoistre quand les choses seront, se Dieu plaist, venuës à plus grande perfection qu'elles ne sont. Cedit Gadifer, si me vouliez baillir les isles qu'autre fois vous ay parlé, ie serois content. Respond Monsieur de Bethencourt qu'il en auoit fait hommage au Roy de Castille, et qu'il ne s'en deferoit point ; et il y eut de grans parolles qui trop longuez seroient à raconter et de quoy je me passe pour le present. Auint dedans huict iours apres que Monsieur Bethencourt eust arruné ses gens et ses besongnes, ledit Bethencourt et Gadifer se partirent des pays des Canares, et s'en allerent en Espagne, non pas fort bien contens l'vn de l'autre ; et se mit Monsieur de Bethencourt en sa nef, et ledit Gadifer en vne autre, et besongnerent ensemble quand ils furent en Espagne, comme vous orrez cyapres.

CHAPTER LXIV.—How the Sieur de Bethencourt and Gadifer arrived
in Spain, and Gadifer, not being able to gain his point against
Bethencourt, returned to France, and Bethencourt to the Islands.

A short time after Monsieur de Bethencourt and Messire
Gadifer de la Salle left Erbanie in no very good humour
with each other. Monsieur de Bethencourt sailed for Spain
in one vessel and Gadifer in another, but when they reached
Seville, M. de Bethencourt took possession of several things
that Gadifer said belonged to him ; and the King of Castile
was informed of the whole dispute, but Gadifer's assertions
were not believed. Whereupon he declared that he would
return to France, where he had much to attend to. In
short, he clearly saw that no other course was open to him.
Accordingly, he left Spain and returned to France, nor did
he ever again make his appearance in the Canary Isles. M.
de Bethencourt had much trouble afterwards in subduing
the said islands, as you will hear more fully by and bye.

[CHAPITRE LXIV.—*Comme le Sieur de Bethencourt et Gadifer
arriuerent en Espagne, et Gadifer ne pouuant gagner autre
chose contre luy, s'en retourne en France et Bethencourt és isles.*]

Dedens ung pou de temps après se partit derbanne Monsieur
de Bethencourt et Messire Gadiffer de la Salle non mye trop
bien dascort. Monsieur de Bethencourt estoit en une barge et
Gadiffer en une autre pour passer la mer en Espaigne ; mais
quant ilz furent en Syville Monsieur de Bethencourt empescha
plusieurs choses que le dit Gadiffer disoit luy appartenir, tant
que le Roy de Castille en eust les nouuelles ; mais rien ne valut
pour ledit Gadifer, et incontinent dit qu'il vouloit aller en France
en son pais et qu'il y auoit bien affaire ; le dit Gadifer voyoit
bien qu'il n'y pouuoit autre chose faire, et pour ce cen vouloit il
aler. Et se partit le dit Gadiffer du royaume d'Espaigne, et
s'en alla en France en son pays, et oncques puis on ne le vit
esdites isles de Canare : et eut depuis Monsieur de Bethencourt
bien à besongner à conquerir ledites isles de Canare ainsi comme
vous orrez plus a plain cy apres. Sy nous tairons de ceste

But for the present we will leave this matter, and will speak of those islands which M. de Bethencourt visited or caused to be visited, and of the manners, customs, and government of the people.

CHAPTER LXV.—Here in the first place the island of Ferro is treated of.

We will first speak of the island of Ferro, which is one of the most distant. It is a very beautiful island, seven leagues in length and five in breadth: it is in the shape of a crescent, and is very difficult of access, for it has no good port or entrance; but it has been visited by the Sieur de Bethencourtand by others, for Gadifer was there a considerable time. Formerly it had been extensively inhabited, but the natives had been captured at different periods and been made slaves of in foreign countries, so that few now remained. The surface of the island is a high table-land, covered with large forests of pine and laurel, bearing wonderfully large and long berries. The ground is good to till and suitable for corn,

matiere quant à present, et parlerons des isles que Monsieur de Bethencourt a visitées et fait visiter, des manieres et des conditions, et gouuernement des isles.

[CHAPITRE LXV.]—*Ycy parle premierement de lille de Fer.*

Si parlerons premierement de l'isle de Fer, qui est vne des plus lointaines, et dit que c'est vne moult belle isle, et contient sept lieuës de long et cinq de large : et est en maniere d'vn croissant, et est tres forte : car il n'y a bon port ne bon entrage, et a esté visitée par ledit sieur et par autres ; car Gadifer y fut bien longuement, et souloit estre bien peuplée de gens, mais ils ont esté prins par plusieurs fois et menez en chetifuoisson en estrangez contrées; et y sont au iourd'hui demourez peu de gens, et est le pays haut et assez plain ; garny de grands bocages de pins et de lauriers portans meures si grosses et si longues que merueilles; et sont les terres bounes pour labourer, pour bleds,

for vines, and all other things. There are many kinds of fruit-bearing trees. There are falcons, hawks, larks, and quails in great numbers; and also a kind of bird with a pheasant's plumage, but of the size of a parrot, and of small flying power. The water is good, and there is great abundance of animals, such as hogs, goats, and sheep. There are lizards as large as cats, but harmless, although very hideous to look at. The inhabitants are a very fine race, both men and women. The men use long lances without iron points, for they have no iron,[1] nor any other metal. They grow a considerable quantity of grain of all sorts. In the highest part of the island are some trees which

---

pour vin et pour toutes autres choses; et si on y trouueroit mains autres arbres portans fruict de diuerses conditions: et y sont faucons, espreuiers, alloüettes et cailles à grand planté, et vne maniere d'oiseaux qui ont plume de faisant, et est de la taille d'vn papegaux, et ont courte vollée. Les eaües y sont bonnes, et y a grand planté de bestes; c'est asçauoir pourceaux, chievres, et brebis, et y a des lesards grandes comme vn chat, mais elles ne font nul mal, et si sont bien hideuses à regarder. Les habitans d'illec sont moult belles gens hommes et femmes, et portent les hommes grēds lances qui ne sont point ferrees: car ils n'ont point de fer ne d'autre metail: et y croit bleds de toutes maniere assez. Et au plus haut du pays sont arbres qui

---

[1] This passage shows that this island did not derive its name, as it would seem to do, from iron. On inquiring why this island was called Hierro or Ferro [i. e. iron], Galindo found that the natives called it Esero, which in their language means "strong"; and as they had no iron in use amongst them, when they saw that it was a "strong" material corresponding to the name of their island, they called iron indifferently by the name of Esero or Hierro, the Spanish word for that metal, so that at last they translated the real name of the island Esero into the Spanish one Hierro, of which Ferro is the Portuguese form. This seems a very unsatisfactory solution. It appears that in the Guanche language "hero" or "herro" means a well or cistern, such as are used in this island for preserving rain-water, and hence the easy lapse into "hierro," "ferro," or, as the French chaplains make it, "fer."

are always dripping with a most clear delicious water, which falls into a pool near the trees formed by the continual dropping ;[1] it is the most excellent for drinking that can

tousiours degoutent eau belle et clere qui chet en fosse aupres des arbres, la meilleure pour boire que l'on sçauroit trouuer ; et

[1] One of these trees, called the "Garoé" or "Holy Tree," has been made famous both by those who have exaggerated its merits, and by its depreciators and those who have denied its existence. All sorts of inaccuracies have been stated both on the one side and the other. Fortunately we possess a detailed description of it by Father Juan de Abreu Galindo, who had the curiosity to pay a visit to this remarkable tree, and whose account may be seen at page 47 of his *Historia de la Conquista de las siete islas de Gran Canaria*, written in 1632, and published at Santa Cruz de Tenerife in 1848. It was a gigantic til (*Laurus fœtens*), standing by itself on the top of a steep rock, about a league and a half from the sea, in the district of Tigulahe. The circumference of the trunk was twelve spans, the diameter four, and its height, to the topmost branch, was forty spans. The circumference of all the branches was 120 feet. The branches were thick and extended, and the leaves distilled sufficient water to furnish drink to every living creature in Ferro. On the north side was a cistern divided into two, each half being twenty feet square and sixteen spans deep. One of these was for the inhabitants, the other for cattle. At this part of the island a cloud or mist arose in the morning, and was carried by the south-easterly winds along a narrow gully which reached from the sea to the cliff, and being there checked by the face of the rock, rested on the thick leaves and wide-spreading branches of the tree, and thence distilled in drops during the day. Of the age of the tree, reputed to be very great, we have no authentic record. The date of its final destruction has been mis-stated by many. Leopold von Buch tells us, without giving his authority, that it still existed in 1689 ; Father Nieremberg places its downfall in 1629 ; and Nuñez de la Peña in 1625. It happens, however. that an official record of the event survives which shows them all to be wrong. In a work entitled *Noticias del Hierro*, by Bartholomé Garcia del Castillo, it is recorded that the tree was overthrown in a hurricane ; and that, at page 184 of the second "Libro Capitular" of the island, stands the following memorandum, made by the ayuntamiento, under date of 12th June, 1612. "Since the Arbre Santo (Holy Tree) has fallen, and the cisterns in which the water used to be collected are blocked up with the trunk and the branches, and as it is necessary that all of it must be removed, and the earth which fell at the same time cleared away: it is ordered and commanded," etc.

be found anywhere. The quality of this water is such that, if any one had eaten till he could eat no more, and were to drink of this water, in one hour the food would be entirely digested, and the man would have as great an appetite as he had before having eaten.

CHAPTER LXVI.—Of the island of Palma, the most distant of all.

The island of Palma, which is farthest out in the ocean,[1] is larger than the map describes it; it is very high and very steep, covered with large forests of various sorts of trees, such as pines and dragon-trees, bearing dragon's blood, and other trees yielding milk of great medicinal value, and fruits of various kinds. There are good rivers flowing through it, and the land is excellent for agriculture of all sorts, and the pastures are excellent. The country is

---

est icelle eau de telle condition que quand on a tant mengé que on ne peut plus, et on boit d'icelle eau, ainchois qu'il soit vne heure la viande est toute digerée, tant qu'on a aussi grand voulenté de menger qu'on auoit auparauant qu'on avoit mangé.

[CHAPITRE LXVI.] —De l'Isle de Palme qui est la plus lointaine.

L'isle de Palme, qui est la plus auant d'vn costé de la mer Oceane, est plus grande qu'elle ne se monstre en la carte, et est tres-haute et tres forte, garnie de grãds bocages de diuerses conditions, comme de pins et de dragonniers portant sang de dragon, et d'autres arbres portant laict de grande medecine, et de fruictage de diuerses manieres, et y court bonnes riuieres parmy, et y sont les terres bonnes pour tous labourages et bien

---

[1] This statement, although nearly correct, is not perfectly so, as the reader will immediately recognise from the early European geographers having made the first meridian to pass through the island of Ferro as being the westernmost of the group.

strong and well peopled, for this island has not been so much visited as the others. The inhabitants are a fine people, and only live upon flesh. It is the most delightful country that we have found amongst all those islands, but it is very much out of the way, being the most distant from the main land. It is only a hundred French leagues, however, distant from Cape Bojador, which is on the main land of the Saracens. The climate of the island, moreover, is extremely good, for, unless by accident, the people are never ill, and they live to a great age.

CHAPTER LXVII.—After that of the island of Gomera.

The island of Gomera is fourteen leagues from the last mentioned. It is a very steep island, in the shape of a trefoil. It is very high and tolerably level, but the gorges are wonderfully wide and deep. This country is inhabited by a tall people who speak the most remarkable of all the languages of these islands, and speak with their lips, as if

---

garnies d'herbages. Le pays est fort et bien peuplé de gens; car il n'a mie esté ainsi foullé comme les autres païs ont esté. Ils sont belles gens et ne viuent que de chair : et est le plus delectable païs que nous ayons trouué és isles de pardeçà, mais il est bien adesmain, car c'est la plus lointainne isle de terre ferme. Toutefois il n'y a du cap de Bugeder, qui est terre ferme des Sarrasins, que cent lieuës Françoises, et aussi c'est vne isle où il y a fort bon air, ne iamais voulentiers on n'y est malade, et les gens y viuent longuement.

[CHAPITRE LXVII.]—*Sy apres de l'Isle Gomere.*

L'Isle de Gomere est quatorze lieuës pardeçà, qui est très forte isle, en maniere d'vne trefle ; et le païs biē-hault et assez plain, mais les baricanes y sōt merueilleusement grandes et parfondes, et est le païs habité de grand peuple qui parle le plus estrange langaige de tous les autres païs de pardeçà ; et parlent

they had no tongues; and they have a tradition that a great prince, for no fault of theirs, caused them to be banished and had their tongues cut out; and, judging by the way they speak, one could well believe it. The country abounds in dragon-trees and other kinds of wood, and in small cattle. There are also many other notable things which it would be tedious to describe.

CHAPTER LXVIII.—Of the island which is called Tonerfiz, but which some call the Island of Hell.

The island of Hell, which is called Tonerfis [Teneriffe], is shaped like a harrow, almost the same as the Great Canary. It is about eighteen French leagues in length and ten in breadth. In the middle there is a large mountain, the highest that there is in all the Canary Islands; and the base of the mountain extends over the greater part of the island, and all round are valleys well wooded and intersected with running streams, and abounding in dragon-trees and many

des baulievres ainsi que si feussent sans langue, et dict on pardeçà que vng grand prince pour aucun meffaict les fit la mettre en exil, et leur fit tailler leurs langues, et selon la maniere de leur parler on le pourroit croire. Le païs est garny de dragonniers et d'autre bois assez, et de bestiail menu, et de moult d'autres choses estranges qui seroient longuez choses à raconter.

[CHAPITRE LXVIII.]—De lille qui sappelle lylle [Tonerfiz] aucuns lappellent lille denffer.

Lille denffer, qui se dit Tonerfis, est en maniere d'vne herche, presque ainsi que la grand' Canare, et contient enuiron dix-huict lieuës Françoises de long et dix de large, et en tour le meilleur a vne grand' montagne la plus haute qui soit en toutes les isles Canariennes, et s'estent la parte de la montagne de tous costez par la plus grand partie de toute l'isle ; et tout entour sont les baricanes garnis de grands bocages et de belles fontaines courantes, de dragonniers et de moult d'autres arbres de diuerses

other kinds of wood.[1] The country is very good for all kinds of agriculture, and numerously inhabited by the hardiest race to be found in all these islands. They have never been run down or carried into servitude like those of the other islands.[2] Their island is ten leagues south of Gomera, and on the other side towards the north it is four leagues distant from the Great Canary; and in those parts it is pronounced to be one of the best islands there is.

---

manieres et conditions. Le pays est mout bon pour tous les labourages, et moult grand peuple y habite, qui sont les plus hardis de tous les autres peuples qui habite és isles; et ne furent oncques courus ne menez en seruage comme ceux des autres. Et marche leur pays près de la Gomere à six lieuës deuers le midy et de l'autre costé deuers le nort à quatre lieuës de la grand' Canare; et dit on par deçà que c'est vne des [plus ?] bonnes isles qui y soit.

---

[1] The Teyde or Peak of Teneriffe, one of the largest volcanic cones known, is more than ten leagues in circumference at the base, and towers 11,430 feet above the level of the ocean. The crater on the summit presents a solfatara of about 300 feet in diameter and 100 feet deep. The view from the top, as described by Sabin Berthelot, took in a range the diameter of which exceeded 100 leagues. Lancerote was seen on the verge of the horizon at a distance of 160 miles. Then Fuerteventura, stretching its length towards the Great Canary. Westward the shadow of the Peak spread itself out in an immense triangle so as to lap over Gomera, while Palma and Ferro showed their scarped summits a little beyond. Thus the entire Archipelago of the Canaries lay like a relief map under his eyes.

[2] Nuñez de la Peña tells us that the natives of Teneriffe called themselves "Guanchinet," which the Spaniards corrupted into "Guanche." "Guan" meant "person," and "Chinet" was the same as "Teneriffe"; so the two words combined meant "a man of Teneriffe." Of all the Canarians, the Guanches of Teneriffe held out the longest against their conquerors. It was not till 1496 that they lost their independence, and were entirely subdued by the Spaniards.

CHAPTER LXIX.—Of the Great Canary and its inhabitants.

The Great Canary is twenty leagues long[1] and twelve broad, and is shaped like a harrow; it is distant twelve leagues from the island of Erbanie. It is the most celebrated of all the islands. On the south side there are large and remarkable mountains, but on the north the country is tolerably flat and good for agriculture. The country is well wooded with pines, firs, dragon-trees, olive-trees, fig-trees, date-palms, and many other fruit-bearing trees. The inhabitants are tall, and look upon themselves as noble,[2] having none of the lower orders amongst them.

[CHAPITRE LXIX.]—*Sy parlle de lille de la Grand' Canarie, et des gens qui y sont.*

La grand' Canare contient vingt lieuës de long et douze de large; et est en maniere de herche, et conte l'on douze lieuës de la grand Canare iusques en l'isle d'Erbannie, et est la plus renommee de toutes les autres isles, et y sont les montagnes grandes et merueilleuses du costé de Midy, et deuers le nort assez plain pays et bon pour labourage. C'est vn pays garny de grand boccages de pins et de sapins, de dragonniers, d'oliuiers, de figuiers, de palmiers portans dattes, et de moult autres arbres portans fruicts de diuerses manieres. Les gens qui y habitent sont grand peuple, et se dient gentilshommes, sans

---

[1] It may be here stated, once for all, that the various measurements and distances given by Bethencourt's chaplains are, as might be expected, very inaccurate: as, for example, in the present instance; the Great Canary, which is nearly round, has for its greatest diameter thirty miles, and is about fifty-five distant from Fuerteventura.

[2] Viera tells us that the nobles of the Great Canary were recognised by special distinctions and enjoyed particular privileges. They wore the beard and hair long. The *faycan* or high priest, whose authority was equal to that of the princes, had the sole right of conferring nobility and arming knights. The law required that the aspirant should be known to possess lands and flocks, should be of noble descent, and in condition to bear arms.

They have barley, beans, and grain of every sort. Everything grows there. They are great fishermen,[1] and net (or hunt) very well. They go quite naked, save for a girdle of palm-leaves. Most of them print devices on their bodies, according to their various tastes, and wear their hair tied behind in the fashion of tresses. They are a handsome and well-formed people. Their women are very beautiful. They wear skins round the middle of the body. The people are well off for animals, such as hogs, goats, and sheep; there is also a kind of wild dog[2] like a wolf, but small. M. de Bethencourt, Gadifer, and several of the company went to the island to study their habits and their government, and to look out for landing places and the entrances into the country, which are good and free from danger, but of which

ceux d'autre condition. Ils ont forment, feuves, bleds de toutes sortes; tout y croit, et sont grands pescheurs de poisson, et noüent merueilleusement bien: ils vont tous nuds fors que les brayez qui sont de feüilles de palmiers, et la plus grand' partie d'eux portent deuises entaillées sur leur chair de diuerses manieres, chacun selon sa plaisance; et portent leurs cheveux liez par derriere ainsi qu'en maniere de tresses. Ils sont belles gens et bien formez, et leurs femmes sont bien belles; affublez de peaux pour couurir leurs membres honteux; ils sont bien garnis de bestes, c'est à sçauoir pourciaux, chievres et brebis, et de chiens sauuages qui semblent loups, mais ils sont petits; Monsieur de Bethencourt, et Gadifer, et plusieurs autres de sa compagnie y ont esté, tout en effet pour voir leur maniere et leur gouuernement, et pour aduiser les descenduës et les entrees du pays qui sont bonnes et sans danger, mais qu'on y tiengne ordonnance,

[1] Viera speaks of two modes of fishing in use by the Canarians: the one spearing by torchlight; the other by poisoning the water with the juice of the "*tabaiba*," a species of *Euphorbia piscatoria*. A species of the same genus, the *Euphorbia hyberna*, is used by the peasants of Kerry for the same purpose. It is so powerful, that a small creel, filled with the bruised plant, suffices to poison the fish for several miles down a river.

[2] Following the narrative of King Juba, Pliny derives the name of Canaria from the great number of dogs that the Mauritanian explorers found in the island.

they took due note, sounding and measuring the harbours and coasts wherever a vessel could put in. Half a league from the sea on the north-east are two towns, two leagues distant from each other, one called Telde and the other Argones, situated on the banks of running streams. Twenty-five miles thence to the south-east is another town, situated on the sea, which beats against it and serves admirably as a fortification on one side, while there is a stream of fresh water on the other. This town is called Arginegy,[1] and a very good harbour might be made of it for little vessels in danger from the fortress. It must be acknowledged that

---

et assonde et mesure les ports et les costieres de la terre par tout où nauire pent approcher. A demy lieuë pres de la mer du costé du nordest sont deux villes à deux lieuës l'vne de l'autre, l'vne nommee Telde, et l'autre Argoné, assises sur ruisseaux courans. Et à vingt-cinq mille de là du costé de suest, si est vne autre ville sur la mer en tres bon lieu pour fortiffier et illec luy bat la mer entres bon lieu pour fortifier et d'un costé a vn ruisseaux d'eauë douce de l'autre costé, laquelle se nomme Argi-negy ; et y pourroit on faire tres·bon port pour petits nauires au danger de la forteresse. Il ne faut point dire que ce ne soit vne

---

[1] Sabin Berthelot, in his *Histoire Naturelle des Canaries*, thus describes the little town of Argyneguy, or rather Arguineguin. He says it might have contained about four hundred houses, the remains of which are seen in a ravine of the same name. They stand in several rows around a great circle, in the centre of which are the ruins of a more considerable building. In front of the entrance to this building is an enormous semicircular seat with a back to it, made of stones joined without cement. The idea suggests itself that this house was the residence of a chief, and that the council assembled in this spot. Long stout beams made of laurel (barbusano), an almost indestructible wood, now extremely valuable for its excellence and rarity, still cover some of these dwellings, the shape of which is elliptical. Inside are seen three recesses sunk into the thickness of the wall, which is eight or nine feet thick. The fireplace is near the entrance-gate, and faces the recesses at the end. The wall is without cement and constructed of stones, rude and unchiselled on the outside, but in the interior perfectly cut and worked to measure. These stones are as well joined together as the best of our masons could do it.

the island is a most excellent one, and replete with advantages ; corn grows twice a year without the land requiring any improvement, and if the land was not so badly cultivated more things would grow than one would be able to mention.

CHAPTER LXX.—Of the island of Erbania, called Fortaventura, in which were two kings.

The island of Fuerteventure, which we call Erbannie, as also do the people of the Great Canary, is twelve leagues from that island on the north-east. It is about seventeen leagues long and eight broad, but in one place it is only a league and a half in breadth from sea to sea. The soil is sandy, and a great stone wall traverses the island right across from one side to the other. The country is varied by plains and mountains, and one can ride on horseback from one end to the other. In four or five places there are running streams of fresh water, which might be made to turn mills ; and on the banks of these streams are large

---

fort bonne isle plaine des tous biēs ; et y viennent les bleds deux fois l'an sans y faire nul amendement, et si ne sçauroit-on trop malaisément labourer la terre qu'il n'y viengne plus de biens qu'on ne sçauroit dire.

[CHAPITRE LXX.]—*Sy parle de lille derbanye dit Fortauenture, en laquelle y avoit deulx Roys.*

L'Isle de Fort auenture, que nous appellons Erbanne, aussi font ceux de la grand' Canare, est douze lieuës par deçà du costé de nort·est, laquelle contient enuiron dix-sept lieuës de long, et huict de large, mais en tel lieu y a qu'elle ne contient qu'vne lieuë d'vne mer à autre. Là est pays de sablō, et est là vn grand mur de pierre qui comprend le pays tout au trauers d'vn costé à l'autre : le païs est garny de plain et de montagne, et peut-on cheuaucher d'vn bout à l'autre, et y trouue l'on en quatre ou en cinq lieuës ruisseaux courans d'eau douce, dequoy moulins pourroient moudre, et a sur ces ruisseaux de grands

groves of trees called *tarhais*,[1] which produce a salt gum,
fine and white, but it is not a wood to be turned to any
serviceable account, for it is twisted, and its foliage is like
heath. The country is plentifully furnished with other
trees, which produce a milk of great medicinal value, like
balm, and there are other trees of marvellous beauty which
contain more milk even than the others. They are divided
into squares, and each square bears a kind of thorn like
brambles. The branches are as large as a man's arm, and
when they are cut the wound is filled with a milk of
marvellous virtue.[2] There are other trees also, such as
date-palms and olives, and mastic trees in great abundance.
A plant also grows there which is very valuable, called
orchil. It is used for dyeing cloth and other things, and
is the best plant for that purpose that is known anywhere;

---

bocages de bois qui s'appellent Tarhais, qui portent gomme de
sel bel et blanc; mais ce n'est mie bois de quoy on peut faire
bonne ouuraige, car il est tortu et semble bruyere, de la feüille.
Le pays est moult garny d'autre bois qui porte laict de grand'
medecine en maniere de baulme, et autres arbres de merueilleuse
beauté qui portent plus de laict que ne fôt les autres arbres, et
sont carrez de plusieres carres; et sur chacune carre a vn rēg
d'espine en maniere de ronces, et sont les branches grosses
comme le bras d'vn hôme, et quand on les couppe tout est plain
de laict qui est de merueilleuse vertu : d'autre bois comme de
palmiers portans dattes, d'oliuiers, et de mastiquers y a grand
plāté, et y croit vne graine qui vaut beaucoup qu'on appelle
orsolle; elle sert à teindre drap ou autres choses, et est la
meillure grayne dicelle que l'on sçache trouuer en nul pais

---

[1] The Rev. R. T. Lowe, author of *The Flora of Madeira*, who has
made the botany of this group of islands a special study, gives me the
following note on this word. " I can find nothing at all like this in my
(carefully identified) vernacular names of Fuerteventuran plants, but
the plant meant was probably *Erica arborea*, L., though now quite
extinct in Fuerteventura, and called in the other islands ' Brezo.' "

[2] The *Euphorbia Canariensis*. When the skin of this plant is in-

and if only this island be once conquered and brought into the Christian faith, this plant will prove of great value to the lord of the country. The people of the country are not very numerous, but very tall, and difficult to take alive; and so formidable are they that, if any one of them is taken by the Christians, and turns upon them, they give him no quarter, but kill him forthwith. They have villages in great number, and they live more closely together than is the custom with the inhabitants of the island of Lanzerote. They eat no salt, and live only on flesh, which they preserve without salt, hanging it up in their houses till it is quite dry, and then they eat it. This meat is much more savoury, and beyond all comparison finer, than any that is prepared in France. The houses smell very bad, on account of the flesh that is hung up in them. They have good store of tallow, which they eat with as much relish as we do bread. They are well off for cheeses, which are superlatively good,

---

pour la condition d'icelle ; et si lille est vne fois conquise et mise à la foy chrestienne, icelle graine sera de grād valeur au sieur du païs : le païs n'est pas trop fort peuplé de gens ; mais ceux qui y sont, sont de grande stature, et a peine les peut-on prendre vifs, et sont de telle condition que si aucun d'eux est prins des chrestiës, et il retourne deuers eux, ils le tuent sans remede nul. Ils ont villages grand foison, et se logent plus ensemble que ceux de l'isle Lancelot. Ils ne mangent point de sel, et ne viuent que de chair, et en font grand garnison sans saler, et la pendent en leur hostieulx, et la font seicher iusques à tant qu'elle est bien fanee, et puis la mengēt, et est icelle chair beaucoup plus sauoureuse, et de meillure condition que celle du païs de France sans nulle comparaison. Les maisons sentent tres·mal, par cause des chairs qui y sont penduës : ils sont bien garnis de suif, et le mangent aussi sauoureusement comme nous faisons le pain. Ils sont bien garnis de formaiges, et si sont

---

cised, an acrid milk exudes which contains active medicinal properties, and, when dried, furnishes the drug known as euphorbium.

the best that are made anywhere about. They are made of
the milk of goats, with which this island is more numerously
stocked than any of the rest. Sixty thousand might be
taken every year, and great profit made of the hides and
fat, of which each animal yields full thirty or forty pounds.
The abundance of the fat and the excellence of the meat
are astonishing, far superior to what they have in France.
There is no good harbour for large vessels to winter in,
but very good ones for small craft. Throughout the whole
of the plain country, wells might be sunk for soft water
for watering the gardens and other purposes. There are
some good districts for agriculture. The inhabitants are of
a resolute character, very firm in their religion, and they
have temples in which they offer their sacrifices.[1] This
island is the nearest to the country of the Saracens, for
there are only twelve French leagues between it and Cape
Bojador, which is the main land of Africa.

---

souuerainement bōs, les meilleures que on sache és parties
d'enuiron: et si ne sont faits que de laict de chieure, dont tous le
païs est fort peuplé plus que nulle des autres isles, et en pourroit-
on prendre chacun au soixante mille, et mettre à profit les cuirs
et graiffes, dont chacune beste rend beaucoup, bien trente et
quarante liures : c'est merueilles de la graisse qu'ils rendent, et
si est merveille que la cher est bonne trop biaucoup meilleur que
ceulx de France sans nulle comparaison. Il n'y a point de bon
port pour niuerner gros nauire, mais pour petit nauire il y a
tres-bons ports : et par tout le plain païs pourroit-on faire puits
pour auoir eauë douce, pour arrouser iardins, et faire ce qu'on
voudroit. Il y a de bōnes veines de terre pour labourages ; les
habitans sont de dur entendement, et moult fermes en leur loy,
et ont esglise où ils font leurs sacrifices. C'est la plus pres isle
qui y soit de terre des Sarrasins, car il n'y a que douze lieuës
Françoises du cap de Bugeder qui est terre ferme.

---

[1] Viera tells us that at Fuerteventura there existed remains of large
circular stone buildings, called "*efequenes*," devoted to worship. They
generally stood on the top of a mountain. The sacrifices were offerings
of butter and libations of goats' milk.

CHAPTER LXXI.—Of the island of Lancerote.

The island of Lancerote lies four leagues north-north-east from the island of Fuerteventura. Between these two is the island of Lobos, which is not peopled, and is nearly round. It is a league in length and the same in breadth ; it is a quarter of a league from Fuerteventura on one side, and three leagues from Lancerote on the other side. On the side of Erbanie there is a very good harbour for galleys. The number of sea-wolves that come there is astonishing, and every year might be got a sufficient quantity of skins and fat to fetch five hundred gold doubloons and more. As for the island of Lancerote, which is called in their language Tite-roy-gatra, it is of the size and shape of the island of Rhodes. It contains many villages and fair houses, and used to be well peopled, but the Spaniards and other corsairs of the sea have so frequently made captures among them, and thrown them into slavery, that now there are but few remaining, for when M. de Bethencourt arrived

[CHAPITRE LXXI.]—Sy parle de lille Lanlot.

L'isle de Lancelot est à quatre lieuës de l'isle de Forte-auenture du costé de nort nort-est; et est entre deux l'isle de Louppes, qui est despeuplee, et est presque ronde, et ne contient que vne lyeuë de long et autant de large, à vn quart de lyeuë derbanne dit Forte-auêture, et de l'autre part à trois lieuëes de l'isle Lancelot. Du costé d'Erbanie est tres-bon port pour galleres. Là viennent tant de Lous-marins que c'est merueilles, et pourroit-on auoir chacun an des peaux et des graiffes cinq cens doubles d'or ou plus. Et quand à l'isle Lancelot, qui s'appele en leur langaige Tite-Roy-gatra, elle est aveques du grant et de la façon de l'isle de Rhodes. Il y a grand foison de villages et de belles maisons, et souloit estre moult peuplee de gens. Mais les Espagnols et autres corsaires de mer les ont par maintes fois prins et menez en seruaige, tant qu'ils sont demeurez peu de gens. Car quand Monsieur de Bethencourt y arriua, ils n'estoient enuiron que

there were scarcely three hundred people. These he conquered, though with great trouble and difficulty, and, by
the grace of God, had them baptized. On the side towards
the island of Graciosa the country is so inaccessible, that it
would be impossible to enter it by force; but on the other
side, towards Guinea, which is the main land of the Saracens,
the country is tolerably flat and free from wood, with the
exception of some brushwood useful for fuel, and a kind
of wood called Hyguerres,[1] with which all the country
abounds from one end to the other. It contains milk of
great medicinal virtue. There is great abundance of springs
and reservoirs of water, as also of pasture land and good
land for tillage. A great quantity of barley grows there,
of which they make excellent bread. The country is well
supplied with salt. The inhabitants are a fine race. The
men go quite naked; excepting for a cloak over their
shoulders, which reaches to their thighs, they are indifferent

---

trois cens personnes qu'il conquesta à grand' peine et à grand
trauail et, par la grace de Dieu, baptisez ont esté. Et du costé
de l'isle Gracieuse, le pays et l'ëtree est si forte que nul n'y
pourroit entrer à force; et de l'autre costé deuers la *Guinoye*,
qui est terre ferme de Sarazins, est plain pays; est asses plain,
et n'y a nuls bois, fors que petits buissons pour ardoir, si ce n'est
vne maniere de bois qui s'appelle *Hygueres*, dequoy tout le pays
est garny d'vn bout à l'autre, et portent laict de grand medecine.
Il y a grand foison de fontaignes et de cisternes, et de pasturages
et de bonnes terres à labourer; et y croist grand' quantité d'orge,
dequoy on fait de tres bon pain. Le pays est bien garny de sel,
les habitans sont belles gens, les hommes vont tous nuds fors
qu'vne mantel par derriere iusques au jaret, et ne sont point

---

[1] I am indebted for the following note to the Rev. R. T. Lowe.
" From one or two herbaceous species of *Euphorbia* being still called in
Lanzerote 'Higuerilla,' it is probable that the two common shrubby
species *E. Regis Jubæ*, Webb, and *E. balsamifera*, Ait., now called
'Tabayba,' were the plants intended. Von Buch says that the closely
allied shrubby *E. piscatoria*, Ait., is called in Palma 'higerilla.'"

to other covering. The women are beautiful and modest. They wear long leather robes, which reach down to the ground. Most of them have three husbands, who wait upon them alternately by months, the husband that is to live with the wife the following month waits upon her and her other husband the whole of the month that the latter has her, and so each takes his turn. The women have a great many children, but have no milk in their breasts; they therefore feed them with their mouths, and thus their under lips are longer than their upper ones, which is an ugly thing to see. The island of Lanzerote is an excellent and charming island, and might well be extensively visited by merchants; and much business might be carried on, for there are two harbours in particular which are exceedingly good and easy of access. Orchil grows here, and a large and profitable trade is carried on in it. But we will dwell no longer on this subject, but return to M. de Bethencourt, who is in the kingdom of Castille, in communication with the sovereign of the country.

---

honteux de leurs membres. Les femmes sont belles et honnestes, vestues de grands houppelandes de cuirs trainans iusques à terre. La plus grand' partie d'elles ont trois maris, et seruent par mois; et celuy qui la doit auoir apres, les sert tout le mois que l'autre la tient, et sont tousiours ainsi à leur tour. Les femmes portēt moult d'enfans, et n'ont point de laict en leurs mammelles, ainsi allectent leurs enfans à la bouche, et pour ce ont elles les boullieuses de dessoubs plus longues que celles de dessus; qui est laide chose à voir. L'isle Lancelot est vne fort plaisante isle et bonne, et y peut arriuer beaucoup de marchands et de marchandises, car il y a par especial deux bons ports et aisez. Il y croit de l'oursolle qui est fort marchande et profitable. Nous laisserons à parler de ceste matiere, et parlerons de Monsieur de Bethencourt, qui est au royaume de Castille deuers le roy du païs.

CHAPTER LXXII.—How M. de Bethencourt took leave of the
King of Spain.

When M. de Bethencourt had got rid of Master Gadifer,
he procured letters patent from the King of Castille, to the
effect that he had done homage for the Canary Isles, and
then took leave of the said king to return to the islands, for
he was wanted there. Gadifer had left his natural son and
several others behind him, and for this reason the Sieur de
Bethencourt was anxious to return with as little delay as
possible. Indeed he would not have gone to Castille had he
not feared that Master Gadifer might steal a march upon him,
and make some statement to the King of Castille which he
would not like. Not that he could say that the Sieur de
Bethencourt had done anything wrong, but, as I have
already said, he was anxious to have his letters all made
out and engrossed and sealed. The king had previously
granted and caused to be delivered to him certain letters
patent in Seville, but they were not as important as these

[CHAPITRE LXXII.]—*Comment Monsieur de Bethencourt prit congé
du Roy d'Espagne.*

Qvand Monsieur de Bethécourt eust faict à Messire Gadifer, il
recueillit lettres au Roy de Castille comme il auoit fait son
hommage des isles de Quenare, et print congé dudit roy pour
s'en retourner és isles ; car il en estoit besoing. Ledit Gadifer
auoit laissé son bastard et aulcuns autres auec luy, pour laquelle
cause ledit Sieur de Bethécourt vouloit retourner le plus brief
qu'il pourroit. Il ne fust ja allé en Castille, si ce n'eust esté
qu'il doubtoit que Messire Gadifer eust entreprins sur luy, et
qu'il eust rapporté quelque chose au Roy de Castille dequoy il
n'eust pas esté content : non pas qu'on luy sceust dire chose que
ledit Sieur eust deseruy ; mais comme i'ay dit par cy-devant, il
desiroit auoir ses lettres toutes faictes, grosses et seellees. Le
roy luy en auoit en parauant baillé et fait bailler lettres en
Siuille, mais ils n'estoient point comme dernieres. Le roy luy

last. In these the king gave him full power to coin money
in the country, and granted him a fifth of all the merchandise which should be imported from the said islands
into Spain. The letters were passed before a notary
named Sariche, living in Seville; and in the said town will
be found all the acts and regulations of the said de Bethencourt. And seeing that the king was highly pleased with him,
several of the citizens of Seville took a great liking to him,
and made him very handsome and gratifying presents in the
way of armour, provisions, money, and gold, to meet his more
pressing necessities. He was very well known in that city,
and greatly beloved. The said Seigneur de Bethencourt took
leave of the king and returned to the islands in high spirits,
like a man who felt that he had managed his matters well.
On reaching the island of Fuerteventura, he was received
by his people with great joy, as you shall presently hear
more in detail.

---

donna plain pouuoir de faire monnoye au païs; et luy donna le
cinquiesme denier de toutes les marchandises qui vendroient des
dites isles en Espagne; et furent les lettres passees deuant vn
tabellion nommé *Sariche* demeurant en Siuille; et en ladite
ville de Seuille on trouuera tout le faict et gouuernement du dit
Bethencourt. Et auecques ce que le roy estoit fort content de
luy aucuns bourgeois de Siuille l'aimoient fort, et luy firent beaucoup de plaisir, côme d'armures, de viures, d'or et d'argent à
son grand besoin. Il estoit fort bien cogneu en la dite ville et
fort aymé. Ledit Seigneur de Bethencourt print congé du Roy,
et s'en retourna aux isles tout joyeux, côme celuy à qui il sembloit qu'il auoit bien fait ses besongnes, et arriua à l'isle de
Forteauenture, là où il fut recueilly de ses gens bien joyeusement,
comme vous orrez cy-apres plus à plain.

CHAPTER LXXIII.—How the Sieur de Bethencourt arrived in the island of Erbanie.

When Monsieur de Bethencourt arrived in the island of Erbania, called Fuerteventura, he found there Hannibal, Gadifer's bastard son, who came forward to greet him; and the Sieur de Bethencourt gave him a very courteous reception. "Sieur," said Hannibal, "what has become of my master?" "He is returned," said Monsieur de Bethencourt, to France, to his own country." "I should much like to be with him," replied Hannibal. "Please God," said M. de Bethencourt, "I will take you thither when my enterprise is completed." "I am very distressed," said Hannibal, "that he has left us without sending us any intimation." "I think," answered M. de Bethencourt, "that he has written to you by my pursuivant." And so he had. The Sieur de Bethencourt then proceeded to a fortress named Richerocque, which he had caused to be constructed, and there he found some of his people. Fifteen of them had that day made a sally against the enemy, but the

---

CHAPITRE LXXIII.—*Comme ledit Seigneur arriua en lille derbane.*

Or est arriué Monsieur de Bethencourt en l'isle d'Erbanne nommee Fort'auenture, et a trouué Hannibal bastart de Messire Gadifer, lequel luy vint au deuant luy faire la reuerence, et ledit Seigneur le receut honnestement. Monsieur, dit Hannibal, qu'est deuenu Monsieur mon maistre, ce dit Monsieur de Bethencourt il s'en est allé en France en son païs. Adonc ce dit Hannibal, je voudrois bien que ie feusse auec luy, ce dit ledit Sieur, ie vous y meneray, si Dieu plaist, mais que i'aye fait mon entreprise : ie suis fort esbahy, ce dit Hannibal, comment il nous a laissez sans nous enuoyer quelque nouuelle : ie pense, ce dit Monsieur de Bethencourt, qu'il vous ait rescript par mon poursuiuant, aussi auoit-il ; ledit Seigneur arriua en vne forteresse nommee *Riche-rocque*, laquelle il auoit fait faire, et trouua vne partie de ses gens en icelle place, il en estoit sailly quinze de la place iceluy iour, et estoient allez courir sur leurs ennemis, et leurs ennemys

Canarians opposed them so vigorously[1] that they killed six outright, and the remainder, much beaten and disheartened, retreated to their fortress. M. de Bethencourt soon devised a remedy for this. There was another fortress there, named Baltarhayz, in which were quartered another portion of the company, and among them Hannibal. Monsieur de Bethencourt took his departure with all his company from Richerocque, which he left empty in order to take the more people with him to Baltarhayz. As soon as he was gone, the Canarians broke into Richerocque and destroyed it,[2] and thence proceeded to the port of Gardins, at a league's distance, where M. de Bethencourt had stored his provisions. They burned a chapel that was there, and seized the supplies, consisting of a great quantity of iron

---

Canariens vindrent sur eux et leur coururent sus vigoureusement, et en tuerent incontinent six et les autres moult batus et froissez se retrairent en la forteresse. Adonc ledit Bethencourt y mit remede bien tost. Or y auoit-il vne autre forteresse là où se tenoit vne partie de la compaignie, et y estoit Hannibal, et se nomme ladite forteresse *Baltarhayz*. Monsieur de Bethencourt se partit à tout sa compaignie, et laissa Richerocque despourveu, pour plus se saisir de gens pour venir à Baltarhays, et incontinent qu'il fut party les Canariens vindrent rompre et destruire Richerocque, et s'en allerent au port des *Gardins* qui est vne lieuë pres de là où estoient les viures de Monsieur de Bethēcourt, et ardirent vne chappelle qui y estoit, et gaignerent de leurs habillemēs, c'est assauoir force fer et canons, et rompirent coffres

---

[1] Father Galindo says that the natives of Fuerteventura are remarkably well built, strong, and courageous; and those in the north part of the island, called Maxorata, were distinguished for their talness. They could, in successive leaps, clear three lances placed parallel to each other at the height of a man, and at different distances. The steepest ravine formed no obstacle to the Guanche shepherd in pursuit of a kid down the mountain's side.

[2] The ruins are still seen. Richerocque is one of ten hamlets in the district of Oliva, in the north part of the island.

and cannons. They burst open chests and barrels, and took
and destroyed everything that was there. Then M. de
Bethencourt mustered together all the people that could be
found in the island, for some were away in the island of
Lancerote, and consequently were not forthcoming. He
took the field and had several engagements with the enemy,
coming off victorious every time. On two days in especial,
a considerable number of Canarians were slain ; and those
whom they succeeded in taking alive, were passed on to
the island of Lancerote with their king, who had remained
with them after the departure of M. de Bethencourt and
Gadifer, for he wished to restore and reopen the fountains
and reservoirs, which, for certain reasons, M. de Bethencourt had caused to be destroyed by Gadifer and his
company during the war, before the country was subdued.
In that part there is such a quantity of cattle, both wild and
domestic, that it is a matter of necessity that these fountains
should be opened, for otherwise the cattle could not live. The
king also desired M. de Bethencourt to send him cloth for

---

et tonneaux, et prindrent et destruirent tout ce qui là estoit. Si
assembla Monsieur de Bethencourt tout tant qu'il peut trouuer
de gens en ladicte isle, car il en auoit en l'isle de Lancelot qui
n'y pourroient estre, et se mit le bon Seigneur sur les champs, et
ont eu affaire auecque leurs ennemis par plusieurs fois, et tousiours ont eu victoire, et specialemēt en deux iournees, esquelles
ont esté morts plusieurs Canariens : et ceux qu'ils ont peu prendre
vifs, ils les ont fait passer en l'isle Lancelot, auecques leur roy,
qui auoit demouré auec eux, depuis que Monsieur de Bethencourt et Gadifer se partirent de là, afin qu'il fist labourer et
rouurir les fōtaines et les cisternes que Monsieur de Bethencourt auoit fait destruire par Gadifer et la compagnie durant la
guerre d'entre eux pour certaines causes parauant qu'il eust le
païs conquis. Et or endroit y a tant de bestiail, tant de priué
comme sauuage, qu'il est de necessité qu'elles soient ouuertes,
car autrement les bestes ne pourroiēt viure. Et a mandé ledit
roy à Monsieur de Bethencourt qu'on luy enuoye draps pour

clothing, and bows and arrows, for all the inhabitants of
the island of Lancerote take readily to archery and warlike
exercises, and behave themselves valiantly in the Christian
ranks against the people of Erbanie. This they do daily,
and several of them have died in the war, fighting for and
helping our people. In order to carry on the contest better
against them, the inhabitants of Erbanie this season mustered
all the youths of eighteen and upwards, so that the war has
occasioned them great losses ; for, although they have the
strongest castles that can be found anywhere, they have
been obliged to abandon them, and dare not take refuge in
them for fear of being shut in ; for, as they only live on
flesh, if they were hemmed in in their fortresses, they could
not subsist, for they do not salt their meat, so that it could
not last long. It is not to be wondered at that we on the
main land, with great multitudes of people and great extent
of country, make war upon one another, when we see these
people, who are thus shut up in islands in the sea, making
war and killing each other. But God allows all these

---

vestir, et artillerie, car tous les habitans de l'isle Lancelot se
prennent à estre archers et gens de guerre, et se sont tres-
vaillammēt maintenus auecque les Chrestiens contre ceux d'Erbannie, et font encor de iour en iour, et ont esté morts plusieurs
d'eux en la guerre combatans et aidans aux nostres ; et ont ceux
d'Erbanne, pour mieux soustenir leur guerre contre eux ceste
saison, mis ensemble tous les hommes de dix-huict ans en sus,
et pert bien qu'ils ont eu guerre contre eux, car ils ont les plus
forts chasteaux que on puit trouuer nulle part, lesquels ils ont
abandonnez et ne se y restrayent plus pour doubte qu'ils ne
soient enclos, car ils ne viuēt que de chair ; et qui les enclorroit
en leurs forteresses, ils ne pourroiēt viure, car ils ne salent point
leur chair, pourquoy elle ne pourroit longuement durer, et ce
n'est mie de merueille se entre nous qui sommes en terre ferme
grand' multitude de peuple, et en grand estenduë de païs, faisons
guerre les ungs les autres lun contre l'autre, puis que ceux qui
sont ainsi enclos és isles de mer se guerroient et occient l'vn
l'autre ; mais Dieu souffre toutes telles choses, afin qu'en nos

L

things, in order that, in our tribulations, we may have the
true knowledge of him; for the more adversity we meet
with in this world, the more we ought to humble ourselves
before him; as in the above-mentioned case of the death of
M. de Bethencourt's people, which happened on the seventh
day of October, 1404.

CHAPTER LXXIV.—How the Lord de Bethencourt restored the castle
of Richerocque, and of his combats with the Canarians.

After this, on the first day of November following [1404],
Monsieur de Bethencourt came back to Richerocque, and
had it carefully restored, and sent for a great number of
his people from the island of Lancerote, both natives and
others, and they came to him. He then sent Jean le Courtois and Guillaume d'Andrac and the people of Lancerote
and several others out to sea, to try and see whether the
enemy would come out at all against them; and while they
were out fishing with the line, sixty Canarians came down

tribulations nous puissions auoir de luy vraye cognoissance, car
de tant que nous aurons plus d'aduersitez en ce monde, de tant
nous deuons nous plus humilier deuers luy; et comme dessus est
dit de la mort des gens de Mōsieur de Bethencourt le fait aduint
le viie iour Doctobre MCCCCIIII.

[CHAPITRE LXXIV.]—*Comme ledit Seigneur fit abiller le chastia
de Richeroque.*

Apres ce, le premier iour de Nouembre ensuiuant, Monsieur
reuint à Richerocque et le fit remettre en poinct, et enuoya
querir grande quantité de ses gens en l'isle de Lancelot, fust de
ceux du pays et d'autres, lesquels vindrent vers luy: et puis
enuoya Jean le Courtois et Guillaume d'Andrac, et iceux de
Lancelot, et plusieurs autres en la mer, pour escouter et pour
voir s'il vendroit rien sur eux: et s'en alloient en peschant à la
ligne, si vindrent sur nos gens soixante Canariens et leur coururent

very sharply upon them, but our people defended themselves
so well and so vigorously that they were able to retreat to their
quarters, which lay at a distance of two French leagues, constantly fighting with their enemies, but without loss. But
had it not been for some darts that they had with them,
they would never have got off uninjured. On the third
day following, some of the company were gone out to the
field together with the men of Lancerote, in as good order
as they could, and had a long encounter with their enemies,
but at last those of Erbanie were discomfited and put to
flight. A short time afterwards, Jean le Courtois and
Hannibal, Gadifer's bastard son, took their departure from
Baltarhayz. Monsieur de Bethencourt was at Richerocque,
which he was having restored. Then Courtois and Hannibal took some companions from the island of Lancerote,
and went out seeking adventures. They came to a village,
where they found a great number of the natives assembled,
whom they attacked so sharply that ten were slain on the

---

sus moult asprement, et nos gens se defendirent si bien et si
vigoureusement qu'ils s'en vindrent à l'hostel qui estoit à deux
lieuës Francoises de la tousiours combatans auec leurs ennemis
sans rien perdre. Mais se n'y eust esté vn peu de trait qu'ils
auoient, ils n'en feussent iamais retournés sans perte. Et le
troisiesme iour ensuiuant estoient allez sur les champs aucuns
des compagnons de la compagnie auec ceux de l'isle Lancelot
les mieux aparliez qu'ils peurent, et s'entre-encontrerent auec
leurs ennemis qui leur coururent sus et combatirent longuement,
mais en la fin ceux d'Erbanie furent desconfits et mis en chasse.
Item tantost apres Jean le Courtois, et Hannibal bastart de
Gadifer, se partirent de Baltarhays. Monsieur de Bethencourt
estoit à Richerocque où il la faisoit rabiller : iceux Courtois et
Hannibal prindrent des compagnons de l'isle Lancelot et s'en
allerent à leur aduanture. Si vindrent à vn village la où ils
trouuerent vne grande partie des gens du pays assemblés, si
leur coururent sus et combatirent à eux bien appertement, en
telle maniere que leurs ennemis furent desconfits, et en mourut

spot, one of them being a giant nine feet high. Monsieur
de Bethencourt, however, had expressly forbidden that any
one should be killed, but that, if possible, they were to be
taken alive. But they said that they could not do otherwise, for he [the giant] was so strong, and fought so well
against them, that if they had spared him they would perhaps have been all defeated and slain. So Hannibal and
those of the company returned much punished and down-
hearted to the dwelling-house, and brought with them
a thousand milch goats.

CHAPTER LXXV.—Various encounters and combats with the Canarians.

At this time and previously, Gadifer's bastard son and
some of his allies were jealous of Monsieur de Bethencourt's
people, although the whole conquest, from first to last, had
been effected by him ; and if they had been the stronger
party, they would have done despite to Monsieur de Bethen-

---

en la place dix, dont l'vn estoit geant de neuf pieds de long ;
nonobstant que Monsieur de Bethencourt leur auoit expresse-
ment defendu que nul ne l'occist, s'il leur estoit possible, et que
ils le prissent vif : mais ils dirent qu'ils ne le pourroient autrement faire, car il estoit si fort, et se combatoit si bien contre eux,
que s'ils l'eussent espargné ils estoient en aduanture d'estre tous
desconfits et morts. Si s'en retourna Hannibal et aucuns de la
compagnie à l'hostel bien battus et navrez, et amenerent auec
eux mille chieure à lait.

[CHAPITRE LXXV.]—(*Diuerses rencontres et combats contre les
Canariens.*)

En ce temps et en par advent, ledit bastart de Gadifer et
aucuns de ses alliez auoiët enuie sur les gës de Mōsieur de
Bethencourt, lequel par luy a esté faite toute la conqueste, et le
commencement et la fin, et non pourtant, s'ils eussent peu estre
les plus forts, ils eussent fait honte aux gens dudit Sieur de Bethen-

court's company. But whatever they might say to him, he always controlled himself, because he had need of them; and as he was in a strange country, he was anxious to avoid causing them any displeasure, unless there were a good reason. Nevertheless, Jean le Courtois and some of his companions of the household of Monsieur de Bethencourt armed themselves well, as if about to engage with the enemy, and took the field early in the morning. It was thought that they were going to effect a surprise; for some four days previously a great number of Canarians had concealed themselves for the purpose of encountering some of us, and a little time before they had beaten a party of our people, and obliged them to retreat to their quarters with their heads bleeding and their arms and legs broken by the stones that were thrown at them. For these people have no other weapons; and, believe me, they can throw and handle a stone much better than a Christian can. It seems like a shot from a crossbow when they hurl it; and they themselves are extremely swift of foot, and run like hares. Thank God, whatever injury they did us, they took none of

court: mais quelque chose qu'on dist au dit Bethencourt, il dissimuloit tousiours pour cause qu'il auoit aide d'eux, et aussi qu'il estoit en estrange pays, et ne vouloit point qu'on leur fist nul desplaisir, si non à raison. Toutefois Jean le Courtois et des compagnons de l'hostel de mondit Seigneur s'armerent tres-bien comme s'ils vouloient aller combattre contre leurs ennemis, et estoit bien matin quand ils vindrent, et cuidoit-on qu'ils allassent en embusche; car il n'auoit pas quatre iours qu'ils s'estoient embuschez moult de Canares pour cuider encontrer aucuns de nous, il n'y auoit gueres de temps qu'ils nous auoient bien battus tant qu'ils nous ont renuoyé à l'hostel les testes sanglantes, les bras et les iambes rompuës de coups de pierre; car d'autres harnois ils n'ont point, et croyez qu'ils iettent et manient beaucoup mieux vne pierre que ne fait vn Chrestien; il semble que se soit vn carreau d'arballestre quand ils la iettent; et sont fort legeres gens; ils courent comme lievres. La mercy Dieu, quelque chose qu'ils nous fissent, ils n'eurent nuls de nous. Si aduint

our people prisoners. It happened, some days afterwards, that the children who had charge of the cattle discovered the places where the Canarians had lain during the night. So they came to the place where Hannibal and Bethencourt's archers and crossbow-men were lodging, to tell them how they had fallen upon the traces of the enemy. Then one named d'Andrac, who had been a servant of Gadifer's, asked the rest if they would go with them to see if they could fall in with the Canarians, but they had other designs and did not go. Then went six of Gadifer's party—for they numbered no more, two remaining to guard the place where they were lodging—and set out at night, each with his bow in his hand, to a mountain in the neighbourhood where the Canarians had been on the night before. D'Andrac started in the morning to join them, together with some companions from M. de Bethencourt's quarters and some from the island of Lancerote, and they took dogs with them as if they were going sporting down the island. When they reached the foot of the mountain where the ambush

---

aucuns iours apres cela que les enfans qui gardoient les bestes trouuerent les lieux où ils auoient couché la nuictée. Sy le vindrent dire là où Hannibal estoit logé, et ceux de Bethencourt estoient qui tiroient de l'arc et de l'arbaleste, et leur dirent comment ils auoient trouué la trace des ennemis : donc demanda vn nommé d'Andrac, qui auoit seruy Gadifer, aux autres ; s'ils vouloient aller auecques eux pour voir s'ils les pourroient encontrer, mais ils auoient autre propos, et n'y allerent point. Adonc y allerent incontinent six des compagnons Gadifer : car ils n'estoient nient plus, sinon deux qui gardoient le logis là où ils se tenoient, et se partirent par nuit chacun son arc en sa main eux embuscher en vne montaigne près de là; où les Canares auoient esté l'autre nuict deuant ; si s'en partit d'Andrac pour aller vers eux lendemain au matin accompagné des compagnons de l'hostel de mõdit Seigneur, et de ceux de l'isle Lancelot; et auoient des chiens auec eux comme s'ils s'allassent esbanoyant à val l'isle. Quand ils furent au pied de la montaigne où l'embusche

lay, they perceived the enemy following them; whereupon
they sent one of their companions to tell d'Andrac to make
for the mountain, for the Canarians were in great numbers.
They gained the mountain, and the enemy drew themselves
out in a line as if they meant to hem them in. Upon this
our people ran down to the encounter. One of our party
closed with them, and with a blow of his sword struck
down a Canarian who had attempted to throw his arms
around him. The others fled when they so clearly saw our
people united against them, and betook themselves to the
mountains, and our men returned to their quarters.

CHAPTER LXXVI.—How the Sieur de Bethencourt sent Jean de
Courtois to speak to Hannibal, who was at Baltharays.

After this, M. de Bethencourt sent John le Courtois and
some others to the tower of Baltharhayz to speak with
Hannibal and d'Andrac, who were of Gadifer's party; for
these latter said many things which were not very agree-

estoit, ils aduiserent leurs ennemis qui les suiuoient. Adonc
enuoyerent vn des compagnons pour dire à Dandrac qu'ils
gagnassent la montaigne: car les Canares estoient grand nombre
de gens. Si monterent amont la montaigne, et les ennemis
les costoyoient comme s'ils les vouloient enclorre. Adonc descendirent nos gens allencontre deux, et se ferit vn des compagnons parmy eux, et emporta ius vn, d'vn coup d'espée, qui
le cuidoit saisir entre ses bras, et les autres s'enfuirent quād ils
virent nos gens assemblés à eux si appertemēt, et se retraïrēt
aux mōtagnes, et nos gens s'en reuindrēt à l'hostel.

[CHAPITRE LXXVI.]—Comment ledit Seigneur enuoia Jean le
Courtois parler à Hanybal, qui estoit à Baltarhays.

Apres Monsieur de Bethencourt enuoya Jean le Courtois et
aucuns autres à la tour de Baltarhays parler à Hanybal et à
Dendrac serviteurs de Gadifer: car ils disoient beaucoup de
paroles qui ne plaisoiēt point fort à mōdit sieur, et leur manda

able to my said lord, and he desired them, by the said
Courtois, to observe the oath which they had taken. They
answered that they would be careful to keep it. Jean le
Courtois then asked Hannibal and d'Andrac why they had
torn in pieces a letter sent by Monsieur de B. They answered that it had been done by the desire of Alphonse
Martin and others ; upon which many words ensued, which
it would be tedious to relate. John le Courtois demanded,
by an interpreter, the Canarian prisoners who were in the
hands of Hannibal; for at least thirty had been entrusted to
his care, who were portioned out to various vocations, such
as minding the cattle, and other things which they were set
to do. When the prisoners arrived, John le Courtois desired his interpreter to conduct them to his lodging, which
was done. At this d'Andrac was greatly enraged, and told
him it was not his business to do this, for he had no
authority to command them, even if Gadifer had. To which
John le Courtois replied that Gadifer himself had no authority. " Suppose," said John, " that you are or have been

---

par ledit Courtois qu'ils tinssent le sermēt qu'ils denoiēt faire et
ils respondirēt qu'ils se voudroiēt garder de mesprēdre. Adonc
demanda Jehan le Courtois à Hanybal et Dendrac pourquoy ils
auoiēt despecé vnes lettres que Monsieur de B. auoit enuoyées ;
ils respondirent que par la volonté d'Alphōce Martin et d'autres,
il auoit esté fait; il y eut beaucoup de paroles qui lōgues seroient
à raconter. Jehan le Courtois manda par vn truchemēt les
Canariēs prisonniers qui estoient és mains d'iceluy Hanybal :
car on luy en auoit baillé en garde bien vne trentaine, lesquels
estoient espartis à faire aucunes vocatiōs, comme à garder bestes,
ou autres choses à quoy on les auoit mis à ce faire. Et quand
ils furent venus, Jehan le Courtois dit à son truchemēt, qu'il les
menast à son logis, et ainsi fut faite. Adōc d'Endrac fut moult
yré et courouceé cōtre luy, et dit qu'il ne luy appartenoit point
de ce faire, et qu'il n'auoit point de puissance de cōmander sur
eux, sois Gadifer. Adōc luy respōdit Jean le Courtois, que
Gadifer n'auoit nulle puissāce ; prenés, dit-il, que vous soyés ou

his servants, neither you nor he have any authority in this place ; it has pleased M. de Bethencourt to appoint me his lieutenant, and unworthy though I am of the honour, still, as it is his pleasure, I shall do my duty in his service to the best of my ability. But I am amazed that you dare act in this manner, for I know well that Gadifer did the best he could against M. de Bethencourt our master, and it has been so arranged that the said Gadifer, whom you call your master, will never return to this country to claim any-thing." D'Andrac was excessively angry at hearing these words, and required that he would desist from doing and saying such dishonourable things with respect to his master, who had not done any injury to M. de B., and he declared that if it had not been for their master the islands would not have been in the advanced state in which they then were ; "but," said he, "I clearly see that I am too weak to resist you, or to refute your words : so I appeal for help to all Christian kings, who shall decide the case." D'Andrac and Hannibal were chiefly enraged at being deprived of their share of the prisoners, which was not the intention of

ayés esté son serviteur, si n'aués-vous ne vous ne luy nulle puissãce en cet endroit ; il a pleu à monsieur de B. que ie sois son Lieutenant, moy indigne, mais puis qu'il luy plaist, ie le seruiray ainsi que ie doit faire. Mais suis esbahy cõme vous osez mouuoir, car ie sçay biē que Gadifer a fait le mieux qu'il a peu enuers mõsieur de B. nostre maistre ; et tãt ont besongné ensemble que ledit Gadifer que vous dites vostre maistre : ne reuendra iamais en ce païs pour y rien demander. Ledit Endrac fut moult courcé d'ouir dire telles paroles ; et luy requerut qu'il se deportast de faire et dire vn tel deshõneur de son maistre, et qu'il n'auoit pas deseruy à monsieur de B. et que ce n'eust esté mõsieur leur maistre, les isles ne fussent pas si auances qu'ils sont, mais ie vois biē que ie suis trop foible de resister cõtre vous, et fais clameur allencontre de vous, et demande l'ayde de tous les Roys Christiens, ainsi que le cas appartient. Ledit d'Andrac et Hãnibal estoient principalemēt courcés de ce qu'on leur vouloit tollir leur part des prisonniers : ce n'estoit pas

M. de Bethencourt, who afterwards appeased them. But d'Andrac and Hannibal were always jealous of the people of my said lord; and had they been the strongest, they would have done them harm and despite, but M. de Bethencourt's people were always ten to one; and when Hannibal and d'Andrac saw that they could do nothing else, and that no notice was taken of what they said, they were compelled to submit. So Jean le Courtois departed with all these prisoners and returned to M. de B. at Richerocque, and began telling him what terrible and proud people he had encountered, and how haughtily they answered. " And who may they be?" asked M. de B. " They are," said John le Courtois, " Hannibal and d'Andrac, and all because I wished to have the prisoners they had in their hands, in whom the others have a share as well as they. It is not their business to have charge of them; but, to hear them talk, one would think they were lords of all the country, and that, had it not been for them, nothing would have been done; and, in good sooth, Monsieur, anybody who believed them would

---

l'entente de monsieur de B. qui depuis les appaisa. Mais de tousiours ledit Endrac et Hanybal auoiët enuie sur les gēs de mōdit Seigneur de Bethencourt; et s'ils eussent esté les plus forts, ils leur eussēt fait desplaisir et déspieça; mais ceux de mōsieur de B. estoient tousiours dix cōtre vn. Quād ledit Hanybal et d'Andrac virent qu'ils ne pourroient faire autre chose, et qu'ils ne tenoient conte de nulles paroles qu'ils dissent, il fallut qu'ils obeyssent. Ledit Jean le Courtois s'en alla à tout ses prisonniers, et s'en vint deuers monsieur de B. à Richeroque, et commença à dire à Monsieur qu'il auoit trouué de terribles gens et de biē orguilleux, et qu'ils ont respondu fort fierement; et qui est-ce, ce dit Monsieur de B. C'est (ce dit Jehan le Courtois) Hannibal et d'Andrac, pource que i'ay voulu auoir les prisonniers qu'ils auoient, les autres y ont part aussi bien qu'eux, et n'appartiēt point qu'ils en ayēt la garde, et semble à les ouïr parler qu'ils doiuēt estre Seigneurs du païs, et qu'on n'eust rien fait se n'eussēt ils esté : et en bonne foy, Monsieur, qui les eût

think that you and your people were far other than what
you are. I wish that you had witnessed the thing yourself." "Silence," answered Monsieur; "you must not
repeat these things to me, for I know well the general discontent. I wish their master had written to them, and
told them how he had fared with the King of Castille. I
am not pleased that you should have acted thus unreason-
ably towards them, and I wish them to have their part and
share in the prisoners like the rest; but, however, I will so
arrange that everyone shall be contented. When I go away,
I will take them with me to their own country, and so we
shall be freed from them. We must not act hastily, but be
always on our guard, and keep in view our honour rather
than our profit."

CHAPTER LXXVII.—How Jean le Courtois retook the castle from
Hannibal and d'Andrac.

After several days, Courtois sent a man named Michelet
Helye and some others of his company to Hannibal and

voulu tousiours croire ne vous ne vos gens ne fussiez pas ainsi
côme vous estes, et ie cuide que vous l'auez bien apperceu
"Taisez vous (ce dit Môsieur) il ne faut point que vous m'en
parliez, car ie sçay bien le cōmun déspieca. Ie cuide que leur
maistre leur ait rescrit de ses nouuelles, et comment il a besongné
en Castille deuers le roy. Se dit Monsieur de Bethencourt: Ie
ne suis pas contēt que vous leur faciez aucune desraisō, et aussi
qu'il ayēt leur part et portion des prisonniers comme les autres,
au surplus i'y mettray si bon remede que chacun sera content;
quand il m'en iray, ie les amencray auec moy en leurs païs, ainsi
on en sera deliuré. Il ne faut pas faire tout tāt que l'on pourroit
bien faire; on doit tousiours dissimuler, et gardor son honneur
plus que son proffit."

[CHAPITRE LXXVII.—*Comment Jehan le Courtois reprit le chastiau
a Hanybal et d'Andrac.*]

Dedans aucuns iours apres ennuoya ledit Courtois vne nōmé
Michelet Helye et autres en sa compagnie deuers Hannibal et

d'Andrac, to tell them that Courtois desired them, on the part of M. de Bethencourt, to send to him all the Canarian women that they had.   To which d'Andrac replied that through him they should have none; but by force and violence, as they had taken the other prisoners, so they might take these, for they had no intention of fighting with him or anybody else.   When Jean le Courtois received this answer, he came to make his attempt, and found his companions more busy than ever covering their dwellings, on account of the bad weather and rain.   There were few people in the house; and so they came, in accordance with the preconcerted plan, and placed themselves between it and them, by the side of a tower which was there.   When d'Andrac saw that, he ran towards them with all speed, and thus addressed them : " What is this, fair sirs, that you propose to do?   Are you not satisfied with what you have done already?   Have you not effected enough mischief, dishonour, and villainy in what you have already done to our master, Messire Gadifer?   Do you not remember the help we have

d'Andrac, qui leur dit, comment Courtois leur mandoit de par Monsieur de Bethencourt que l'on luy enuoyast toutes les femmes Canares qu'ils auoient.   Adonc respõdit d'Andrac, que par luy n'en auroit il point : mais à force et outrage, comme ils auoient prins les autres prisonniers, le pourroient ils faire : car ils ne s'en pensoiët point à cõbatre contre luy ne autre.   Apres ce que Jean le Courtois eust eu la responce il vint et y fit son effort, et trouua les compagnons plus embesongnez que pieça n'auoient esté, qui couuroient leurs maisons pour la force du temps et de la pluye qu'il faisoit.   Ils estoient peu de gens à l'hostel.   Si vindrent ainsi qu'ils auoient entreprins, et se mirent entre l'hostel et eux.   Il y auoit vne tour, et là se mirent à costé ; et quand d'Andrac vit cela il y accourut tant qu'il peut courre, et leur commença à dire : Et qu'est-ce cy, beaux Seigneurs, que nous pensez-vous faire ? ne vous suffit il pas ? ne nous auez-vous pas fait assez de mal, du deshonneur et villenie que auez fait à nostre maistre Messire Gadifer ? ne vous souuient-il pas de l'aide que

afforded you in times past, a matter which it seems to us that you do not take into any account?" To which John le Courtois replied: "Have those women fetched out to us;" and he commanded his people to break through everything until they got them. Then a German called out in his language for fire, to burn the tower. D'Andrac understood him perfectly, and said, "Fair sirs, you can burn everything down if you will;" and said much more to them which it would take long to relate; but he told them that they were doing great dishonour to M. de la Salle in thus seizing his house and possessions," which he left," he said, "in our charge, and you are not doing honourably, and I call all present to witness the outrage which you are perpetrating upon us." To this John le Courtois replied, that the house, as well as all the country, belonged to Monsieur de Bethencourt, and that the said Sieur was lord and king of the whole, and that before Messire Gadifer left the islands he was aware of that fact. "I am amazed," continued Courtois, "that you should venture to rebel against M. de Bethencourt,

---

nous vous auons faite au tēps passé, de laquelle chose il nous sēble que vous ne faites point de compte? Adonc dit Jehan de Courtois : faites nous mettre ces femmes dehors, et commenda à ses gens que l'on rompist tout, et l'on fit tant qu'on les eust. Adonc demanda vn Allemant en son langage, du feu pour ardoyer la tour, et d'Andrac l'entendit bien : et dit, beaux Seigneurs vous pouuez bien tout ardoyer si vous voulez, et leur dit beaucoup de paroles qni seroiēt longues à dire et raconter. Mais il leur dit qu'ils faisoient grand deshonneur à Monsieur de la Salle de prendre ainsi son hostel et ses besongnes qu'il nous auoit laissez en garde, et ne faites pas bien, et ceux icy ie les en en appelle à tesmoings de l'outrage que vous nous faites. Adonc dit Jean le Courtois, que l'hostel estoit à Monsieur de Bethencourt, non pas seulemēt le païs, et que ledit sieur en estoit roy, seigneur et maistre, et que diés deuāt que Messire Gadifer se partist des isles, il le sçauoit bien. "Je suis bien esbahy, cedit Courtois, comme vous osez rebeller à l'encontre de Monsieur de

who is even now at this time in this country, and when he
hears of it will be very displeased, whereas your master is
in his own country far away from here.   Moreover he had before leaving used all his endeavours with the King of Castille,
but in vain, so that he returned to France and parted with M.
de Bethencourt on fair terms.   If you will believe me, you will
do well to come to my lord, who is a man to treat you better
than you have deserved."   Then said d'Andrac and Hannibal,
" We will go gladly, for we firmly believe that he will listen to
reason and will restore us our prisoners, or such portion of
them as is due to us."   Le Courtois then went into the tower
and the house, and took the women and brought them with all
the other Canarians to the island of Lanzerote, and so they
departed and went their way.

Bethencourt qui encore de present est en ceste isle, et quãd il
le sera, jagré ne vous en sçaura, et encore plus y a vostre maistre
est en son pays qui est si loing d'icy ; et encores y a-il plus,
qu'il en a fait tout son effort enuers le Roy de Castille, tant
qu'il s'en est allé comme jay dit en son pais et si est party assez
d'accord de Monsieur de Bethencourt.   Se me croyez, vous
vẽdrez vers Monsieur de Bethencourt, il est tel qu'il vous fera
mieux que ne l'auez deseruy.   Ce dirent d'Andrac et Hannibal,
nous irons voirement, et croy fermement qu'il nous fera raison,
et qu'il nous fera rendre nos prisonniers, ou telle part que nous
deurõs auoir.   Le dit Courtois entra dedans la tour et hostel, et
print les femmes et les amenerent avec tous les autres Canares
en l'isle Lancelot, et à tant se partirent et s'en allerent.

CHAPTER LXXVIII.—How the two Saracen Kings of Fuerteventura agreed to surrender and become Christians, for they saw that they could hold out no longer.

Some little time afterwards, when the people of the island of Erbanie, who were unaware of the discord that existed between the Christians, saw the war that M. de Bethencourt had carried on against them, and considered that the Christians were armed with arrows, which they were not (for, as we have elsewhere said, they had no armour and were only clothed in goat-skins and leather, and could only retaliate with stones and wooden lances untipped with iron, although they did a good deal of mischief), they began to perceive clearly that they could not hold out long. And when they heard from those who had been made prisoners their report of the government and the conduct of the Christians, and how considerately they treated those who consented to be subject to them, these islanders determined

---

[CHAPITRE LXXVIII.]—*Comment les deux Roys Sarrazins de l'Isle d'Arbanye parlementerent pour eux rendre et faire Crestiens, car ilz voient que ilz ne povent plus durer.*

En aucun pou de temps apres, ceux de l'isle d'Erbanne, non sçachant le discord d'entr'eux, voyans la guerre que Monsieur leur auoit raite, considerans qu'il ne la pourroient longuement maintenir allencontre d'iceluy seigneur et les Chrestiës, et que les Chrestiens estoient armés et artillés, ce qu'ils n'estoient pas : car comme autre fois i'ay dit, ils n'ont nulles armures, et si ne sont vestus que de peaux de chievres et de cuirs, et si ne se reuengēt que de pierres et de lances de bois non ferrées qui faisoient beaucoup de mal : ils sont surges et allegres, ils voyent bien qu'ils ne pourroient longuement durer : et veu la relation d'aucuns de la part qui ont esté prisonniers entre eux, qui leur ont raporté la maniere du gouuernement des Chrestiens et de leur emprinse, et comme ils traictent gracieusement tous ceux qui veulent estre leurs subgiets. Et pour ce ont eu en leur

in council that they would present themselves before the said Sieur de Bethencourt, as the chief of the company, and king and lord of the country, and as the first conqueror of these unbelievers; for they had never been Christians, nor had any other Christian before him been known to undertake this enterprise. Now in this island of Erbanie were two kings who had made war upon each other for a long period, during which many lives had been lost, and both sides had become much enfeebled; for, as has been said before, they had suffered great losses from intestine wars, for they have the strongest castles, built after their fashion, that could be found anywhere, and in the middle of the country there is also a very strong stone wall, which extends from one sea to the other.

---

cōseil qu'ils vendroiēt par devers le dit Sieur de Bethencourt qui estoit le chef de la compagnie, roy et seigneur du païs, cōme tout nouuel conquesteur sur les mescreans, car oncques ils ne furēt Chrestiēs, ne iamais navoit Chrestien que on puisse sçauoir ne l'auoit entreprins : et est de vray qu'ils sont en icelle isle d'Erbanie deux roys qui long-temps ont eu guerre ensemble, en laquelle guerre il en y a eu par plusieurs fois beaucoup de morts, tant qu'ils sont bien affoiblis, et, comme deuāt est dit, il y pert bien qu'ils ont eu guerre entre-eux, car ils ont les plus forts chasteaux edifiez selon leur maniere qu'on pourroit trouuer nulle part, et ont aussi comme au milieu du païs vne tres-grand mur de pierre qui comprend là endroit tout en trauers de l'vne mer à l'autre.

CHAPTER LXXIX.—How the two Kings of Fuerteventura sent
a Canarian to the said Sieur de Bethencourt.

Now there came to M. de Bethencourt a Canarian, who
was sent by the two pagan kings of Erbanie, with a request that he would be pleased to allow them to appear
before him on pacific terms, for they wished much to see
and speak with him, their wish and desire being to become Christians. When M. de Bethencourt understood this
through the medium of his interpreter, he was overjoyed,
and replied to the Canarian, through his interpreter, that
whenever it should please them to come for the purpose
which he announced, he would be rejoiced to receive them
with all hospitality, and make them right welcome. On his
return, the said Canarian was accompanied by the Canarian
Alphonse, who had become a Christian, and who was received with great cordiality. When they presented themselves before the two kings, the latter rejoiced greatly on

[CHAPITRE LXXIX.]—*Comment les deulx Roys derbanye enuoyerent ung Canare uers ledit sieur de Bethencourt.*

Or est venu deuers Monsieur vng Canarien qui a esté envoyé par
les deux Roys d'Erbanne Payens, lesquels mandent à Monsieur de
Bethencourt qu'il luy plaise qu'ils viennent parler à luy à treues,
et qu'ils auoient grand desir de le voir, et de parler a lui et leur
vouloir estoit d'estre crestiens ; et a ceste cause cestoit quil
avoit desir de parler au dit Seigneur. Et quand Monsieur de
Bethencourt eust ce entendu, par vng truchement qu'il auoit dit
que cestoit la voulonté de yceulx deulx Rois de venir vers lui
pour eulx faire crestiens, il fut bien fort ioyeux, et rendit response
audit Canarien, et lui fit dire par son truchement, que quãd
il leur plaira à venir pour faire ce qu'il rapportoit et disoit, que
il leur feroit tres-bonne chere, et ioyeuse, et seront les tres-bien
venus quand ils vendront. Et s'en retourna auecques ledit Canarien vng nommé Alfonce, Canarien, qui s'estoit faict Chrestien,
auquel l'on fit tres-bonne chere. Quand ils furent venus deuers
les deux Roys lesquieulx furent fort ioyeux quand ils ouyrent la

M

receiving the answer of M. de Bethencourt. They wished to retain Alphonse the interpreter, in order that he might be their guide when they came to present themselves before M. de Bethencourt; but he would not remain, not having received orders to that effect. Then the two kings had him conducted in safety to M. de Bethencourt's house, and he related to him all they had said and done, and was the bearer of a handsome present of I do not know what fruit, which grows a great way off, and its odour is wonderfully fragrant.

CHAPTER LXXX.—How the Saracen King of the Island of Lancerote came to be baptized.

The king who came first to M. de Bethencourt was the one who ruled that part of the island towards Lancerote; and he was baptized, and all the people he brought with him, on the eighteenth day of January, one thousand four hundred and five. He received the name of Lewis; and

response que auoit fait Monsieur de Bethencourt. Les deulx Rois voulurent retenir Alfonce le truchement pour et afin qu'il les conduisist quand ils vendroient vers mondit Sieur de Bethencourt, mais il ne le voulut pas, car on ne luy auoit pas commandé. A donc les Roys le firent conuoyer seurement iusques à l'hostel de mondit Sieur, et raporta au dit Sieur de Bethencourt toute la maniere qu'ils auoient dit et fait, et vng beau present de ie ne sçay quel fruict qui croist en païs bien lointain, et odoroit si tres-bon que c'estoit merueille.

[CHAPITRE LXXX.]—Comment le Roy Sarazin de lille lancclot vint et se fit crestien.

Il est venu premieremēt vng des Roys deuers Monseigneur de Bethencourt, celuy du costé de l'isle Lancelot soy quarante-deuxiesme, et fut baptisé luy et ses gens qu'il auoit amenez auec luy, le dix-huictiesme iour de Januier mil quatre cens et cinq, et fut nommé Louys, et trois iours apres vindrent vingt-deux per-

three days afterwards came twenty-two persons, and they were baptized on the day of their arrival. On the twenty-fifth day of January, the king of that part of the island which lies towards the Great Canary presented himself to M. de Bethencourt with forty-seven of his people, but they were not baptized until the third day from their arrival. The king received the name of Alphonse. From that time forward all the people came to be baptized; some now, some then, according as their dwellings might happen to be scattered about the country; so that by this time, thank God, they are all Christians, and bring their little children, as soon as they are born, to the court of Baltarhayz, where they are baptized in a chapel that M. de Bethencourt has had built; and they mingle with his people and share all their comforts. The said Lord de Bethencourt has commanded that they should be treated with the utmost gentleness; and he issued an order, in the presence of the two kings, that John le Courtois should continue to be his lieutenant as he had hitherto been, for he himself wished to

---

sonnes et furent baptisez iceluy iour mesmes. Le vingt-cinquiesme iour de Ianuier ensuiuant vint le Roy qui estoit du costé deuers la grand' Canare, deuers ledit Seigneur soy quarante-septiesme de ses gēs, et ne furent mie baptiser celuy iour ; ils le furent le tiers iour apres, et fut ledit Roy nommé *Alfonce*. Et de là en auant se venoient tous baptisez, puis les vns, puis les autres, ainsi comme ils estoient logez et espars parmy le païs, tant que auiourd'huy, la mercy Dieu, ils sont tous Chrestiens, et apporte len les petits enfans, tantost qu'ils sont nez, à la court de Baltarhays, et là sont baptisez en une chappelle que Monsieur de Bethencourt a fait faire ; et vont et viennent auecques les gens de Monsieur de Bethencourt, et qui leur administrent ce qui leur faut de tout ce que l'on peult finer. Ledit Seigneur a commandé qu'on leur face la plus grand' douceur que l'on pourra; et ordonna en la presence des deux Roys que Jean le Courtois seroit tous-iours son Lieutenant cōme il auoit esté, et que il s'en vouloit aller

visit his own country of France, where he proposed to stay as short a time as possible. He kept his word ; for he had such favourable weather, that he only spent four months and a half from the time of his departure till his return. He desired Messire John le Verrier and Messire Pierre Bontier to remain, in order to explain and teach without intermission the Catholic faith. He took as few people as possible with him; but among them were three Canarian men and one Canarian woman, as he wished them to see for themselves the manners and customs of the kingdom of France, and to give an account of them when he brought them back to the Canaries. So he left the island of Erbanie on the last day of January with tears of joy ; and all those whom he left behind wept on account of his departure, and the Canarians even more than the others, for the said lord had always treated them with great kindness. He took also with him some of Gadifer's people, but not d'Andrac or Hannibal, and so he took his leave. May God protect him and bring him safely back.

---

vn tour en Frāce en son païs, et qu'il demouroit tout le moins qu'il pourroit, et aussi fit-il; car il eut si bon temps, qu'il n'y demoura, que d'aller que de venir, que quatre mois et demy. Il ordonna à Messire Jean le Verrier, et Messire Pierre Bontier qu'ils demou-reroiēt, pour tousiours monstrer et enseigner la foy Catholique, et amena le moins qu'il peut de gens auec luy, sinon qu'il en amena trois Canariens et une Canarienne avec lui pour veoir le pais de France, pour rapporter quād il les ramenroit au païs de Canare. Et se partit le derrain iour de Ianuier Monsieur de Bethencourt de l'Isle d'Erbenne en pleurant de ioye, et tous les autres de lille derbanne pleuroient de ce qu'il s'en alloit, et plus encor les Canariens que les autres, car ledit Seigneur les auoit doucement traictez : le dit Monsieur de Bethencourt amena auec lui aucuns des gens de Gadifer, non pas d'Andrac ne Hannibal, et se partit : Dieu le veuille conduire et reconduire.

CHAPTER LXXXI.—How the Sieur de Bethencourt left the Island of
Lancerote and arrived at Harfleur.[1]

The said Lord de Bethencourt left the island of Erbanie
and set sail, and in twenty-one days he reached the port of
Harfleur. There he found Messire Hector de Bacqueville,
who made him very welcome, as also did several others of
his acquaintance. He passed only two nights at Harfleur,
and then proceeded to his own house at Grainville, where he
found Messire Robert de Bracquemont, knight, his near relation, in fact his uncle. M. de Bethencourt had let to him, for
a certain time, the lands of Bethencourt and the barony of
Grainville, and received from him a certain yearly rent. The
said Braquemont did not know of his arrival until he was
informed that he was at the end of the town of Grainville,
and then he left the chateau and met him on the road. It is
needless to ask whether their greeting was a warm one.

CHAPITRE LXXXI.—*Comment le dit Sieur se partit de lille lancelot
et arriua a herfleu.*

Ledit Seigneur de Bethencourt partit de l'isle d'Erbenne, et se
mit en mer, et singla tant qu'en vingt et vng iour il arriua au
port de Herfleur, là où il trouua Messire Hector de Bacqueuille,
lequel luy fit grand' bienvenüe et plusieurs du païs qui le cognoissoient, et ne fut que deux nuicts à Herfleur qu'il vint à Grainuille son hostel, et là trouua Messire Robert de Bracquemont
Cheualier et proche parent, oncle dudit sieur. Ledit Seigneur luy
auoit baillé pour aucun certain temps la terre de Bethencourt et la
Baronnerie de Grainuille, et luy en faisoit certaine somme de
deniers jus chacun an jusquez au bout du terme. Ledit Bracque-
mōt ne sceut oncques riens tant qu'on luy dit qu'il estoit au bout
de la ville de Grainuille, et adonc saillit hors du Chastel, et
s'entre encontrerent sur le marche ; il ne faut pas demander s'ils
firent grand chere l'vn à l'autre. Les Gentils hōmes d'autour y

---

[1] It will be seen that the heading of the chapter makes Bethencourt
sail from Lancerote, and the text from Fuerteventura. The discrepancy
appears to occur in the early MS.

The noblemen of the neighbourhood and the townsfolk, who were dependents of the said Lord de Bethencourt, came to meet him ; and it is impossible to describe the hearty reception they gave him every day. Members of his family and other noblemen were continually arriving from the country. There were Messire Ystace d'Erneville and his son Ystace d'Erneville, the Baron de la Heuse, and several other great lords whose names I cannot mention. They had heard speak of the conquest of the Canary Islands, and of the labour and toil which the said lord had undergone; for Madame de Bethencourt, whom her lord had sent back from Spain, had brought the first news of the conquest. Bertin de Berneval also, who had come without permission, had also brought some news : he was not very well received, as you may have heard already. Moreover, M. de Bethencourt himself wrote often, so they had received constant news.

---

vindrēt, et les hommes de la ville, qui estoiēt hōmes dudit Seigneur de Bethēcourt ; il ne faut point demander la chere qu'ō luy faisoit tous les iours. Il ne cessoit de venir de ses parens et autres Gentils-hommes du pais. Il y vint Messire Ystace d'Erneville, and Ystasse derneville son filz; le Baron de la Heuse le vint voir, et plusieurs autres grands Seigneurs que il ne sçaurois dire ; ils auoient bien ouy parler de la conqueste des Isles de Quenare, et de la grand' peine et trauail que ledit Seigneur de Bethencourt yauoit euë; car premièrement Madame de Bethencourt, que ledit Seigneur auoit renuoyée du Royaume d'Espagne, auoit apporté les premieres nouuelles de la conqueste ; et aussi auoit fait Bertin de Berneual qui s'en estoit venu sans congé, et n'y a pas eu fort grand honneur comme vous auez peu oüyr cy deuant ; aussi ledit Seigneur rescripuoit fort souuent, parquoy on auoit tousiours des nouuelles.

CHAPTER LXXXII.—How Bethencourt engaged several nobles and
workmen to go out to the Canaries.

M. de Bethencourt did not find his wife at Grainville, for
she was at Bethencourt; he sent for her, and when she
arrived we need not say how joyous was their meeting.
Never had Monsieur rejoiced so much at meeting Madame, for
whom he had brought many curiosities as presents from those
distant countries. With the said lady came Messire Renault
de Bethencourt, my lord's brother. After a stay of about
a week at Grainville, Messire Ystace d'Erneville and others
proposed to take leave of M. de Bethencourt. He then informed them that he meant to return to the Canaries as
soon as possible, and to take as many people as he could from
Normandy; and that it was his intention to conquer the
Great Canary if possible, or at least to have a touch at it.
Messire Ystace, who was present, said that, with his leave,
he would go with him. "My nephew," answered de Bethencourt, "I will not give you this trouble : I will take less

[CHAPITRE LXXXII.]—[*Comment Bethencourt engagea plusieurs
gentilz hommes et gens de mestiers pour les amener aux Canaries.*]

Mōsieur de Bethencourt ne trouua point sa femme à Grainuille, car elle estoit à Bethencourt. Il l'enuoya querir, et quand
elle fut venuë, il ne faut point demander la chere qu'ils firent
ensemble; oncques mais Monsieur ne fit si grand chere à Madame,
et luy demanda et apporta des nouueautez du païs de par delà ;
et vint auec ladite dame Messire Renault de Bethencourt son
frere : et quand le seigneur eust esté à Grainuille enuiron huict
iours, ledit Messire Ystasse d'Erneville et autres voulurent
prendre congé du dit Sieur. Adonc il leur dit que le plutost
qu'il pourroit il retourneroit en Canare, et qu'il amenoit le plus
des gens du pays de Normandie qu'il pourroit, et que son
intentiō estoit qu'il cōquerroit, s'il pouuoit, la grand' Canare, au
moins il luy bailleroit vne touche. Le dit Messire Ytasse, qui
present estoit, dit que "s'il luy plaisoit il iroit. Mon nepueu
(ce dit Monsieur de Bethencourt) ie ne vous veux pas donner

important persons than you." Upon this several noblemen then present volunteered their services ; for example, one named Richard de Grainville, a relative of de Bethencourt's, one named Jean de Boville, another named Jean de Plessis, as well as Maciot de Bethencourt and some of his brothers : indeed, the greater part of the company, consisting of people of various stations in life, were willing to go. M. de Bethencourt then said : "I wish to take with me people of all the different trades that can be mentioned or thought of; and when they arrive there they need have no doubt of finding a profitable country and one easy to live in without hard labour ; and to those who come I will give sufficient land to till, if they will only undertake the trouble. There are many mechanics in this country who have not a foot of ground of their own, and who live very hardly ; now if they will come with me yonder, I promise them that I will do the best for them that I can, better than for any others that may come in future, and much better even than for the

---

ceste peine, ie prendray auec moy de plus legeres gens que vous."
Aussi plusieurs gentils-hommes, qui là estoiēt, s'y offrirent, il si offrit vn nommé Richard de Grainuille parēt dudit Seigneur ; vng nommé Jehan de Bouille lequel y fut, vng nommé Jehan du Plessis qui y fut, ung nommé Maciot de Bethencourt, et aulcuns de ses freres ; lesquieux y furent, et plusieurs autres quilz soffrirent audit Seigneur, desquels y eut grand' partie qui y furent auec ledit Seigneur de Bethencourt, et des gens de plusieurs conditions ; car, cedit Monsieur de Bethencourt, "i'y veux mener des gens de tous mestiers que l'on sçauroit dire ne deuiser ; et quand ils y seront, il ne faut point doubter qu'ils seront en bon pays pour viure biē-ayses, et sans grand' peine de corps ; et ceux qui y vendront ie leur donneray assez de terre pour labourer s'ils veulent prendre celle peine : il y a beaucoup de gens mechanicques en ce pays qui n'ont pied de terre, et qui viuent à grand' peine, et s'ils veulent venir par delà ie leur promets que ie leur feray tout le mieux que ie pourray, et mieux que à nuls autres qui y sçachent venir, et beaucoup plus que aux gens du

natives who have embraced Christianity." Every one then
took leave of the said lord, except Messire Renault de
Bethencourt his brother, and Messire Robert de Bracquemont, who was residing in the chateau of Grainville at the
time of his arrival. Before long all the country became
aware that M. de Bethencourt intended to return to the
Canary Islands, and wished to take with him people of
various trades, both married and marriageable, as many as
were willing to go; so that you might see every day arrivals
of first ten, then a dozen, and at length thirty in a day,
who offered to accompany him without asking for wages.
Some even were willing to bring their own provisions.
Thus M. de Bethencourt mustered a good many people of
position, as well as others of various grades. He took
eight score people of position, of whom twenty-three brought
their wives. First, John de Boville, John du Plessis,
Maciot de Bethencourt and several of his brothers, all
noblemen, accompanied the said lord; the remainder were

---

païs qui sont du pais mesmes faits Chrestiens." Chacun print
congé dudit sieur, fors Messire Renault de Bethencourt son
frere, et Messire Robert de Bracquemont qui estoit demourant
au chasteau de Grainuille quand Monsieur arriua. Et tantost
apres tout le pays sceut que Monsieur de Bethencourt vouloit
retourner esdites isles de Canare, et vouloit mener gens de tous
mestiers et gens mariez et à marier, ainsi qu'il les pouuoit
trouuer, et qui auoient bonne voulenté d'y aller, et tant que vous
eussiez veu tous les iours venir puis x, puis xii [xx?], puis xxx pour
vng iour, qui soffroient a Monsieur de Bethencourt à lui tenir
compagnie sans demander nuls gages quelsconques; encore y en
auoit-il qui estoient contens d'y porter leur prouision de viures.
Ledit Seigneur y assembla beaucoup de gẽs de bien et d'vne
maniere et d'autre. Il y mena huict vingts hommes de deffence
dõt il y en eut vingt et trois qui y menerent leurs femmes.
Premierement Jean de Bouille, Jehan du Plessis, Maciot de
Bethencourt, et aucuns de ses freres, qui tous estoient gentils-
hommes, vindrent auec ledit Seigneur, et le demourant estoient

all mechanics or labourers. Eleven came from Grainville :
one was named Jean Anice, and another Pierre Girard.
Three came from Boville, from d'Hanouard, and from Beuze-
ville; many from the villages of Caux; from Bethencourt
Jean le Verrier; Pierre Loisel, and four or five others from
Picy and the country round. There were amongst them all
sorts of handicraftsmen, so that the Sieur de Bethencourt,
having now got together the number that he required,
made his preparations for returning to the Canaries. He
bought a vessel belonging to Messire Robert de Bracquemont: he had already two ships of his own, and he devoted
all his attention to the preparations for his return to the
Canaries. When his arrangements were completed, he
ordered all those who intended to accompany him to be
ready to start on the sixth of May, and to meet at Harfleur,
where the two barges were. He then intimated to all his
friends and neighbours the day of his intended departure,
and announced that on the first of May he would take leave
of all his friends, and wish them " God speed." On the

---

tous gens mechaniques et gens de labour. Il y en eut vnze de
Grainuille, dont l'vn auoit nom Jehan Anisse, et vng autre
Pierre Girard. Il y en eut trois de Bouille et de Hanouart, de
Beuzeuille ; de beaucoup des villages de Caux ; de Bethencourt,
Jean le Verrier, Pierre Loisel, et quatre ou cinq aultres de Picy,
et du pays enuiron, et y en auoit de tous metiers, tant que ledit
Seigneur eut le nombre qu'il vouloit auoir ; et quant il vit quil
eut son nombre quil vouloit avoir il fit les aprestes pour s'en
retourner en Canare. Il achepta vne nef qui estoit à Messire
Robert de Bracquemont, et auoit deux nefs au voyage, lesqieulx
estoient siennes, et fit la plus grand' diligence qu'il peust pour s'en
retourner en Canare. Et quand il eust fait les apprestes, et qu'il
eut mandé à tous ceux qui vouloient venir auecques luy, que ils
fussent prez de partir le sixiesme iour de May ensuiuant, et qu'ils
se trouuassent à Herfleur là où estoiët les deux barges, il māda à
tous ses amis et voisins qu'il se partiroit audit iour, vi^e iour de
May, et que le premier de May il prendroit congé de ses amis,

appointed day, the knights and nobles presented themselves at Grainville, and were received with great hospitality by the Sieur de Bethencourt. Many a lady and fair maiden was there beyond my power to name, and for three days the feasting and rejoicing lasted. On the fourth day the Sieur de Bethencourt took his departure from Grainville, and went to join his company at Harfleur on the appointed sixth of May, and on the ninth they set sail with a favourable wind.

CHAPTER LXXXIII.—How Monsieur de Bethencourt, on his return from Normandy, arrived at Lancerote, where he was received with great demonstration.

Thus M. de Bethencourt started on the ninth of May, 1405, and continued his voyage until he reached the island of Lancerote, where he landed. In the island of Fuerteventura he was welcomed with the music of trumpets,

---

et payeroit sa bien allee. Les sieurs cheualiers et gentils-hommes se trouuerent à iceluy iour à son hostel à Grainuille, et là furent receuz dudit sieur qui leur fit grand chere, et y eut dames et damoiselles plusieurs que ie ne sçaurois dire ne escrire, fors que ledit Seigneur leur fit la plus grant chere que ilz peut; et dura la feste et la chere trois iours accomplis, et au quatriesme iour ledit sieur se partit de Grainuille et s'en alla attendre sa compagnie à Herfleur; ledit sixiesme iour de May se comparrurent a herfleu, et le neufiesme iour se mit en mer ledit Sieur et sa compagnie, et eurent vent à desir.

CHAPITRE LXXXIII.—*Comment Monsieur de Bethencourt à son retour de Normandie arriva en lille Lancelot, où il fut recuelli à grand chose.*

Or se partit Mōseigneur de Bethencourt le neufiesme iour de May mil cccc et v, et singla tant qu'il descendit en l'isle Lancelot, et en l'isle de Fort' auenture; trompettes sonnoient et clerons,

clarions, drums, harps, rebecks, bassoons, and all sorts of
musical instruments to announce his arrival. God's thunder
would have been drowned in the noise of the music that
they made, so that the people of Fuerteventura and Lancerote,
and especially the Canarians, were astounded. The Sieur
de Bethencourt had no idea that so many instruments had
been brought, but there were a number of young people who,
without his knowing it, were musicians, and had brought
their instruments with them. Maciot de Bethencourt,
who was one of those whose business it had been to ascertain the characters of the volunteers, advised M. de Bethencourt to take those, as they seemed to him to be fit and
able men. When M. de Bethencourt landed, banners and
standards were unfurled, and all the company were in their
best dress, and presented a very creditable appearance. To
each man he had given a *hocqueton*, and six gentlemen who
were with him were *argentés* [*i.e.*, wore the jacket of a king's
guard] at the expense of the said lord; many others also wore
silver lace, but such as wore it paid for it. They all looked

---

tabourins, menestrés, herpes, rebequets, busines, et de tous instrumens. On n'eut pas ouy Dieu tonner de la melodie qu'ils
faisoient, et tant que ceux d'Erbannie et de Lancelot furent tous
esbays, et specialement les Canariens : nouobstant que ledit Seigneur ne cuidoit point auoir amené tant d'instrumens ; mais il y
auoit beaucoup de ieunes gens de quoy ledit Sieur ne se guett-
toit point, qui en iouoyent, et auoient apporté leurs instrumens
auec eux. Aussi Maciot de Bethencourt, qui en partie auoit eu
la charge de s'enquerir quels compagnons c'estoient, conseilloit
ledit Sieur de les prendre ainsi qu'il luy sembloit qu'ils estoient
propres et habiles ; bannieres et estendars estoient estendus ; et
estoient tous les compaignons en leur habillement quand ledit
Seigneur descendit à terre ; ils estoient assez honnestement habillez. Monsieur de Bethencourt leur auoit donné à chacun vng
hocqueton, et à six gentils-hommes qui estoient auec luy, ils
estoient argentez, que ledit Sieur paya : nonobstant qu'il y en
auoit beaucoup d'autres argentez ; mais celuy qui le portoit le

very well. Never had M. de Bethencourt been received with such distinction. When his vessel was within half a league's distance, the inhabitants of Lancerote perceived that it was indeed their king and sovereign, and you might see from the ship the Canarians, men, women, and children, coming to the beach to meet him; and they cried out in their language, "Here is our king coming!" and so great was their joy that they leaped and danced and kissed each other, so that it was very evident that they were delighted at his arrival; nor can it be doubted that his own people, whom M. de Bethencourt had left in the islands of Lancerote and Fuerteventura were equally glad. As I have said, the instruments in the barges made such grand melody that it was a fine thing to hear; and the Canarians were utterly amazed, for the music both pleased and frightened them. When Monsieur landed, we need not ask what sort of welcome he received. The Canarians prostrated themselves on the ground, believing that to be the highest honour they could pay him,

---

payoeit. Ilz estoient tous fort honnetes. Onques Monsieur de Bethencourt n'y alla si honnestement; et quand le nauire fut à demy lieuë prez, les gens de l'isle de Lancelot virent et apperceurent bien que c'estoit leur Roy et leur Seigneur : vous eussiez veu de la nef les Canariens, femmes et enfans, qui venoient au riuage au deuant du dit Seigneur, et disoient et crioient en leur langaige ; Voicy nostre Roy venir ; et estoient si joyeux qu'ils sailloient et s'entreboutoient de ioye, et s'entre accolloient, et paroist bien clairement qu'ils auoient grand' ioye de la venuë de leur Roy ; aussi il ne faut point doubter que ceux que Monsieur de Bethencourt laissa és dites isles de Lancelot et Fort' auenture, qu'ils n'auoient pas moins de ioye ; et, comme i'ay dict, les instrumens qui estoient és barges faisoient si grand' melodie que c'estoit belle chose à ouïr, et les Canariens en estoient tous esbahys, et leur plaisoit terriblement ; et quand Monsieur fut arriué à terre, il ne faut pas demāder si tout le peuple luy fit grand chere ; les Canariens se couchoient à terre, en luy cuidant faire le plus grand houneur qu'ils pouuoient, c'estoit à dire

for they implied by that act of prostration that their bodies and goods belonged to him. The said lord raised them and greeted them with all possible warmth of manner, and especially the king who had become a Christian. The people of the island of Fuerteventura were well aware that their king and sovereign had arrived in the island of Lancerote, and accordingly Jean le Courtois, lieutenant of the said lord, took a boat and six companions with him, one of whom was Hannibal, and another named de la Boëssiere, and four others, and came to the island of Lancerote, into the presence of their said master, and rendered him due homage. Then M. de Bethencourt inquired of Jean le Courtois how everything was going on? He answered, " Sir, all is going on well, and better and better, and there is every prospect of all your subjects becoming good Christians, for they have made a fair beginning, and they are as delighted at your return as ever people could be. The two Christian kings wished to come with me, but I told them that you would be soon coming, and that I should not return without you." " Nor shall you," answered he. " I shall go to-morrow,

quilz se couchoient que corps et biens estoient à luy. Ledit Seigneur les receuillit, et leur fit la plus grand' chere qu'il peut, et par especial au Roy qui s'estoit fait Chrestien. Ceux de l'isle de Fort' auenture sceurent bien que leur Roy et Seigneur estoit venu et arriué en l'isle de Lancelot. Jean le Courtois, Lieutenant dudit Seigneur print vng bastel et six compagnons auecques luy, dont Hannibal estoit vng, et vng nommé de la Boëssiere, et quatre autres, et vindrent en l'isle de Lancelot deuers leur dit Seigneur, et luy fit la reuerence ainsi qu'il appartenoit. Adonc Monsieur de Bethencourt demanda à Jean le Courtois comme tout se por- toit? ce dit Jean le Courtois, Mōsieur tout se porte bien et de mieux en mieux, et cuide et croy que tous vos subjets seront bōs Chrestiens, car ils ont beau commencement, et sont si ioyeux de vostre venuë, que iamais nulles gens ne pourroient plus estre ; les deux Roys Chrestiens vouloient eux en venir auec moy, mais ie leur ay dit que vous y vendrez bien-tost, et que ie ne retournerois point que ce ne fust auecques vous ; n'aussi serez vous, ce dit ledit

please God." The Sieur de Bethencourt took up his abode
at Rubicon in the castle with most of his company. You
must not ask if the people whom M. de Bethencourt had
brought with him from Normandy were much astonished at
sight of the country and of the Canarians, dressed as they
were, for, as I have said before, they wore no clothing except a goat-skin behind, while the women wore robes of
leather which reached to the ground. The newcomers were
much pleased with the country, which fulfilled their expecta-
tions and pleased them more the more they looked at it.
They ate of the dates and other fruits of the country, which
they thought very good, and there was nothing that did
them any harm. Indeed, they were very pleased to find
themselves in such quarters, and they felt they could live
very happily there. I could not tell you how pleased
they were, and they will be more so when they see the
island of Fuerteventura. Monsieur asked Hannibal how he
was, and what he thought of his company, and Hannibal
replied: "Sir, it seems to me that if you had come with a like
company in the first instance, our progress would not have

Sieur; j'iray demain, se Dieu plaist. Ledit Sieur fut logé à Rubicon
au chasteau ; et la plus part au chastiau. Il ne faut pas demander
si les gens que ledit Seigneur auoit amenez derrainement de
Normandie estoient esbays de voir le païs et les Canariens ainsi
habillez qu'ils estoient ; car comme i'ay dit cy-deuant, ils ne sont
vestus que par derriere, et de cuir de chieure. Et les femmes sont
vestuës de houpelādes de cuir iusques à terre. Ils estoient bien
ioyeux de voir le païs et leur plaisoit fort, et plus le regardoient
et plus leur plaisoit. Ils mangeoient de ces dattes et des fruits
du païs, qui leur sembloient fort bons, et rien ne leur faisoit nul
mal ; mais estoient fort ioyeux d'eux y trouuer, et leur sembloit
qu'ils viuroient bien au pays : ie ne vous scaurois que dire fors
qu'ils estoient fort contens, et encore le seront-ils plus quand ils
verront l'isle d'Erbenne dit Fortaventure. Monsieur demanda à
Hannibal comme il le faisoit, et qu'il luy sembloit de sa compagnie ; Monsieur, ce dit Hannibal, il me semble que si du premier on y fust venu par telle maniere, les choses n'eussent pas

been so slow as it has been, and things would have been in a greater state of advancement. It is a very fair and noble company; and when the other Canarians in the other islands, who have not yet become Christians, see such a company in such fine order, they will be more easily daunted than they have hitherto been. "It is my intention," said Monsieur, "to go and see the Grand Canary, and to give them a touch."

CHAPTER LXXXIV.—How the Sieur de Bethencourt arrived in the Island of Fuerteventura, and the two Kings came forward expressly to pay him respect.

Monsieur de Bethencourt left the island of Lancerote and proceeded to Fuerteventura, taking with him all his company. On his arrival, there were to be seen a great number of Canarians, who had come down to the seashore to greet their king and sovereign, and there also were the two kings who had embraced Christianity. No need to ask if they and the rest of the people of the country were glad. It is

duré si longuement qu'ils ont fait, et si on fust encore plus auant que l'on n'est ; c'est vne fort belle compaignie et bien honneste ; et quand les autres Canares des autres isles qui ne sont point Chrestiens verront si belle ordonnance, ils esbahiront plus qu'ils n'ont faict ; c'est bien mon intention, ce dit Monsieur, d'aller voir la grand' Canare, et de leur bailler vne touche.

[CHAPITRE LXXXIV.]—*Comment ledit sieur aryva a lille de fort-auenture, et la les deulx rois vindrent au devant, et tout ce pour faire reverence.*

Monsieur de Bethencourt se partit de l'isle Lancelot pour aller en l'isle de Fortauenture, et print tous ses gens qu'il auoit amenez. Là vissiez quant Monsieur fut arriué grand nõbre des Canariens qui estoient arriués à la riue de la mer à l'encontre de leur roy et seigneur ; et là estoient les deux rois qui s'estoient faits Chrestiens. Il ne faut pas demander s'ils estoient ioyeux

impossible to describe the joy which they testified after their fashion; they seemed to fly with joy. When M. de Bethencourt arrived at Richerocque, he found it strong and well restored, for Jean le Courtois had devoted great care to this after his master's departure for Normandy, and pleased him very much. The two Christian kings came to do homage once more to M. de Bethencourt, who gave them the best welcome in his power, and kept them to supper. He did not understand them, but he had an interpreter who spoke both their language and French, so that they understood each other very well. While M. de Bethencourt was supping there were minstrels playing, which prevented the two kings from eating, from the pleasure they took in listening to these minstrels and in gazing on the embroidered dresses, there being at least fifty-four richly decorated with silver lace, for there was rivalry amongst some of the company and anxiety to outvie one another in dress, especially amongst the sons of the principal dependents of M. de Bethencourt from Grainville and from Bethencourt. The two kings declared that if they

---

et tous les autres du pays. On ne sçauroit dire la ioye qu'ils en menoient selon leur façon et maniere; ils voloient tous de ioye. Ledit seigneur arriua à Richerocque qu'il trouua moult fort et bien rabillé; car Jean le Courtois y auoit fait fort besongner depuis que ledit seigneur s'estoit parti pour aler en Normandie et hesta fort audit Seigneur. Lesdits deux roys Chrestiens se vindrent encor offrir audit Seigneur, lequel leur fit la plus grand' chere qu'il peut, et les retint à soupper auec luy. Ledit Seigneur ne les entendoit point, mais monsieur auoit vn truchement qui parloit le Français et leur langage, parquoy on entendoit ce qu'ils disoient. Et tandis que ledit Sieur souppoit, il y auoit des menestrés qui iouoyent, dequoy iceux roys ne pouuoient manger, du plaisir qu'ils prenoient à ouyr lesdits menestrés; et aussi de voir ces hoquetons brodés; car il y en auoit bien cinquante et quatre fort chargéz d'orfauerie; car il y auoit d'aucuns qui s'abilloient à l'enuie à qui mieux mieux, et par especial aucuns fils des hommes dudit Seigneur de Bethencourt de Grainuille, et de Bethencourt. Et dirent lesdits roys que si du premier ils fussent venus en ce

had made their first appearance in such guise, they should have been conquered at first sight, and that it only depended on the king to achieve the conquest of many countries. The said Canarians never called M. de Bethencourt anything but king, and treated him as such. "As to that," said M. de Bethencourt, "my intention is to make an expedition to the Great Canary and to investigate its resources." Then said Jean le Courtois, "Sir, it will be a good thing to do, and I think it will not be long before, please God, we shall be able to ascertain the point of entrance and to learn something about the country." Then said Hannibal, "I intend to make my fortune and to gain much booty; I have been there already, and it does not seem to me that it will be so serious an undertaking as you anticipate." "Ha!" answered Monsieur, "but it is a serious undertaking. I am informed that there are ten thousand nobles there, which is no trifle, and we are no match for them. But in order to reconnoitre the country with reference to the future, we will make an effort to go there, if only to become acquainted with the harbours and roads of the country;

---

poinct, ils eussent esté pieçà vaincus, et qu'il ne tendroit au roy s'il ne conqueroit encores beaucoup de pays. Lesdits Canariens n'appellent autrement Monsieur de Bethencourt que le roy, et pour tel le tenoient. Or ça, ce dit Monsieur de Bethencourt, mon intention est de faire vne course à la grand' Canare, et de sçauoir que c'est. Ce dit Jean le Courtois, monsieur, ce sera bien fait; il me semble qu'ils ne dureront gueres, mais qu'il plaise à Dieu qu'on puisse sçauoir l'entrée et cognoistre aucunement le pays. Ce dit Hanybal qui y estoit, i'ay l'intention d'y mouiller mes souppes, et d'y gagner bon butin; i'y ay autrefois esté, il me semble que ce n'est pas si grand' chose qu'on dit. Ce dit monsieur, si est, c'est grand'chose, si suis aduerty qu'ils soit dix mille gentilshommes qui est bien grand chose, et ne sommes pas gens pour eux. Mais pour cognoistre le pays pour le temps aduenir nous ferons nostre effort d'y aller, et ne fust que pour sçauoir les ports et passages du pays; et se Dieu plaist il vendra quelque bon

and, please God, some good prince may come from some other country and conquer them, and who knows what besides; and God grant it may be so. However, I must consider when I can go, and whom I shall leave here, for as for you, Jean le Courtois, you will come with me on this expedition." "Good, Monsieur," said le Courtois, "I am very pleased to hear it." Then said M. de Bethencourt, "I shall leave Maciot de Bethencourt here, in order that he may make himself acquainted with the country, as my intention is that he shall not return to France, for I do not wish this country to be without one of the name of Bethencourt and of my lineage in occupation." Then Jean le Courtois said, "Please God, I should like, Sir, to return with you to France. I am a bad husband, for it is five years since I have seen my wife." But, to tell the truth, it did not seem to trouble him much. When Monsieur had supped, every one repaired to his own quarters. Next day M. de Bethencourt went to Baltarhayz, and there a Canarian infant was baptized, by way of welcome to him : the Sieur stood godfather to it, and named it Jean. He had brought

---

prince de quelque pays qui les conquerra et autres choses avec ; et Dieu par sa grace le vueille ainsi faire. Se dit Monsieur de Bethencourt, il fault regarder quand i'y pourray aller, et qui ie laisseray par deçà ; car quant au regard de vous, Jean le Courtois, vous en vendrez auec moy au voyage ; et bien, monsieur, ce dit le Courtois, i'en suis tres-fort ioyeux. Ce dit Monsieur de Bethencourt, ie laisseray Maciot de Bethencourt, affin qu'il cognoisse le pays, car mon intention n'est point de la remener en France, car je ne veux plus que ce pays soit sans le nom de Bethencourt, et sans vn de mon lignage. Ce dit Jean le Courtois : Monsieur, se Dieu plaist, ie m'en retourneray avecquez vous quand vous retourneres en France. Ie suis vn mauuais mary, il y a cinq ans que ie ne vis ma femme, et à la verité il ne luy en faisoit point trop de mal ; et quand monsieur eut souppé, chacun s'en alla là où ils deuoient aller. Le lendemain ledit seigneur s'en alla à Baltarhays et là fut baptisé vn enfant Canarien, à la bien venue dudit seigneur et ledit seigneur fut le parrain et le nomma Jehan ; il fit apporter en la

into the chapel some vestments, an image of our Lady, and other church furniture, as well as a very beautiful missal, and two little bells, each weighing a cent. He ordered the chapel to be called "The Chapel of our Lady of Bethencourt;" and Messire Jean Verrier was the curé of the country, and spent the remainder of his life there very happily. After M. de Bethencourt had been a short time in the country, he started on his expedition to the Great Canary. He arranged for it to take place on the 6th of October, 1405, and by that time he was ready to start with all the fresh people he had brought and with several others, and they set sail on that day in three vessels, two of which belonged to the Sieur, and one had been sent to him by the King of Spain. Adverse winds separated his vessels, and all three came ashore near the country of the Saracens, very near to Cape Bojador; and M. de Bethencourt and his people landed and remained a week in the country, and took and carried away men and women, and more than three thousand camels, but they could not take them on board, so they

chappelle des vestemens, vne image de nostre Dame, et des veste- mens d'église, et vn fort beau messel et deux petites cloches chacune d'vn cent pesant; et ordonna qu'on appellast la *Chap- pelle nostre Dame de Bethencourt;* et fut Messire Jean Verrier curé du pays, et y vescut le demourant de sa vie bien aise. Et Monsieur de Bethencourt eust esté vne piece de temps au pays, il print iournée d'aller à la grand' Canare. Il ordonna que ce seroit le sixiesme iour d'Octobre mil cccc et v ; et en icelle iournées il fut prest pour y aller à tout les nouueaux hommes qu'il auoit amenés et plusieurs autres, et se mirent en mer iceluy iour, et se partirent trois galeres, dont les deux estoient audit seigneur, et l'autre estoit venue du royaume d'Espaigne que le Roy luy auoit enuoyée. Fortune vint dessus la mer que les barges furent departis, et vindrent tous trois pres des terres Sarrazines bien près du port de Bugeder, et là descendit Monsieur de Bethen- court et ses gens, et furent bien huict lieux dedans le pays, et prindrent hommes et femmes qu'ils emmenerent auec eux, et plus de trois mille chameaux ; mais ils ne les peurent receuiller au

killed and potted some of them, and then they made their way back to the Great Canary, as M. de Bethencourt had arranged; but fortune interfered with their course in such a manner, that of the three vessels one reached Erbanie, the second came to the island of Palma, and there remained until the arrival of the third, in which was M. de Bethencourt, under great opposition from the people of the country.

CHAPTER LXXXV.—How Monsieur de Bethencourt went to the Great Canary, and of the great battle of his people, who, by their presumption were defeated by the Canarians.

Soon afterwards M. de Bethencourt proceeded to Great Canary, and several conferences took place between him and King Artamy. Now there came there one of the vessels which had been on the coast of Bojador, in which were some of my lord's people, namely, Jean le Courtois, Guillaume d'Auberbosc, Hannibal, d'Andrac, and several other companions. When they arrived, they were somewhat proud of having advanced so far on the mainland of

nauire, et en tuerent et iarerent, et puis s'en retournerent à la grand' Canare, comme Monsieur de Bethencourt l'auoit ordonné. Mais fortune les print au chemin, que des trois barges l'vne arriua en Erbanie, et l'autre deuziesme en l'isle de Palmes, et la demourerent iusques à tant que l'autre barge, là où estoit Monsieur de Bethencourt, fust arriuée en faisant guerre à ceux du pays.

[CHAPITRE LXXXV.]—(*Comme ledit Sieur ala à la grant Canare.*)

Tantost apres Monsieur de Bethencourt s'en alla à la grand' Canare, et par plusieurs fois parlerent ensemble luy et le Roy Artamy, et là arriua vne des barges qui auoit esté à la coste de Bugeder, en laquelle estoit des gens de mondit Sieur de Bethencourt, vn nommé Jehan le Courtois, Guillaume d'Auberbosc, Hanybal, Dendrac, et plusieurs autres compagnons. Quand ils furent là arriuez ils furent vn peu orguillieux de ce qu'ils estoient si autant entrez en terre ferme au pays des Sarrazins; là dit vn

the Saracens. Then boasted a Norman, named Guillaume
d'Auberbosc, that, with twenty men at most, he could
easily cross the entire island of Great Canary, in spite of
all the Canarians, although they were stated to be full ten
thousand fighting men; and, contrary to the wish of M. de
Bethencourt, they commenced their skirmish, and landed
at a village called Arguyneguy, in two boats, containing
forty-five men, amongst whom were some of Gadifer's people,
and drove the Canarians well back into the country, but
were themselves very disorderly. When the Canarians
observed this want of order amongst them, they rallied and
fell upon them and defeated them. They gained possession
of one of the boats, and slew two-and-twenty men. In that
affair died Guillaume d'Auberbosc, the originator of the
skirmish, Geoffry d'Auzonville, Guillaume d'Allemagne, Jean
le Courtois, the Sieur de Bethencourt's lieutenant, Hannibal,
Gadifer's bastard, one named Seguirgal, Girard de Sombray,
Jean Chevalier, and several others.

Normant nommé Guillaume d'Auberbosc que à tout vingt hommes
il cuideroit biē trauerser toute l'isle de la grand' Canare, malgré
tous les Canariens, lesquels se dient bien dix mil hommes de
deffence ; et contre la volonté de Monsieur de Bethencourt, commencerent l'escarmouche, et descendirent à terre, à vn village
nommé *Arguyneguy*, en deux bateaux quarante-cinq hommes,
et y eu auoit de ceux qui estoient à Gadifer, et rebouterent les
Canares bien auant à la terre, et se desordonnerent moult. Quand
les Canares virent leur desarroy, ils se relierent et leur coururent
sus, et les desconfirent, et gagnerent l'vn des basteaux, et tuerent
vingt-deux hōmes ; là mourut Guillaume d'Auberbosc, qui auoit
fait et commencé l'escarmouche, Geuffroy d'Auzonuille, Guillaume
d'Allemagne, Jehan le Courtois lieutenant dudit Sieur de Bethencourt, Hanybal bastart de Gadifer, vng lecto[1] nommé Seguirgal,
Girard de Sombray, Jehan Chevalier, and plusieurs autres.

---

[1] Unintelligible, but so in the MS.

CHAPTER LXXXVI.—How the Sieur de Bethencourt left the Great
Canary.

After this M. de Bethencourt took his departure from the
Great Canary with both his vessels, and such of his people
as had escaped from that day's conflict, and proceeded to
the island of Palma, where he found his other vessel, the
crew of which had landed and made severe war upon the
natives. He also landed, and advanced into the heart of
the country, and had several encounters with the enemy,
and losses ensued on both sides, but much more among the
Canarians than among us. Five of our people died, and
more than a hundred of theirs. After they had remained
six weeks in the country, they returned to their vessels,
which were awaiting them. Then two vessels were directed
to go to the island of Ferro, and there they remained three
months; and when they had been there for that length of
time, Monsieur determined to send an interpreter to the
inhabitants of the island, by name Augeron, who came from

[CHAPITRE LXXXVI.]—*Comme ledit Sieur se partit de la grant
Canare.*

Apres se partit Monsieur de Bethencourt de la grand' Canare à
tout ses deux barges qui là estoient, auec aucuns qui estoient
eschappés d'icelle iournée, et passa outre iusques en l'isle de
Palmes, là où il trouua l'autre barge qui estoit descenduë à terre,
et faisoient grosse guerre à ceux de l'isle : si dessendit Monsieur
de Bethencourt à terre auec eux, et lui et ces gens entrerent bien
auant au pays et eurent à faire par plusieurs fois à leurs ennemis,
et en furent de morts de costé et d'autre, et beaucoup plus de
Canares que des nostres. Il mourut cinque de nos gens, et il en
mourut des leurs plus de cent; apres qu'il eurēt demouré six
sepmaines au pays, ils se recueillirent aux barges qui les attendoient. Adonc fut ordonné deux barges pour aller en l'isle de Fer,
là où ils demourerent bien trois mois; et quand ils eurent esté
si longuement, monsieur s'aduisa qu'il enuoyeroit à ceux du pays
vn truchement nommé Augeron, lequel estoit de Gomere, et

Gomera, and who had been with M. de Bethencourt in Arragon before he started for the present expedition, having been provided for him by the King of Spain, named Don Enrique, *i.e.*, Henry, and Queen Catherine. This interpreter, Augeron, M. de Bethencourt sent to the inhabitants of this island of Ferro, he being brother to the king of the island; and he managed so well, that he decoyed the king his brother, and a hundred and eleven persons with him, by means of his assurances, and brought them into the presence of M. de Bethencourt, who kept for his own share thirty-one of them, of whom the king was the first: the rest were divided as spoil and sold for slaves. This Monsieur did for two reasons: to appease his companions, and also to provide dwellings for those whom he had brought from Normandy, by way of not causing displeasure to the inhabitants of Lancerote and Fuerteventura. For it was necessary that he should establish these people in these islands; and, in fact, he settled there a hundred and twenty households, consisting of those who were best acquainted with agriculture, while the rest

l'auoit eu ledit seigneur en Arragon dés deuant qu'il vint à la conqueste, et luy fit auoir le Roy d'Espagne qui s'apelloit le Roy Donnerique cest à dire Henry, et la Royne s'appelloit Katheline. Ledit seigneur enuoya iceluy truchement aux Canares d'icelle isle de Fer, et estoit iceluy Augeron frere du roy de ceste isle; et tant feit iceluy truchement, qu'il amena son frere roy du pays, et cent et onze personnes soubs celle asseurance, et furent amenez deuers Monsieur de Bethencourt, et en retint Monsieur de Bethencourt pour sa part trente et vn, dont le roy estoit le premier, les autres furent departis au butin, et y en eut de vendus comme esclaues; et ce fit monsieur pour deux causes, pour appaiser les compagnons, et aussi pour y bouter des mesnages que ledit seigneur auoit amené de son pais de Normandie, à celle fin qu'il ne fist pas si grand desplaisir à ceux de Lancelot et de Fortauenture. Car il eust fallu qu'il eut mis esdits compaignons et mesnagiers aux dites isles de Lancelot et fortauenture, desquels il y en eut six vingts mesnages de ladite compagnie, et de ceux qui cognoissoient mieux le labour, et le demourant fut

were placed in the islands of Fuerteventura and Lancerote. But for these people thus established there by M. de Bethencourt, the island of Ferro would have been left utterly deserted, without a living creature in it. On other occasions it has been several times depopulated, and the natives taken prisoners. However, it is one of the pleasantest islands in those parts, considering its size.

CHAPTER LXXXVII.—How the Sieur de Bethencourt arranged the apportionment of the land, and of the administration of justice and the government of the country.

After that M. de Bethencourt had conquered the islands of Palma and of Ferro, he returned to Fuerteventura with his two vessels, and took up his quarters in the tower of Baltarhayz, which Messire Gadifer had commenced building while he was in Spain; and he arranged many things in this country which it would take a long time to describe. He established, as I have stated, a hundred and twenty

---

mis és isles de Forte-auenture et lille de Lancelot; et se n'eust esté icelles gens que Monsieur de Bethencourt y mist, l'isle de Fer eust esté deserte, et sans creature du monde. Autrefois et plusieurs fois elle à esté desheritée de gens, et les a en prins tousiours, et toutes fois c'est vne des plus plaisantes isles qui soit en pays par deça, d'autant de pays qu'elle contient.

[CHAPITRE LXXXVII.]— (Comment le Sieur de Bethencourt ordonne du departement des terres, et de la iustice et police du pays.)

Appres que Monsieur de Bethencourt eut conquis l'isle de Palme et celle de Fer, ledit seigneur s'en reuint en l'isle de Forte-auenture auec ses deux barges, et se logea à la tour de Baltarhays que Messire Gadifer auoit commencé à faire tandis qu'il estoit en Espagne, et ordonna beaucoup de choses en ce pays qui longues seroient à raconter : Il logea ceux qu'il auoit amenés, comme i'ay dit, six vingts en l'isle de Fer, et le demourāt en lille de Forte-

households in the island of Ferro, and placed the remainder in Fuerteventura and Lancerote. To each he allotted portions of land, manors, and houses, and dwellings, to every one as it seemed good to him, and managed so well that every one was satisfied, and he decreed that none of the people whom he had brought from his own country should pay anything whatever for nine years, but at the end of nine years they were to pay like the others, that is to say, a fifth—the fifth head of cattle, the fifth bushel of corn ; in fact, a fifth of everything. With respect to the orchil, nobody was to dare to sell any without the leave of the king and sovereign of the country : it is a plant which may prove of great value to the lord of the land, and grows without cultivation. As for the two priests of Erbanie and Lancerote, it is quite clear that they have a right to their tithes ; but inasmuch as there are many people and little ecclesiastical help, they will only receive a thirtieth when a prelate is appointed ; "and please God, when I leave this," said Monsieur, "I will go to Rome and obtain for this country a bishop, who shall uphold the

auenture et en lisle Lancelot ; et leur bailla à chacun part et portion de terres, de manoirs, maisons et logis a chacun selon qu'il luy sembloit bon et qu'il luy appartenoit ; et fit tant qu'il n'y eut nul qui ne fust contēt, et si ordonna que ceux qu'il auoit amenés de son pays ne payeroiēt quelque chose du monde iusques à neuf ans : et au bout de neuf ans ils payeroient comme les autres ; c'est à dire qu'ils payeroient le quint denier, la cinquiesme beste, le cinquiesme boissel de bled, et de tout le cinquiesme pour toutes charges : et quand au regard de l'oursolle, nulluy ne l'osera vendre sans le cōgé du roy et seigneur du pays : c'est vne graine qui peut valoir beaucoup au seigneur du pais et qui vient sans main mettre. Quand au regard des deux curés d'Erbanie et Lancelot, il est tout notoire qu'ils doiuent auoir le dixiesme : mais pour ce qu'il y a beaucoup de peuple et peu de secours d'Eglise, ils n'auront que le trentiesme, tant qu'il y ait prelat : "et au plaisir de Dieu, quand ie partiray d'icy, i'iray à Rome requerir que vous ayez prelat euesque en ce pais, qui ordonnera et magnifira la foy

discipline and the dignity of the Catholic faith." M. de
Bethencourt then appointed his nephew to be lieutenant and
governor of all the islands which he had conquered, and
commanded him to look to the due observance of God's laws
and to give all possible honour to Him ; and he desired that
the people of the country should be treated with gentleness
and affection. He further directed him to appoint two ser-
geants to each island, who should administer justice under
him and subject to his decisions, and he was to see justice
done to the best of his knowledge, as the case might require.
The gentry who remained behind should be well regulated
in their lives ; and if any judgment had to be given, these
gentlemen should be first summoned, in order that a decision should be come to after great deliberation by several
people chosen as the wisest and most notable amongst them.
This decree I have made, he said, in accordance with God's
commandments, and with a view to the increase of the
population. "And I command that every year, at least
twice, you send news to me in Normandy of the welfare of
the islands ; and that the revenues derived from the islands

Catholique." En apres ledit seigneur ordonna son lieutenant et
gouuerneur de toutes les isles, que ledit seigneur a conquestées,
et luy commenda comment il feust, que Dieu y soit seruy et
honnoré tout le mieux que l'on peut, et que les gens du pais
feussent tenus doucement et amoureusement ; et si luy commanda
qu'il fist à chacune isle deux sergens qui aucunement auroient le
gouuernement de iustice soubs luy et soubs sa deliberatiō : et
qu'il fist iustice ainsi qu'il pourra congnoître que le cas le requert ;
que les gentilshommes qui y demeureront soient de bon gouuernement, et que s'il y auoit aucun iugement à faire, que premier
iceux gentilshommes y soient appellez, à celle fin que le iugement
soit fait par grande deliberation de plusieurs gens, et des plus
sçachāts, et des plus notables ; et tant que Dieu y ait ordonné, et
que le pays soit plus peuplé, i'ordōne qu' ainsi soit fait. "Aussi
i'ordōne que tous les ans du moins deux fois enuoyez en Normandie vers moy, et m'enuoyez des nouuelles de par deça ; et que
le revenu qui sera desdites isles Lancelot et Forteauēture soit mis

of Lancerote and Fuerteventura shall be applied to the
erection of two churches, such as my gossip Jean, the
mason, shall design and construct; for I have already explained to him how I should like them built, and I have
brought carpenters and masons sufficient to perform the
work well. With respect to your own provision and allowance
for maintenance, it is my wish that whereas five deniers belong
to me, you are to have one of those five as long as you shall live
in the country acting as my lieutenant. The rest of the re-
venue for five years from this time is to be devoted to the
churches and other such edifices as you and the said Jean, the
mason, may plan, whether it be for repairs or for new buildings. Furthermore, I give you full power and authority to
command and to have put into execution all things that you
shall see to be for the profit and honour of all, but having
regard, in the first instance, to my honour and profit. As
near as you possibly can, observe the customs of France and
of Normandy in the administration of justice and all other
points, where you see it advisable. And I beg and charge
you to do all in your power to preserve peace and unity

à faire deux églises telles que Jehan le Masson mon compere
ordōnera et edifiera; car autre fois ie luy ay conté et dit comme
je les veux auoir. Car i'ay amené charpentiers et massons assez
pourquoy on le peut bien faire; et quant est de vostre prouision
et pour vos gages pour vous viure, ie veux que s'il m'appartiēt
5. deniers de la reuenuë qui issira desdites isles, que vous en ayez
vn à tousiours tāt que vous viurez et ferey en ce pays mō lieu-
tenāt: et du surplus de la reuenuë, que de cy à cinq ans il soit
mis aux eglises, et l'autre part en edifices tel que vous et le dit
Jean le Masson ordōnerez, soit en reparatiō ou en nouueaux
edifices; et outre ie vous ōdne pleine pouuoir et auctorité que en
tout choses que vous verrez qu'il sera profit et honneste, vous
ordōniez ou faciez faire, en sauuant mon honneur premier et
profit. Et qu'au plus pres que vous pourez que vous teniez les
coustumes de France et Normādie, c'est à dire en iustice, et en
autre chose que vous verrez bō faire. Aussi ie vous prie et charge
que le plus que vous pourrez vous ayez paix et vnion ensēble, et que

amongst you, and that you love one another as brothers, and especially amongst you gentlemen let there be no feelings of envy or rivalry. I have appointed to each your part. The country is large enough ; conciliate one another, maintain good relations one with the other, and help one another. I know not what more to say to you, except that above all things you keep at peace amongst yourselves, and then all will go well."

CHAPTER LXXXVIII.—How Monsieur de Bethencourt rode about the country, and re-explored it.

The Sieur de Bethencourt had two mules which had been given to him by the King of Spain, on which he rode when he paid his visits to the different islands. He remained three months in the country after his return from the Great Canary, and he rode about the islands, speaking very kindly to the natives through three interpreters who accompanied him ; for by that time there were a good many who spoke and understood the language of the country, especially those

---

vous entreaimiez tous cōme freres, et specialemēt entre vous gentiles hōmes n'ayez point enuie les vns sur les autres. Je vous ay à chacun ordonné vostre fait, le païs est assez large, appaisez l'vn l'autre et vous apparentez de l'vn l'autre, et aidez l'vn à l'autre. Ie ne vous sçaurois plus que dire, fors que principalement vous ayez paix ensemble, et tout se portera bien.'

[CHAPITRE LXXXVIII.] — (Comme Monsieur de Bethencourt chevauches par le pais en le revisitant.)

Le dit Seigneur auoit deux mules que le Roy d'Espagne luy auoit donnés, qu'il cheuauchoit parmy les isles. Si fut trois mois en iceluy païs apres qu'il fut venu de la grant' Quenare, et en icelles isles il cheuaucha et chemina par tout en parlant bien doucement au peuple du païs auecques trois truchemens qu'il auoit auec luy. Iaçoit qu'il y auoit desia beaucoup de gens qui parloient et entendoient le langage du païs, parespecial ceux qui

who had come first at the beginning of the conquest. During his progresses he was accompanied by Maciot, and by the other gentlemen whom he wished to take up their residences in the country, as well as Jean the mason, and other mechanics. There were carpenters and people of all trades, who thus rode about with him, and he showed and explained to them all his plans, and heard their opinions ; and when he had explored the whole country as far as he was able, and had explained all his plans and wishes, he caused it to be proclaimed everywhere that he intended to start on that day month, which would be the 15th day of December ; and that if any had requests to prefer to their king and sovereign, they were to come to him, and he would do whatever was necessary to meet their wishes. He then proceeded to Rubicon, in the Island of Lancerote, and remained there until his departure, which took place on the day above mentioned. Several people of different grades came to him belonging to the islands of Lancerote and Fuerteventura ; but as for the island of Ferro none came from thence, for there

---

y estoient venus au premier de la conqueste ; et là en cheuauchant le pays estoit auec luy ledit Maciot et les autres gentils-hommes, lesquels il vouloit qu'ils demourassent au pays, et si y estoit Jehan le Masson et autres du mestier ; il y avoit charpetiers et gens de tous mestiers qui cheminoiēt auec luy, et ledit seigneur leur monstroit et deuisoit ce qu'il vouloit en les oyant et escoutant parler. Et quand il eust esté par tout le païs au mieux qu'il peut, et qu'il eut devisé ce qu'il luy sembloit estre bon de faire, il fit crier par le païs qu'il se partiroit à d'auiourd'huy en vn mois, qui seroit le quinziesme iour de Decembre ; et que s'il y auoit nul qui vouloist rien deuers le roy et sieur du païs, qu'ils vinssent vers luy, et qu'il fairoit tant que chacun seroit content. Ledit seigneur vint à Rubicon en l'sle Lancelot, et se tint là iusques à son partement, qui fut le iour deuant dit xvᵉ jour de Decembre, il luy vint plusieurs gens, et de plusieurs façons dela dite isle de Lancelot et Fort-auenture. Quand au regard de l'isle de Fer, il n'y en vint nuls ; car il n'y en estoit point demouré si peu que

were hardly any left, and such as were there had completely submitted to the people M. de Bethencourt had left there; nor did any come from Gomera. As for the island of Lobos, it has no inhabitants; there are only some animals called sea-wolves, but which, as I have elsewhere said, are very valuable. The King of Lancerote, who was a Saracen, came to Monsieur de Bethencourt, and besought him, as his true lord and sovereign, to grant him a place to live in, with a certain quantity of land for tillage and sustenance. Monsieur de Bethencourt answered that it was his earnest wish that he should have a larger mansion and homestead than any other Canarian in that island, with a sufficiency of land attached thereto, but that neither he nor any other should hold fortresses therein. M. de Bethencourt then assigned to him a residence which he had asked for in the middle of the island, with about three hundred acres of wood and land round it, subject to the tax which the said lord had decreed; namely, one-fifth of everything. The Canarian king was very contented, for he had never expected so much, and, to

non, et ce qui estoit demouré n'estoit point pour resister à l'encontre de ceux que Monsieur de Bethencourt auoit ordonné d'y aller et demourer. Aussi de la Gomere il ne vint nuls. Au regard de l'isle de Louppes, il n'y demeure personne, et n'y a que bestes qu'on appelle loups marins qui vallēt beaucoup, comme autrefois i'ay dit. Il luy vint le roy qui estoit Sarrazin, de l'isle Lancelot, qui demanda son vray seigneur et roy du pais Monsieur de Bethencourt, s'il luy plaisoit bailler et donner le lieu là où il demourroit, et certaine quantité de terres pour labourer et pour uiure. Monsieur de Bethencourt luy octroya qu'il vouloit biē qu'il eust hostel et mesnage plus que nul autre des Canariens d'icelle isle, et des terres suffisamment; mais de forteresse il n'auroit point ny nul du païs. Ledit seigneur luy bailla vng hostel qu'il demanda qui estoit au milieu de l'isle, et si luy bailla enuiron trois cens acres que bois que terre au tour de son hostel, en faisant le truage que ledit seigneur auoit ordonné, c'est à dire le cinquiesme de toutes choses. Le dit roy Canarien fut fort content : il ne cuidoit iamais auoir si bien ; et à dire vray il eut

tell the truth, he had the best land in the whole country for tillage, so that he knew well what he was about when he asked for that spot. Several others came—both Normans and Canarians—and were well satisfied with their allotments. The two kings of Fuerteventura, who had been baptized, came to the Sieur de Bethencourt, and, in like manner, he assigned them localities according to their demands ; and allotted to each of them four hundred acres of wood and land, and they were very contented. The nobles from his own country he located in the fortresses, so that they were well satisfied.   Those, also, who came from Normandy were domiciled as each thought right and fit. It was reasonable that they should be better accommodated than the Canarians of the country. M. de Bethencourt succeeded in pleasing every one ; he arranged a great number of other things which it would take long to describe, and therefore I will pass them by, and speak of his return, and how he commanded all the gentlemen whom he had brought back with him, as well as those who were in the country before, to

tout des meilleures terres du païs pour labourer ; aussi il cognois-soit bien le lieu qu'il demandoit. Plusieurs autres y vindrent et de ceux de Normandie et des Canares d'icelle isle, et chacun fut contenté selon ce qu'il le valloit. Les deux roys qui s'estoient fait baptiser de l'isle Fort'-auenture vindrent vers ledit Sieur de Bethencourt, et pareillement le dit seigneur leur bailla lieu et place, ainsi que aucunement le requeroient, et leur bailla à chacun quatre cens acres que bois que terres, et furent fort conteus dudit seigneur. Ledit Seigneur logea les gentilshommes de son païs és fortes places, et fit tant qu'ils furent contens, et les autres pareillement du païs de Normandie, furent logez chacun selon qu'il sembloit estre de raison et de faire. C'estoit bien raison qu'il fussent mieux que les Canariens du pays : le dit Seigneur fit tant que chacun fut content ; il ordonna plusieurs choses qui longues seroient à raconter, et partant ie m'en tais, et veux parler de son retour, et comme il commanda à tous les gentils-hommes qu'il auoit amenez, et ceux qui estoient auparauant au

present themselves before him two days before his departure, as well as all the masons and carpenters; and he also
invited the three Canarian kings to be present on that occasion, when he would announce to them his last wishes,
and commend them to God's care.

CHAPTER LXXXIX.—How Monsieur de Bethencourt gave a banquet
and festival to all his friends in that country by way of farewell.

On the second day before his departure M. de Bethencourt was at the castle of Rubicon, and there made a great
feast to all the gentlemen and to the three kings who had
come at his invitation. There were present also Jean the
Mason, and all the other masons and carpenters, and several
other people from Normandy, as well as natives of the
country, who all dined and feasted on that day in the castle
of Rubicon. After M. de Bethencourt had dined, he seated
himself upon a slightly raised chair, at that end of the room
from which it was easiest to make himself heard, for there

pays, qu'ils fussent deux iours deuant son partement deuers luy;
et aussi que tous les massons et charpentiers y fussent, et si
voulut que les trois Roys Canariens y fussent, et que à iceluy
iour il leur diroit sa volonté et les recommanderoit à Dieu.

[CHAPITRE LXXXIX].—*Comment ledit Sieur a tous ces amis du
pais pour leur dire a Dieu leur donna a diner et les festia.*

Le deuxiesme iour deuant le partement de Monsieur de Bethencourt, lequel estoit au chasteau de Rubicon, là où il fit icelle
iournee fort grand' chere à tous les gentils-hommes, et à iceux
trois roys lesquels s'y trouuerent, ainsi qu'il auoit commandé;
et y estoit iceluy Jean le Masson, et autres massons et charpentiers, et plusieurs autres du pays de Normandie et du pays
mesmes; lesquels tous disnerent et mangerent iceluy iour au
chastel de Rubicon. Et quand ledit Seigneur eut disné il s'assit
en vne chaire vng peu haut a celle fin qu'on l'ouït plus aise, car

were more than two hundred persons present, and he
addressed the company in the following words: "My friends
and Christian brethren, it has pleased God our Creator to
pour out his mercy upon us and upon this country, which
at this moment is Christian and converted to the Catholic
faith, which faith may He graciously vouchsafe to maintain,
and may He grant to me and to you all to know how to conduct the affairs of this country so that what we do shall
redound to the glory and advancement of Christianity. In
order that you may know why I have summoned you all
here to-day, I will tell you that my main object is to bind
you together in brotherly affection, and I have called you
together that you may know from my mouth the orders
which I wish to give, and which I desire may be faithfully
carried out. First, I appoint my relative, Maciot de Bethencourt, to be my representative and governor of all these
islands, and controller of all my affairs, whether in matters
of war or justice, the erection of buildings and repairs, or
the formation of new laws, according as he shall see that

---

il y auoit plus de deux cens personnes; et là ledit Seigneur
cōmença à parler: " Mes amis et mes freres Chrestiens, il a pleu
à Dieu nostre Createur qu'il a estēdu sa grace sur nous et sur
cestuy païs, qui est à ceste heure Chrestien, et mis à la foy
Catholique; et Dieu par sa digne grace le veüille maintenir, et
moy dōner pouuoir et à vous tous de s'y sçauoir si bien conduire,
que ce soit l'exaltation et augmentation de toute Chrestienté : et
pour sçauoir pourquoy i'ay voulu que vous soyez cy tous en
presēce; ie le vous diray: il est vray que pour vous tenir tous
ensemble en amour, ie vous ay assemblez, à celle fin que vous
sçachiez de par ma bouche ce que ie veulx ordonner et ordonneré,
et ce que i'ordonneray ie veux qu'ainsi soit fait. Et premierement i'ordōne Maciot de Bethencourt, mon cousin et mon parent,
mon lieutenant et gouuerneur de toutes les isles, et de toutes mes
affaires, soit en guerre, iustice, en edifices, reparations, nouuelles
ordonnances, selon qu'il verra qni se pourra ou deura faire, et en

such may or ought to be made, and in such manner as he shall see fit to do or cause to be done or to be devised, without any reservation whatever, provided always that first the honour and then the profit of myself and of the country be kept in view. And I entreat and charge you all to obey him as if he were myself, and to have no jealousies amongst you. I have ordered a fifth portion to be reserved for my own benefit, that is to say, the fifth kid, the fifth lamb, the fifth bushel of corn, the fifth of everything. Of these levies and dues, two-fifths shall be reserved for the erection of two fair churches, one in the island of Fuerteventura, the other in the island of Lancerote. Another fifth shall belong to my said cousin Maciot; and, when five years have expired, I shall, please God, do the best that shall lie in my power. And touching what I leave to the said Maciot, I desire that he shall have for his own use a third of the revenues of the country as long as he shall live; and at the expiration of five years he shall be bound to send the surplus of the third of the revenues to my house in Normandy. He shall also

---

quelque maniere qu'il le voudra faire, ou faire faire, ou deuiser sans y rien reseruer, en tousiours gardant l'honneur premier et profit de moy, et du pays. Et à vous tous ie vous prie et charge que vous luy obeyssiez comme à ma personne, et que vous n'ayez point d'enuie les vngs sur les autres; j'ay ordonné et si ordonne que le cinquiesme denier soit à moy, et à mon profit; c'est à dire la cinquiesme chievre, le cinquiesme aignel, le cinquiesme boisel de bled, le cinquiesme de toutes choses; et dessus iceux deniers et debuoirs on prendra iusques à cinq auec les deux parts pour faire deux belles églises, l'vne en l'isle de Fort' auenture, l'autre en l'isle Lancelot; et l'autre part sera audit Maciot mon cousin, et quand ce vendra au bout des cinq ans, ce Dieu plaist, ie feray tout le mieux que ie pourray. Et quand est de ce que ie laisse audit Maciot, ie veux qu'il ait le tiers de la reuenuë du païs à tousiours tant qu'il viura; et au bout de cinq ans il sera tenu de m'enuoyer le surplus du tiers de la reuenuë à mō hostel en Nor-

be bound to send me every year a report of the progress of the country. Furthermore, I pray and charge you all that you be good Christians, that you serve God well, that you love Him and fear Him, that you attend church, and promote and observe the laws to the best of your knowledge and abilities, until God shall give you a pastor, I mean a prelate, who shall have the direction of your souls, and, please God, I will take pains that there shall be such an one; and when I leave this I will, if God permit me, go to Rome and entreat the Pope to send you one. God grant that I may live to do this. And now," said M. de Bethencourt, "if any one wishes to say anything to me, or to ask my opinion on any point, I pray him to speak now, without omitting any point, whether small or great, and I will attend to him most willingly." Nó one had a suggestion to make, but all said unanimously, " We have nothing to say. You, sir, have so well spoken, that it is impossible for us to offer any idea or remark by way of improvement." Every one was contented, and very pleased that Maciot

---

mandie. Et si sera tenu tous les ans de m'enuoyer des nouuelles de ce pays. En outre, ie vous prie et charge que tous vous soyez bons Chrestiens, et seruiez bien Dieu ; aymez-le, et le craignez, allez à l'eglise, et augmentez, et gardez les droits au mieux que vous sçaurez, et pourrez ; en attendant qne Dieu vous ait donné vn pasteur, c'est à dire vng prelat, qui ait le gouuerne-ment de vos ames ; et, se Dieu plaist, ie mettray peine qu'il y en aura vng ; et quand ie me partiray à Rome requerir au Pape que vous en ayez, jay dit ung pateur cest a dire ung evesque qui ara le gouuernement de vos ames. Et Dieu me doint la grace de tant viure de ce faire. Or çà, ce dit ledit Seigneur, s'il y a quelque vng qui me veüille dire ou aduiser de quelque chose, ie luy prie que à ceste heure il le dise, et qu'il ne laisse point soit petit ou grand, et ie l'orray tres voulontiers." Il ny eust nulluy qui disist mot, mais disoient tous ensemble, nous ne sçaurions que dire, Monsieur a si bien dit que l'on ne sçauroit ne penser ne dire mieux. Chacun estoit content, et si estoient bien ioyeux que

should have the government of the country. M. de Bethencourt had made this appointment because he was of his
name and lineage. He then selected those whom he wished
to take with him to Rome. Messire Jean le Verrier, his
chaplain, curé of Rubicon, wished to go with M. de Bethencourt, who would have been very glad that he should remain behind, but he prayed to be allowed to accompany
him. He took Jean de Boville, his squire, and six others
of his household, and no more. One was his cook, another
his valet de chambre, and another his groom; each had his
office. At length, on the fifteenth day of December, M. de
Bethencourt set sail in one of his vessels. The other he
left at Rubicon, and charged Maciot to send it as soon as
possible after Easter to Normandy, to the port of Harfleur,
and that he would load it with native productions and
despatch it without fail.

Maciot auoit le gouuernement du pays, et ledit Seigneur le fit
pour ce qu'il estoit du nom et de la ligne. Ledit Seigneur
ordonna ceux qu'il vouloit auoir auecques luy à Rome; Messire
Jehan le Verrier son chapellain, curé de Rubicon, voulut aller
auecques ledit Seigneur, jaçoit que ledit Seigneur eust bien voulu
qu'il fust demeuré, mais il pria Monsieur qu'il luy tinst compagnie.
Il print Jean de Bouille escuyer, et six autres de sa maison, et
non plus; l'vn estoit cuisinier, et lautre estoit varlet de chambre
pallefrenier; chacun auoit son office. Et quand ce vint au quinziesme iour de Decembre ledit Seigneur se mit en mer en l'vne
de ces barges, et l'autre barge il la laissa à Rubicon, et chargea
ledit Maciot que le plutost qu'il pourroit apres Pasques passez,
il renuoyast ladite barque en Normandie à Herfleur; et qu'il la
chargeast des nouueautez du pays, et qu'il n'y eust point de
faute.

CHAPTER XC.—How the Sieur de Bethencourt left the Canary Islands
to go to Normandy, never again to return.

After Monsieur de Bethencourt had taken leave of all his
people, and of the whole country, and had set sail, all the inhabitants were to be seen weeping and lamenting, the Canarians more bitterly than the Normans; but the grief and
lamentations of both were distressing to witness. Their
hearts told them that they would never see him again, and that
he would never return to the country; and they were right,
for he never came back again. But though these dreaded
it, they prayed him to return without delay. Others threw
themselves into the sea, holding on to the vessel in which
M. de Bethencourt was. No one would suppose to what an
extent they took it to heart. "Our leader and master," they
cried, "why do you leave us? We shall never see you again!
Alas, what will the country do, deserted by a sovereign so wise
and so prudent, who has put so many souls into the road of

[CHAPITRE XC.]—Comment ledit sieur se partit des Ysles de Canare
pour sen venir en Normandie, et onquez plus ny retourna.

Apres que Monsieur de Bethencourt eut prins congé de tous
ses gens et de tout le païs, et se mit en mer, vous eussiez veu
tout le peuple crier et braire, et plus encore les Canariens que
ceux du païs de Normandie; c'estoit pitié des pleurs et des
gemissemēs que les vngs et les autres faisoient. Leurs cœurs
leur disoient qu'ils ne le voirroient iamais plus, et qu'il ne
vendroit james plus au pays: et il fut vray, car iamais oncques
plus n'y fut. Si ne luy estoit par aduis qu'il n'y reuint, et le
plus bref qu'il pouuoit. Il y en eut aucuns qui se bouterent en
la mer iusques aux aisselles en tirant à la barque là où Monsieur
estoit. Il leur faisoit tant de mal que ledit Seigneur s'en alloit
que nul ne sçauroit penser, et disoit ainsi nostre droicturier
Seigneur, pourquoy nous laissez vous? nous ne vous verrons
iamais! Las! que fera le pays, quãd il faut que vng tel Seigneur
si sage et si prudent, et qui a mis tant d'ames en voye de salua-

eternal salvation! We should like it much better were it otherwise, and if such had been his pleasure." But if the people of the islands were grieved at M. de Bethencourt's departure, it was more painful to him to go away and leave them, for he felt inwardly sure that he should never return. His heart was so full that he could not speak, even to bid them farewell. Not to any one, whether relative or friend, did he find it in his power to utter the word adieu, for when he tried to say it his heart was so full that he could not speak. And now that he is starting, and that they have hoisted sail, may God of his grace be pleased to guard him from evil and disaster. He had a tolerably fair wind, and in seven days reached Seville, where he received a hearty welcome, and remained three or four days. He inquired where the King of Spain then was, and they told him he was at Valladolid, and he went thither to him. The King of Spain received him even more graciously than he had ever done before; for he had heard a good deal about the conquest, and how M. de Bethencourt had

---

tion eternelle, qu'il nous laisse; nous aymissiōs biē mieux qu'il fust autremēt, si c'estoit sō plaisir : et se le peuple des dites isles leur faisoit mal de son allee, encore faisoit plus de mal audit Seigneur d'en partir et de les laisser : car le cœur luy disoit bien qu'il n'y viendroit iamais, il auoit le cœur si serré qu'il ne pouuoit parler, et ne leur pouuoit dire à Dieu, ne il ne fut oncques en la puissance dudit Seigneur qu'il sceust proferer de la bouche de dire à nul quelconque, tant fut son parēt et amy, adieu; et quand il vouloit dire ce mot, il auoit le cœur si tres-estreint qu'il ne le pouuoit dire. Or se part ledit Seigneur de Bethencourt, et est le voile leué; Dieu par sa grace le veüille garder de mal et d'encombrié. Ledit Seigneur eut assez bon vent, et arriua en sept iours à Siuille, là où on luy fit fort grand' chere, et y fut trois ou quatre iours. Il s'enquerut là où estoit le Roy d'Espagne; on luy dit qu'il estoit à Valladolid, et là s'en alla vers luy : lequel Roy d'Espagne luy fit encores plus grand chere qu'il n'auoit oncques fait : car ledit roy auoit bien ouy parler de sa

had the natives baptized, and all by fair and honourable means. When M. de Bethencourt came into the presence of the King of Spain and had made his obeisance to him, the king received him very graciously; if he had formerly welcomed him warmly, he now did so in a yet more marked manner. The king inquired of him how the act of conquest had been brought about, and of the manner and fashion of it. Monsieur de Bethencourt related everything as well as he could, and the king took so much pleasure in listening to his narrative that he never got tired. M. de Bethencourt remained fifteen days at the court of Spain. The king gave him great presents, sufficient to enable him to accomplish the journey which he contemplated, and gave him two handsome jennets, and an excellent and very handsome mule, which carried M. de Bethencourt all the way to Rome. When he left the island of Lancerote he had given one of his mules to Maciot de Bethencourt, and had only brought away one. When he had stayed sufficiently long at the court of Spain, and felt that it was time for him to take his departure, he went to take leave of the king,

---

conqueste, et comme il auoit fait tout baptiser, et tout par beaux et bons moyens. Quand Monsieur de Bethencourt vint deuers le Roy d'Espagne, et qu'il luy eut fait la reuerence, ledit roy le recueillit fort honnestement, et si autrefois il luy auoit fait grand' chere, encore luy fit-il plus grande: le roy luy demanda comment le faict de la conqueste auoit esté, et la maniere et la façon; et ledit Seigneur luy raconta tout le mieux qu'il peut, et tant que roy fut si aise de l'ouïr parler qu'il ne luy enuuyoit point. Ledit Seigneur fut quinze iours à la cour du Roy Despagne. Le roy luy donna de grands dons assez pour aller au voyage là où il vouloit aller; et luy donna deux beaux genets et vne mule fort bonne et bien belle, qui porta ledit Seigneur iusques à Rome. Quand il partit de l'isle Lancelot, il donna vne de ses deux mulles à Maciot de Bethencourt et n'en ramena qu'vne. Et quand ledit Seigneur eut esté assez longuement à la cour du Roy d'Espagne, et qu'il estoit temps qu'il se partist, il voulut

and thus addressed him: " Sire, with your permission, I would wish to beg of you one favour." " Name it," said the king. " Sire, it is very true what I have told you about the conquest of the country of the Canary Islands, which extend over more than forty French leagues,[1] and the inhabitants are a very fine race; but it is very requisite that they should receive exhortation and instruction from a man of dignified bearing and position, who should be their pastor and bishop; and I think he would live very well there, and he would have enough to occupy him; and, besides, the whole country will graduallysubmit, and so, please God, the domain will constantly be on the increase. If you would be graciously pleased to write to the Pope to ask for a bishop, to you will be due the bringing of these people to a state of great perfection, and the salvation of the souls of these as well as of those who are to come hereafter." The king replied: " M. de Bethencourt, it will not be my fault if I do not write. What you say is excellent, and could not be better. I will do it most willingly, and

---

prendre congé du roy, et luy dit: " Sire, s'il vous plaist, ie vous veux requerre d'vne chose. Or dites, ce dit le roy: Sire, il est biē vray que comme ie vous ay raconté la conqueste du païs des isles de Canare, qui contiennent en tout plus de quarāte lieuës Frāçoises, et y a de beau peuple: il est besoin qu'ils soient exhortez et monstrés par vng homme de biē qui soit leur pasteur et leur prelat; et il me semble qu'il y viura bien, et qu'il y aura assez de quoy pour soy entretenir; et aussi le païs se rendra, et se sera et augmentera, se Dieu plaist, tousiours de mieux en mieux. S'il vous plaist de vostre grace en rescrire au Pape qu'il y ait vng euesque, vous serés cause de leur grād perfection et saluation de leurs ames, de ceux qui y sont à present, et de ceux qui sont encore à venir." Respondit le roy, " Monsieur de Bethencourt, il ne tendra pas à moy ne à en rescrire, et dites tres bien, l'on ne sçauroit mieux dire, ie le feray tres-voulontiers,

---

[1] This only refers to the four islands conquered.

I will even write for the individual whom you may wish
to see appointed, if such is your desire." " As to that,
Sire, I know no one to whom to give a preference.
But it is necessary that they should have a bishop who
is a good scholar and who knows the language of the
country. The language of this country [of Spain] is very
similar to that of the country of Canary." The king
answered : " I will send with you a worthy man to accompany you to Rome, who is a very good scholar, and both
speaks and understands the Canary tongue well ; and I will
write to the Pope and explain your case as it stands
and as you have described it to me, and I think and believe
that he will not refuse you, but give you a very favourable
reception. Indeed, I think he ought to do so." The king
wrote the letters to the Pope as he had promised, and gave
them to M. de Bethencourt. The priest whom the king
had mentioned was called *Alure de las Casas*, that is to say,
Albert of the Houses. M. de Bethencourt was now ready to
start on his voyage to Rome, and he took leave of the king
and went all the way by land with ten others, in handsome

---

et encore ie rescriray pour celuy que vous voudriez qui y fust
mis, se c'est vostre volōté." " Sire, au regard de ce, ie ne sçache
nulluy pl' à l'vn que à l'autre. Mais il est besoing qu'ils ayēt
vng prelat qui soit bō clerc, et qu'il sçache la lāgue du païs, le
lāgage de ce païs approche fort de celuy du païs de Canare." Ce
dit le roy, ie vous bailleray vng hōme de bien auec vous qui vous
cōduira à Rome, et c'est vn tres bon clerc, et si parle bien le
lagage de Canare et les entēd bien ; et ie rescripray au Pape
vostre faict, et tout ainsi qu'il est, et que vous me l'auez conté,
et ie cuide et croy qu'il ne le vous refusera pas, et qu'il vous
receura honnestemēt : car il me semble qu'ainsi le doit-il faire.
Le roy rescript les lettres du Pape ainsi qu'il auoit dit, et les
bailla audit Seigneur, et iceluy clerc que le roy auoit dit, lequel
se nomme *Alure des Cases*, c'est à dire *Albert des Maisons*. Ainsi
ledit Seigneur fut prest de s'en aller en son voyage de Rome, et
print cōgé du roy, et s'en ala ledit Scigneur a Romme tout par

style enough, for he had liveries made for all his people as soon as he arrived in Seville, before he had spoken to the King of Spain, and so he rode on muleback until he reached Rome, as you will hear presently.

CHAPTER XCI.—How Monsieur de Bethencourt presented himself before the Pope to ask for a prelate for the Canary Islands, which request was granted.

Monsieur de Bethencourt arrived at Rome and remained there three weeks; he presented himself before the Pope, and gave him the letters sent by the King of Spain; and when His Holiness had caused them to be read twice over, and had comprehended the substance thoroughly, he summoned M. de Bethencourt, who kissed the Pope's feet, and was thus addressed by him : " You are one of our children, and as such I hold you. You have achieved a goodly deed, and have made a goodly beginning, which will be the forerunner, by God's grace, of a still greater conclusion.

---

terre luy vnziesme assez honnestement, car il fit liurées à tous ses gens des qu'il arriua en Siuille et du deuāt qu'il eust parlé au Roy d'Espagne, et cheuaucha tant qu'il arriua à Rome comme vous orrez cy-apres.

[CHAPITRE XCI].—Comme Monsieur de Bethencourt vint devers le pappe lui requerir quil eut prelat es isles de Canare, laquelle chose luy fut octroyée.

Monsieur de Bethencourt arriua à Rome, et là fut l'espace de trois sepmaines; il se presenta au Pape, et luy bailla les lettres que le Roy d'Espaigne luy enuoyoit; et quand il les eut faire lire par deulx fois, et il eut entendu bien la matiere; il appella Monsieur de Bethencourt, lequel baisa le pied au Pape, qui luy dit: " Vous estes vn de nos enfans, et pour tel ie vous retiens; vous auez fait vng beau faict et vng beau commencemēt, et serez premier cause, se Dieu plaist, de paruenir et faire paruenir

The King of Spain writes me word that you have conquered
certain islands, whose inhabitants have now embraced the
faith of Jesus Christ, and that you have caused them all to
be baptized; for which cause I wish to hold you as my son
and as a son of the Church, because you are the originator
of conquests which other sons [of our Holy Church] shall
hereafter achieve, for, from what I gather, the main-land of
Guinea and Barbary is not far distant from the islands,
indeed only twelve leagues from them. Furthermore, the
King of Spain informs me that you penetrated ten leagues
into the land of Guinea, and that you killed and brought
away Saracens from that country. You are indeed a man
worthy of honour, and it is my wish that you may not be
forgotten, but that you may have now a place amongst
other kings and be mentioned in their list. With respect
to your desire for the appointment of a prelate and bishop
over the country, your reason and your wish are both
praiseworthy, and I consent to appoint whomsoever you
may name, provided he be suitable for the office." M. de

à vne plus grand' chose. Le Roy d'Espaigne icy me rescript
que vous auez conquis certaines isles, lesquelles sont de present
à la foy de Jesus Christ, et les auez faict tous baptiser; pourquoy
ie vous veux tenir mon enfant, et enfant de l'eglise, et serez
cause et cōmencement qu'il y aura d'autres enfans qui conquer-
ront apres plus grand' chose, car ainsi que i'entens le païs de
terre ferme n'est pas loing d'y là, le pays de Guynee, et le pais
de Barbarie ne sōt pas à plus de douze lieuës; encore me rescript
le Roy d'espagne que vous auez esté dedans ledit païs de Guynee
bien dix lieuës, et que vous auez tué et amené des Sarrazins
d'iceluy pays; vous estes bien hōme de quoy on doit tenir cōte,
et veux que vous ne soyez pas mis en oubly, et que vous soyez
mis en escript auec les autres roys, et en leur catalogue; et ce
que vous me demādez que vous ayez vng prelat et euesque au
pays, vostre raison et voulente est honneste, et celuy qui vous
voulez qu'il le soit, puis qu'il est homme suffisant à l'office, ie le
vous octroye." Monsieur de Bethencourt le mercia humblement,

Bethencourt humbly thanked His Holiness, and rejoiced greatly at his success. The Pope asked him several questions as to how he had the courage to go to such a distance from France; to which he made such replies as won the Pope's entire approval; indeed, the more he heard the better pleased he was. His Holiness received him with distinction in his palace and made him handsome presents. After he had been about fifteen days at Rome, he desired to take leave of the Pope. The Bulls were drawn up in due form, and Albert de las Casas was appointed Bishop of all the Canary Islands. Monsieur de Bethencourt then took his leave of the Pope, who gave him his blessing, and desired that he should not hesitate to ask of him whatever might give him pleasure, and that it should be willingly conceded.

---

et fut fort ioyeux qu'il faisoit si bien ses besognes. Le Pape araisonna le dit Seigneur de plusieurs choses; comment son courage luy mouvoit d'aller si loing côme du pays de France? Ledit Seigneur luy respondit tellement que le Pape estoit si content, que tant plus il l'oyoit, et plus ayse estoit: le Pape le fit recuellir honnestement en son hostel, et luy eslargit de ses biens. Et quand il eut esté enuiron quinze iours à Rome, il voulut prendre congé du Pape; les Bulles fuerent faictes ainsi qu'il falloit qu'elles fussent; et fut Monsieur Albert des Maisons Euesque de toutes les Isles de Canare; ledit Seigneur print congé du Pape, lequel luy donna sa benediction, et luy dit qu'il n'espargnast point chose qu'il luy peust faire plaisir, et qu'il le feroit volontiers.

CHAPTER XCII.—How Monsieur de Bethencourt took leave
of the Pope.

When Monsieur de Bethencourt had taken leave of the
Pope, he set out for his own country, although he did not
know what to do about returning to Spain with his bishop.
He returned, however, straight to France to his house in
Normandy. His bishop took leave of him at Rome, and M.
de Bethencourt wrote to the King of Spain : he also commanded the master of the vessel, which had brought him
from Canary to Seville, as soon as he could make up his
cargo, to sail for Harfleur. The vessel set sail, but it was
never known what became of her, except that M. de Bethencourt was informed that some were of opinion that it
foundered at sea near La Rochelle, but that it was laden
with cargo and was making for Harfleur. It was never
heard of afterwards, however, and thus the vessel was lost.
On the bishop's arrival in Spain, he presented himself
before the king and delivered Monsieur de Bethencourt's

[CHAPITRE XCII]—*Comme Monsieur de Bethencourt print congé du
Pappe.*

Quand Monsieur de Bethēcourt eut prins congé du Pape, il
print son chemin à s'en retourner en son pays ; jaçoit qu'il ne
sçavoit que faire de retourner en Espaigne auecques son euesque :
mais il s'en retourna en France et en Normandie à son hostel.
Son euesque print congé de luy à Rome, et ledit Seigneur rescript
au Roy d'Espaigne ; et si manda au maistre de la nef qui l'auoit
amené de Canare en Siuille, que le plutost qu'il pourroit trouuer
sa charge, il amenast son nauire à Herfleur, et le nauire estoit
desja party, et on ne peut oncques sçauoir qu'il deuint, fors qu'on
dit audit Seigneur qu'il estoit aduis à aucuns qu'il s'estoit noyé
en la mer enpres la Rochelle, et qu'il estoit chargé, et qu'il venoit
pardessa ainssi fut son navire perdu ; onques on n'en oüyt
parler plus avant, et fut la barge perduë. Or est venu l'Euesque
en Espagne deuers le Roy, et luy a apporté lettres de Monsieur

letters to His Majesty, who rejoiced greatly at his success. M. de Bethencourt had also written by this same bishop to Maciot de Bethencourt, who, after the departure of Monsieur, had himself raised to the rank of knighthood. We will now leave M. de Bethencourt and speak of the said Messire Maciot and of the bishop, who is now arrived at the Canary Islands.

CHAPTER XCIII.—How Bishop Albert arrived in the Canary Islands, where he met with a joyful reception.

Messire Albert de las Casas arrived in the Canary Islands at the island of Fuerteventura, where he found Messire Maciot de Bethencourt, and delivered to him the letters which his uncle had sent to him, which gave Maciot great pleasure; while all the country was delighted at having a prelate and bishop, and, as soon as they became aware of his arrival, they all made him very welcome, more especially when they found that he understood the language of the country. The bishop gave directions in the church as to his wishes

---

de Bethencourt, desquelles il fut ioyeux qu'il auoit fait ses besongnes. Aussi Monsieur de Bethencourt rescript par iceluy Euesque à Messire Maciot de Bethencourt, lequel se fit faire cheualier depuis que Monsieur se partit. Or nous laisserons à parler de Monsieur de Bethencourt et parlerons dudit Messire Maciot et de l'euesque qui est arriué és isles de Canare.

[CHAPITRE XCIII.]—*Comme lesvesque ariva en Canare, la ou il fut receulli joyeusement.*

Messire Albert des Maisons est arriué és isles de Canare en l'isle de Fort'auenture, la où il a trouué Messire Maciot de Bethencourt, et luy a baillé les lettres que Monsieur de Bethencourt luy enuoye, desquelles fut fort joyeux et tout le pays d'auoir Prelat et Esvesque au pais; et tant que tout le peuple le sçeut, ou luy fit fort grand'chere, et plus encore pour ce qu'il entendoit le langage du pays; iceluy euesque ordonna en l'eglise ce qu'il voulut et

and what was to be done, and he demeaned himself so well, so graciously, and in such a pleasant manner, that he found favour with all the people, and was the cause of many great blessings to the whole country. He preached very often, now in one island and now in another. There was no pride in him, and whenever he preached he caused a prayer to be said for M. de Bethencourt, their king and sovereign lord, who was the cause of their life, that is of life eternal, and of the salvation of their souls. Thus, at the sermon, prayer was always offered for M. de Bethencourt, who had made them Christians. The bishop's conduct was so perfect that none could find any fault with him.

CHAPTER XCIV.—Of the good qualities and virtues of Messire Maciot de Bethencourt, and of the progress of the faith in the Islands.

As for Messire Maciot, it is needless to say that he is all goodness. There is neither king nor prince, nor great nor small, who does not speak most highly of him ; he makes

ce qu'il estoit de faire, et se gouuerna si bien et si gratieusement, et si debonnairement, qu'il eut la grace du peuple, et fut cause de bien grands biens au pays. Il preschoit bien fort souvent, puis en vne isle, puis en vne autre, et n'y auoit point d'orgueil en luy ; et à chacun preschement il faisoit faire priere pour leur roy Monsieur de Bethencourt, leur souverain seigneur, qui estoit la cause de leur vie, c'est à dire de la vie eternelle, et de la saluation de leurs ames. Aussi au prosne de l'eglise tousiours on prioit pour ledit seigneur qui les auoit faits Chrestiens. Ledit euesque se gouverna si bien que nul ne le sçauoit reprendre.

[CHAPITRE XCIV]—(*Des bonnes qualitez et vertus de Messire Macyot de Bethencourt, et du progrés de la foy és isles.*)

Quant au regard de messire Maciot, il ne faut point dire, qu'il est tout bon ; il n'y a ue roy, ne prince, ne grand, ne petit, qui ne dise de grands biens de luy, il se fait amer à grans et à petis, et

himself beloved by all, and especially by the natives, who
are beginning in earnest to work in the fields, to plant and
to build. They are making a very good beginning. May
God, in his mercy, be pleased to direct them so that they
may work for the welfare both of their souls and of their
bodies. Messire Maciot interests himself very much about
the building of churches, which is a source of great joy to
the bishop. There is not one, either great or small, who
does not do all in his power for the good of the church. It
cannot be said that the native Canarians fail in their part,
for they bring stones, they work and help to the best of
their ability and with a hearty good will, as one can plainly
see. Those also whom Monsieur de Bethencourt brought
over with him the last time are perfectly contented, and
would on no account change their condition, for they pay
no taxes of any sort, and live in the greatest harmony together. We will now take leave of them, and speak of
Monsieur de Bethencourt, who is on his road home from
Rome to his native country of Normandy.

principalement à ceux du pays, et ceulx du pais commencent fort
à labourer, planter et edifier. Ils prennent vn tres-bel commencement : Dieu par sa grace les veuille entretenir, qu'ils
puissent faire le profit de leurs ames et de leurs corps. Ledit
Messire Maciot fait fort besongner és Eglises, dont l'Euesque est
moult ioycux : il n'y a ne grand ne petit qui ne face de tout son
pouvoir bien à l'Eglise. Ce n'est pas les Canariens du pays
qu'ils n'en facent leur deuoir; ils apportent pierres, ils besongnent,
et aident de ce qu'ils sçauroient faire, et ont un grand et bon
vouloir, ainsi que l'on peut aperceuoir. Aussi ceux que Monsieur
y mena dernierement, ils sont bien aises, et ne voudroient pour
rien estre autre part, car ils ne payent nuls subsides ne autres
choses, et viuent en vne grande amour ensemble. Nous laisserons
à parler de ceste matiere, et parlerons de Monsieur de Bethencourt,
qui est en chemin de retourner de Rome en son pays en Normandie.

CHAPTER XCV.—How Monsieur de Bethencourt arrived at Florence.

Monsieur de Bethencourt rode as far as Florence, where he found some merchants, who had previously heard speak of him and of his doings. When he arrived some people asked who this grandee was, and some of his people answered that he was the King of Canary. It soon became common talk that a king had arrived in the city who was called the King of Canary, and that he was lodged at the sign of the " Stag" in the High Street. The news soon reached the Town Hall, where was a merchant who had once seen M. de Bethencourt at Seville, and had heard of the Canary Isles, and that the Sieur de Bethencourt had conquered them, and this merchant related this to the mayor of the town, who was at the time in the Town Hall ; whereupon they immediately sent to the inn to ask if the stranger were indeed Monsieur de Bethencourt. When it came to the mayor's knowledge that such was the case, a

[CHAPITRE XCV.]—*Comme le dit Sieur (de Bethencourt) est arrivé à Fleurance.*

Monsieur de Bethencourt a tant cheuauché qu'il est arriué à Florence, et là a trouué aucuns marchands qui auoient autre fois ouy parler de luy et de ses faits. Quand il vint à la ville de Fleurance, aucuns demanderent quel Seigneur c'estoit : il y eut aucuns de ses gens qui dirent que c'estoit le Roy de Canare ; il estoit tantost tout commun qu'il estoit arriué vn Roy à la ville qu'on appelloit *le Roy de Canare*, et qu'il estoit logé à l'enseigne du Cerf en la grand' rüe ; et tant que les nouvelles vindren t à l'hostel de la ville ; il y auoit vn marchand qui autrefois auoit veu Monsieur de Bethencourt en Siuille, et auoit bien autrefois ouy parler des isles de Canare, et que ledit Sieur de Bethencourt les auoit conquises, et le contoit iceluy marchand au maire de la ville qui là estoit en l'hostel de la ville : et tantost ils enuoyerent au logis pour sçauoir si c'estoit Monsieur de Bethencourt, et trouuerent que c estoit-il : et quãd le maire le sçeut, on luy

very handsome present of meat and wine of excellent quality
was sent to M. de Bethencourt on the part of the mayor and
dignitaries of the city. The presentation was made by the
same merchant who knew him, and who detained Monsieur
de Bethencourt in the city of Florence, entertaining him in
the most generous manner, and defraying all his expenses.
Nor would he take any refusal from him, for he was a very
wealthy man. This same merchant had dined with him in
his lodging at Seville, and they had had a private conversation together, so that from some words which the merchant
let fall, M. de Bethencourt recognised him. On the fourth
day of his sojourn in this city he took his departure, and
the merchant accompanied him for more than two leagues.
He then made all speed until he reached Paris, where he
found many acquaintances. He remained a week in Paris
to rest and refresh himself, and after eight days came to
Bethencourt, where he found Madame de Bethencourt, and
spent some time there : it is needless to ask what welcome
was given him. All the noblemen and gentry came to see

enuoya vn bien honneste present de par le maire et seigneurs de
la ville ; il y auoit vin et viande bien honneste, et le vint presenter
iceluy marchand qui le cognoissoit, lequel fit demourer ledit
sieur en la ville de Florence, et le festoya si honnestement qu'on
ne vous le sçauroit dire, et defraya ledit seigneur de toutes choses :
pour quelque chose que ledit Seigneur vouloit ou non, il falut
qu'ainsi fust fait ; aussi c'estoit vn fort riche marchād. Ledit
marchand auoit disné auec luy en son logis en Siuille, et auoiēt
priuette ensemble ; et par aucunes paroles que ledit marchand
luy dit, Monsieur le Bethenconrt le recognut. Le quatriesme
iour qu'il fut en icelle ville, il se partit et le conuoya iceluy marchand plus de deux lieuës ; et s'en vint ledit Seigneur, et
cheuaucha tant qu'il arriua à Paris, là où il trouua de la cognoissance assez, et fut huict iours dedans Paris pour se rafraichir ; et
apres les huict iours il s'en vint à Bethencourt, et là il trouua
Madame de Bethencourt, et vescut vn espace de temps : il ne
faut point demander la chere qu'on luy fit. Tous seigneurs et

him, as well as the relatives of those whom he had taken to
the Canary Islands, who inquired, How is my brother?
how is my nephew, my cousin? etc. : people came from all
parts. When M. de Bethencourt had spent a little time at
Bethencourt, he went to his house of Grainville la Teinturière en Caux, and took up his abode in his own chateau,
where he was received with the usual enthusiasm. If great
people had come there on the former occasion, they came
now in greater numbers : presents and friends poured in,
and M. de Bethencourt stayed a long time at Grainville,
and Madame de Bethencourt joined him there. Some time
afterwards Messire Regnault de Bethencourt returned from
the household of Duke John of Burgundy, the one who was
killed at Montereau-faut-Yonne. This Regnault had been
for a time the comptroller of his household, and he came to
visit his wife, Dame Marie de Briauté, who was at Rouvray;
and when he learned that his brother was arrived, he went

---

gentils-hommes le venoient voir, et aussi les parens de ceux
qu'il auoit amenés és isles de Canare, qui vendoient;[1] comme le
fait mon frere? côme le fait mon neueu? mon cousin, etc., il
venoit gens de tous parts; et quand ledit seigneur eut esté vn
peu de temps à Bethencourt, il s'en alla en son hostel de Grainuille la Teinturiere en Caulx, et se logea en son chasteau ; il ne
faut pas demander se on luy fit grand'chere. S'il y estoit venu à
l'autre fois des gens de bien, il en vint encore plus, vous
n'eussiez veu que gens et presens venir et apporter, et se tint
ledit seigneur audit lieu de Grainuille bien fort longuement, et
fit venir Madame de Bethencourt à Grainuille. Et dedans vne
espace de temps Messire Renault de Bethencourt reuint de
l'hostel du Duc Iean de Bourgongne, celuy qui fut tué à Monte-
riau faut-Yonne; iceluy Regnaut estoit son grand-maistre
d'hostel pour l'heure, et vint voir sa femme qui estoit à Rouuray,
laquelle se nommait Dame Marie de Briauté : et quand il sçeut
que Monsieur son frere estoit venu, le plustost qu'il peût, il s'en

---

Sic in MS. Bergeron has more correctly " demandoient."

to him with all speed, and they met with tender affection, as was only natural, for they were the only children of the same father and mother, issue of the Sieur Jean de Bethencourt and of Dame Marie de Bracquemont. Monsieur Bethencourt, King of Canary, had no children ; his wife was a young and beautiful lady, whereas he was now an old man. She was of the house of Fayel, of the neighbourhood of Troyes, in Champagne. Unhappily, however, Monsieur de Bethencourt and Regnault de Bethencourt his brother had a great quarrel together about a nothing at all, which caused great distress to Madame de Bethencourt and to the said Messire Regnault, surnamed Morelet.

[CHAPTER XCVI.—Of the quarrels which took place between Monsieur de Bethencourt and Messire Regnault his brother.]

It happened that the said Regnault came to see his brother Monsieur de Bethencourt at Grainville la Teinturière, and great was the festivity and mirth. And Madame de Bethencourt, who was a young and merry lady, was enjoy-

alla vers luy, et firent grand chere l'vn à l'autre, et aussi deuoient-ils bien faire : car ils n'estoient qu'eux deux de pere et de mere, issus de Messire Jean de Bethencourt et dame Marie de Bracque-mont, et n'auoit Monsieur de Bethencourt Roy de Canare nuls enfans, si estoit sa femme belle et ieune Dame, et il estoit ja fort ancien : elle estoit issuë de ceux de Fayel d'entour Troyes en Champaigne. Il ne demoura quyere que le dit seigneur et Regnault de Bethencourt son frere grosse noise en semble et pour vng nyent, laquelle noyse fit beaucoup de mal a Madame de Bethencourt et audit Messire Regnault dit Morelit.

[CHAPITRE XCVI.]—(Des noises qu'il y eut entre Monsieur de Bethencourt et Messire Reynault son frère.)

Avint que a Grainville la tainturiere ledit Regnault essoit venu veoir son frere Monsieur de Bethencourt et fesoit grand chere et joyeuse. Et Madame de Bethencourt, qui essoit joyne et joyeuse

ing herself in the company of Monsieur de Bethencourt and Messire Regnault his brother, when it happened that she thus addressed herself to her husband Monsieur de Bethencourt. " It would have been a more correct and proper thing if I had had in marriage Messire Morelet your brother, and that you should have had my sister, who is his wife, for she is much older than I am, and your brother is much younger than you." But this she said in nothing but simple merriment. Monsieur de Bethencourt, however, did not take it in this light, and from that speech arose very serious evils, for, to begin with, his wife lost her husband's love, and she very soon perceived it. Monsieur Regnault his brother also was compelled to quit the house, and Monsieur de Bethencourt would not see him on account of those words, which he could not away with. He had not given occasion for them to be said to him, and he was quite astounded. But if he was so, how much more was Madame de Bethencourt ! It was a terrible thing for a man to put himself into so furious a passion for a word which was only

---

dame, se jouet a Monsieur de Bethencourt et a Messire Regnault son frère, avint que elle dit a Monsieur de Bethencourt son mary : Si eut este une chose plus licite et plus propre que je eusse eu en mariage Messire Morelet vostre frère, et vous eussies eu ma seur sa fame ; car elle est biaucoup plus vielle que je ne suis et monsieur vostre frere est plus joune que vous. Et icelle parolle quelle dit elle ne le disoit que en joyeusete. Mais Monsieur de Bethencourt ne luy print pas. Et pour ycelle parrolle en auint de bien grans maulx ; car tout premierement elle ne fut a lamour de son mary, et elle saparceut bien tost, et aussi fit Messire Regnault son frere, lequel il falut quil sen allast hors de son hostel et ne vouloit Monsieur de Bethencourt veoir son frere pour yceulx parrolles dont il nen pouet mes. Il ne luy auoit pas fait dire. Il estoit tout esbahy. Et sil estoit bien esbahy encore lestoit plus ladite dame de Bethencourt. Aussi cestoit une bien vne terrible chose a ung homme de se corrosser si terriblement pour une ytelle parolle quil ne se faisoit que par joyeuseté. Ledit

said from light-heartedness. But he fell into such a state of jealousy of his own brother by the same father and mother, that all the most beautiful robes that she possessed, of which there was a great variety and very rich of silk brocade, he burned in the fire before her eyes. You may easily suppose the distress she suffered, not so much for the robes only, but for the conduct of Monsieur de Bethencourt. He further had her taken to Bethencourt and placed her in a walled prison, and put her on rations of meat and drink. She suffered very great hardship without having deserved it, for she was a lady of extremely good reputation, and Monsieur de Bethencourt was not justified in treating her so badly. As to Messire Morelet, he dared not approach his brother; but one day Madame de Bethencourt sent for Messire Morelet, who came to Bethencourt, and, to his amazement, found her immured in a prison. She said to him : "Ah, my brother! I am suffering great sorrow and distress on account of you, while both you and I are blameless. I

---

seigneur entra en une si grant jalouzie de son propre frere de pere et de mere, que toutes les plus belles robbes de ladite dame, dont il y en auoit de dras de soye de plusieurs sortes et de bien riches, il brula au feu tout deuant elle. Vous pouez bien pensser quil lui deut bien faire mal non pour tant pour les robbes seullement mas pour la maniere de faire ledit seigneur. Ledit seigneur la fit mener a Bethencourt et la il la mist en une prison tout amurée et la fasoit pensser de boire et menger. Elle eust biaucoup de mal sans lauoir dasseruy, car cestoit une dame de fort bonne renommee. Ledit sire nauoit nulle cause de lui faire si grant tort. Quant au regart de messire Morellet frere dudit seigneur il neut ose vertir autour monsieur son frere. Une journée auint que Madame De bethencourt enuoia querir messire Morellet, lequel vint vers elle a bethencourt et là la trouua amurée et en prison, dont il fut tout esbahy, et elle luy a dit : A mon frere, je seuffre beaucoup de mal et de destresse a cause de vous, dont vous ne moy non pouons mas. Je uous prie mettes y

pray you effect my release." " My sister," said he, " my
brother has told me that I shall never succeed to anything
of his, and declares that he will sell everything in order to
spite me.   If he does so, he will do wrong, for I have done
him no wrong.   I am quite overwhelmed at his having taken
such a fancy into his head.   It is the enemy from hell who
is irritated at the good things which he has done.   He has
been the cause of the salvation of many souls, and the
enemy from hell is angry thereat, and is striving hard to
have his ; for, if he does not control himself and should die
in this state of mind, he places his soul in great danger."
" My brother," said Madame, " I pray you take measures
for getting me removed from this place, and speak to him,
if you possibly can."   " I will do so, my sister," said
Messire Regnault : " he threatens me, but I am not afraid
of him."   It so happened once that Monsieur de Bethencourt
came from Grainville to Bethencourt, and Messire Regnault
started from Bethencourt with the view of meeting his
brother, and so he did.   They met in a spot named the
Valley of Bethencourt, within the woods of Bethencourt,

---

remede. Ma seur, se dist il, mon frere ma mande que james je
namendere de chose quil ait et quil vendra tout pour despit de
moy. Sil le fait il fera mal, car je ne lui ay pas desseruy. Je suis
tout esbahy de se quil a boute vng ytelle fantazie en sa teste.
Cest lanemy denffer qui est marry des biens quil a fait. Il est
cause dauoir sauue maintes ames et lanemy denffer en est
corrosse, et mest paine dauoir la sienne, car si ne sa modere et il
meurt en se point il mest son ame en grant danger. Mon frere,
se dit madame, Je vous prie metes paine de moy mestre hors
dicy et parles a lui se vous poues. Ma seur, se dit Messire
Regnault, je le feray. Il me menasse mais je nay pas pour de lui.
Il aduint que une fois Monsieur de Bethencourt venoit de
Grainuille a bethencourt et messire Regnault partoit de bethencourt et sen aloit cuidant encontrer Monsieur De bethencourt
son frere, et aussi fit il. Ils sentrencontrerent en ung lieu que
on appelle le val de bethencourt dedans les bois De bethencourt et

and passed close by one another. When Monsieur de Bethencourt came near to his brother, he opened his breast with both his hands, and said, "Hold, my brother, strike there!" and no more. It must be confessed that he must have been sorely troubled in his mind to utter such words. His brother passed on without saying a word, for he could not speak. It is needless to say that they were both deeply affected. Subsequently, Regnault de Bethencourt found means to make peace for himself and Madame de Bethencourt, but not until he himself had received great injury, for Monsieur de Bethencourt mortgaged and sold a great portion of his lands, so that Regnault was all but disinherited, and succeeded to next to nothing from his elder brother, whose rightful heir he was and ought to be, for Monsieur de Bethencourt died without heirs of his body. The quarrels were settled, because they were really groundless. So the said Lord of Bethencourt, conqueror of the Canaries, lived for a certain time, and received news of the said islands,

---

passerent a res lun de lautre. Et quant Monsieur De bethencourt vint bien pres de son frere ledit sieur de bethencourt ouurit a deulx mains sa pourtrine et dit a son frere, tieng mon frere, frappe la, et non autre chose lui dist. Il fault bien dire que ledit sieur estoit fort trouble en son esperit quant il dit icelle parolles. Son dit frere passa oultre sans lui mot dire car il ne seut parler. Il ne faut pas demander se tous deulx estoient bien troubles. Autre fois ledit Regnault De bethencourt trouua maniere de faire la paix de lui et de Madame de bethencourt, mais se ne fut pas que ledit Regnault ny eut grant dommage, car ledit Seigneur de bethencourt engagea et vendit plusieurs de ces terres tant que ledit Regnaut de bethencourt fut pres que tout desherite, et namenda de guiere de chose de son frère aysne, lequel Regnaut estoit et deuoit estre son propre heritier, car il mourust sans nuls hoiers de son corps. "Les noises furent appaisees car il ny auoit nulle rayson." Or vescut ledit Seigneur de Bethencourt conquereur des Isles de Canare vne espace de temps ; il eut des nouuelles desdites isles, et s'attendoit

and intended to return to them, but he never did return.
He received intelligence that his two vessels were lost at
sea, laden with merchandise and curiosities of the country.
He would have received earlier news than that which came
from Messire Maciot, had it not been for the misfortune of
the loss of these two vessels.

CHAPTER XCVII.—Of the illness, last words, and death of Monsieur
de Bethencourt, the conqueror of the Canary Islands.

One day the Sieur de Bethencourt fell ill in his castle of
Grainville, and perceived clearly that he was about to die.
He sent for several friends, and especially for his brother,
who was his next of kin and his heir, and intended to
say many things to him. Madame de Bethencourt was
already dead: he asked several times for his brother;
and when he found that he did not come, he declared
to all present that the thing which lay most upon his
conscience was the wrong and despite which he had done

qu'il y retourneroit de bref: Mais oncques puis n'y retourna. Il
eut nouuelles que ses deux barges estoiēt perdues en la mer, qui
apportoient marchandises et nouueautés du pays: il eust eu des
nouuelles plustost qu'il n'a eu de messire Maciot, ce n'eust esté
l'auenture desdites barges qui ont esté perduës.

[CHAPITRE XCVII.]—(De la maladie, derniers propos et mort [de
Monsieur de Bethencourt, conquereur des Yles de Canare.])

Vng iour aduint qu'il fut malade en son Chasteau de Grainuille, et voyait bien qu'il se mouroit. Il enuoya querir plusieurs
de ses amis, et specialement son frere qui estoit son plus prochain
et son heritier, et auoit intention de luy dire beaucoup de choses.
Madame de Bethencourt estoit ja pieça trespassée: il demandoit
par plusieurs fois où estoit son frere il ne venoit point. Et
quand il vit qu'il ne venoit point, il dit en la presence de ceux
qui y estoient que c'estoit la chose qui plus luy touchoit sa
conscience que le tort et desplaisir qu'il auoit fait à son frere, et

to his brother, which he knew he had not deserved. "I am sure," said he, "that I shall never see him again, but I charge you to tell him that he must go to Paris, to the house of a man named Jourdain Guerard, and demand from him a packet of letters which I have given him to keep, and on the outside of which are written the words 'These are the letters of Grainville and de Bethencourt.'" Not long after he had said this he expired. His brother arrived as he was dying and could no longer articulate. There is no room to doubt that he had as good an end as one could speak of. He made his will and received all the sacraments. Messire Jean le Verrier, his chaplain, whom he had taken with him and brought back from the Canary Islands, wrote his will, and was with him throughout his last illness. The said lord died possessed of the lordships of Bethencourt, of Grainville la Teinturière, of Saint Saire sous Neufchatel, of Lincourt, of Riville, of Grand Quesnay, and Hucquellen, of two fiefs at Gourel en Caux, and the barony of St. Martin le Gaillard, in the conté d'Eu. He is dead and gone from

qu'il sçauoit bien qu'il ne l'auoit point deseruy; "ie voy bien que ie ne le verray iamais plus; mais ie vous charge que vous luy disiez qu'il voyse à Paris chez vn nommé Jourdain Guerard, et qu'il luy demāde vn coffret de lettres que ie luy ay baillé, en ces enseignes qu'il y a dessus escrit, Ce sont les lettres de Grainuille et de Bethencourt." Tantost apres ces paroles, il ne fut gueres qu'il ne rendist l'ame. Son dit frere vint ainsi qu'il se mouroit, et ne pouuoit ja parler, il ne faut point douter qu'il a eu aussi belle fin qu'on sçauroit dire; il fit son testament et eut tous ses Sacremens. Messire Jean le Verrier son chappellain qu'il auoit mené et ramené des isles de Canare, escriuit son testament, et fut à son trespas tout du lōg. Ledit sieur mourut saisi et Seigneur de Bethencourt, de Grainuille la Tainturiere, de sainct Sere soubs le Neuf-chastel, de Lincourt, de Riuille, de Grand Quesnay, et Hucquellen, de deux fiefs qui sont à Gourel en Caux, et Baron de sainct Martin le Gaillart, en la conté d'Eu. Il est trespassé et allé de ce siecle en l'autre, Dieu luy vueille

this world to the next. May God vouchsafe him pardon for his misdeeds. He lies buried in the church of Grainville la Teinturière, just in front of the high altar. His decease took place in the year one thousand four hundred and twenty-two.

---

pardonner ses meffaits; il est enterré à Grainuille la Tainturiere, dans l'église de ladite ville, tout deuant le grand autel, et trespassa l'an mil CCCCXXII.

CEST LIVRE EST A JEHAN DE BETHENCOURT ESCUIER SEIGNEUR DE BETHENCOURT.

THE END.

INDEX.

Q

CORRIGENDA.

Page 70, for Feldes, read Telde. In headings of Chapters LXXX and LXXXI, for Lancerote (sic in MS.), read Fuerteventura.

CPSIA information can be obtained
at www.ICGtesting.com
Printed in the USA
FSHW021112150720
72184FS